Nationalism
and Communism
in Asia
The American Response

**PROBLEMS IN
AMERICAN CIVILIZATION**

Nationalism and Communism in Asia

The American Response

Edited and with an introduction by

Norman A. Graebner
University of Virginia

D. C. HEATH AND COMPANY
Lexington, Massachusetts Toronto

Published simultaneously in Canada.

Printed in the United States of America.

International Standard Book Number: 0-669-00683-1

Library of Congress Catalog Card Number: 76-26357

CONTENTS

INTRODUCTION

This nation's response to Asia's postwar upheaval produced its most demanding, divisive, and unsatisfactory policies. As late as mid-century the exorbitant price which its Asian involvements would exact of the United States was not apparent. Since the 1920s two forces—nationalism and communism—had threatened European colonial rule throughout Asia without provoking any official American concern. But with the onset of the Cold War the presence of Marxist leadership in the key Chinese and Indochinese revolutionary movements raised troublesome questions about the relationship of Asian communism to Soviet power and purpose: Was Asian communism, where it existed, an indigenous, pragmatic, and fundamentally nationalist movement seeking independence and a new order for Asia? Or was it a universal, ideological force, one element in a global conspiracy directed from Moscow, skimming the Asian landscape in search of nations to conquer and add to the international Communist bloc? It could not be both. Asian Communists in authority could not sustain their local bases of power by pursuing programs of national concern and simultaneously respond to the dictates of an international movement, issuing demands that had little or no relationship to their countries' established interests. Governing a nation and serving an externally directed international cause are not compatible enterprises. Yet ultimately American officialdom could make no distinction between them at all.

Earlier the revolutionary pressures in Asia appeared understandable enough. Long before the twentieth century, South, Southeast, and East Asia, with the exception of China and Thailand, had become the exclusive domain of the European imperial nations. Through the imposition of the unequal treaties, the major Western powers had reduced China to a colonial status as well. It was this massive, and generally unchallenged, Western dominance that gave the Orient its internal stability. If the European presence in Asia defied the principle of self-determination, it guaranteed political and economic arrangements that served Western interests admirably.

Colonial rule survived in an aura of white invincibility. Everywhere in the colonial world whites formed a privileged class, commanding the most prestigious positions and enforcing social distinctions that placed all white men above the most distinguished natives. Asia's political awakening had its inception in the resulting dichotomy between the wealth, education, and intelligence of the foreign-trained national elites and their subordinate political and racial status. Native leaders, in their opposition to colonial rule, often acted from self-interest and desired only to break the white monopoly on the high offices and to obtain the power and perquisites which such offices bestowed. Few had any interest in social revolution.

But Asia's leaders, in their struggle for recognition and power, searched for those popular appeals which could excite in their backward populations the fundamentally European emotion of nationalism. This emotion they could then employ in the name of the masses to strengthen their onslaught on the old order, whether that order were identified with European colonialism or indigenous feudalism. Nationalists generally discovered their emotional and intellectual resources in Western liberal thought—the principles of racial equality, self-determination of peoples, and social justice. During the Great War, Woodrow Wilson proclaimed the goal of self-determination for all peoples. To the disappointment of Asia's elites, he failed at Versailles to apply the principle to the victorious European empires of Britain, France, Belgium, and the Netherlands.

One significant Asian minority, characterized by such revolutionary leaders as Mao Tse-tung and Ho Chi Minh, found their intellec tual authority in Marxism. Following the failure of revolution across Central Europe in the wake of Germany's collapse in 1918, Lenin, the spokesman for Russia's new Bolshevik regime, turned to the more volatile Orient with the expectation of greater success. What made communism and nationalism natural allies in Asia was the fact that both were anti-imperialist and authoritarian. Both harbored a profound distrust of the white race. In Europe Communists appeared to be cosmopolitan, at least in their professions, for nationalism, in practice, had often been reactionary. In Asia, however, nationalism was a liberating force. Thus Lenin, in his new strategy of world revolution, supported Asian nationalism as a popular, revolutionary pressure for change aimed largely at the goal of national independence. By championing the liberation of colonial peoples, the Socialists had no choice but to patronize Asian nationalism as the only force available to effect that liberation. Yet Soviet influence faced resistance in that very nationalism which it encouraged, even when Asian independence movements came under Marxist leadership, for nationalism, not communism, gave every independence movement its fundamental purpose and character.

Ho Chi Minh, as the spokesman for Indochinese independence, traveled to Paris as early as the Versailles conference. With the failure of self-determination for the French Empire in Asia, Ho found his support for Indochinese liberation in the anti-imperialism embodied in socialist doctrine. It was Lenin's writing especially, he recalled, that gave him the courage after Versailles to pursue the cause of Indochinese independence. He recalled many years later:

> *The reason for my joining the French Socialist Party was that these "ladies and gentlemen"—as I called my comrades at that moment—had shown their sympathy toward me, toward the struggle of the oppressed peoples. But I understood neither what was a party, a trade-union, nor what was Socialism nor Communism. . . . What I wanted most to know— and this was not debated in the meetings—was: which International sides with the peoples of colonial countries? I raised this question . . . and a comrade gave me Lenin's "Thesis on the national and colonial questions," published by l'Humanité to read. There were political terms difficult to understand in this thesis. But by dint of reading it again and again, finally I could grasp the main part of it. What emotion, enthusiasm, clear-sightedness, and confidence it instilled in me! I was overjoyed to tears. Though sitting alone in my room, I shouted aloud as if addressing large crowds: "Dear martyrs, compatriots! This is what we need, this is the path to our liberation!"*

Later Ho organized the Communist Party of Indochina as the agency, not of an international conspiracy, but of Indochinese independence and state-building. Its program favored a body of economic, social, and educational reforms designed to serve the masses; nothing in it acknowledged the allegiance to any ideal or movement which transcended the interests, as Ho perceived them, of a free Indochina. Even as the Marxists took control of the Indochinese nationalist movement, they abstained from making any doctrinal claims. Orthodoxy yielded to national need; communism assumed a traditional nationalist role.

For Mao Tse-tung the challenge of revolution was that of making China strong and resistant to external pressure so that European power would not reduce it totally to the condition of Indochina or Korea. The May 4, 1919, student uprising in Peking was no less than a nationalistic response to China's failure to recover the Shantung Peninsula at Versailles. The "May Fourth Movement" could not touch the weaknesses of Chinese society; nor did it have the support of the peasants and soldiers. But it established the foundations of a Chinese revolutionary movement. By 1920 Mao had become a convert to communism. In June of that year the Soviets dispatched a Commintern agent to China to form a Communist party. Initially the Chinese Communists, under Kremlin direction, attempted to build their power on an urban-labor foundation. Dr. Sun Yat-sen, the leader of China, soon came to terms with them, for Chinese nationalism and Chinese communism shared the goal of building China into a strong, unified country by eliminating domestic warlordism and foreign intervention. Despite the pervading influence of Borodin, the Soviet revolutionary expert, in the Chinese Nationalist Government (Kuomintang), Chinese communism had no future as a fundamentally proletarian movement.

General Chiang Kai-shek seized control of the Kuomintang in 1926 and promptly drove the Communists from key positions within the Chinese government. This isolation of the Communists catapulted Mao into a position of leadership. Conscious of the nationalistic outburst among the Chinese peasants which followed the massacre of Chinese citizens by foreign police in Shanghai in May 1925, Mao, having lost his urban base of support, concluded by 1927 that China's fate would be decided in the countryside. The peasants, he wrote that year, were "like a tornado or tempest—a force so extraordinarily swift and violent that no power, however great, will be able to suppress it." After 1927 the Chinese revolution, whatever its leadership, was in large measure a peasant uprising which sought to cleanse China of the foreign and domestic enemies of the Chinese masses.

Defying the Soviets, who favored urban insurrections, Mao focused his attention on the rural areas. Following the Long March to Shensi, Mao became, by 1935, the acknowledged leader of the Chinese Communist movement. Thereafter he proclaimed that movement unique and created his own theoretical formulations to guide it. For Mao China's future had to be distinctly Chinese and human as well as Marxist; China's mission would remain essentially Chinese and Asian. To such observers as the Jesuit scientist Teilhard de Chardin, Mao's forces comprised "the only coherent grouping where one perceives any kind of common soul, any kind of ideal." The Communist movement, he believed, was the one catalyst capable of bringing China into the modern world. Increasingly during the Sino-Japanese war, which began in 1937, Mao extended the area of his control and asserted his independence of both the Kuomintang and the Kremlin. His strength lay in the Chinese peasantry and flowed from the opportunities for successful civil war created by China's struggle against the Japanese. At the end of the war in 1945 the Kremlin's alienation from the Chinese Communists was almost complete.

Faced with growing resistance among native populations, the colonial governments put down revolts in India, Indonesia, and Indochina with a level of repression that seemed disproportionate to the threat. In Indonesia colonial officials found it politically advantageous to designate all enemies of the Dutch regime as Communists. Soetan Sjahrir, the Indonesian nationalist, argued in his memoirs that nationalists were indistinguishable from Communists in the anti-Dutch vanguard. But as a consequence of Dutch policy, Sjahrir recalled, even moderate, middle-class nationalists, often as thoroughly addicted to middle-class values as the Dutch officials themselves, faced imprisonment as radicals. Among the prisoners arrested in the Indonesian uprising of 1927, wrote Sjahrir, "I recognize a part of our ordinary Indonesian people; and they are absolutely 'ordinary' regardless of whether they are called communists or rebels. They are, simply and fundamentally, Indonesians. . . ." All Asian Communist leaders before Pearl Harbor were nationalists. It was not conceivable that they would serve any interest except Asian independence from colonial rule. But whether nationalist or Communist, Asia's leaders as late as World War II had achieved little against the reluctance of the Western powers to part with their imperial structures.

II

Japan's successful invasion of Southeast Asia in 1942 instilled new courage in native nationalists and brought the underlying revolution to a new stage of insistence. As the war progressed, the Japanese assigned many occupation tasks to Asians. One Malay leader acknowledged the result: "Yes, I worked for the Japanese during the war. They did more to awaken my country than all the years of English rule. They showed us what Asians could accomplish." One month after the fall of Singapore the astute London *Economist* warned: "There can be no return to the old system once Japan has been defeated. . . . The need is for entirely new principles or rather the consistent application of principles to which lip service has long been paid." Similarly journalist Nathaniel Peffer wrote in 1942: "That which was known as the white man's prestige, something apart from and beyond his intrinsic power, has passed. The glow of invincibility is no longer about the white empires. They will . . . hold only such position as they can prove their capacity to hold." Political settlements following the war, ran such admonitions, would embody the concept of Asiatic equality or there would be no security for the West in the Orient; white armies on Asian soil fighting to reestablish colonial rule against native forces, whatever the justice of their cause, would become *ipso facto* the aggressors. Later, as the Japanese began their long retreat, they handed arms and other military equipment to the increasingly well-organized and determined Asian nationalists. The first reading of this book is a warning from G. W. Seabridge, given as early as 1944, that Europeans would restore their former empires in Asia with difficulty if at all.

Washington viewed the changes being wrought by war in the Far East with decided ambivalence. The European empires had served the interests of the United States, and this nation had long deserted its earlier identification with revolution. But President Franklin D. Roosevelt took the doctrine of self-determination seriously and argued that the Atlantic Charter of August 1941, which proclaimed self-determination as the political objective of the Allied war effort, be applied universally. He was concerned especially that the French give up their empire in Southeast Asia. He approved a State Department memorandum of September 1944 that favored "early, dramatic and concerted announcements by the nations concerned making definite commitments as to the future of the regions of Southeast Asia . . . [including] specific dates when independence or complete self-government will be accorded. . . ." At his press conference of February 23, 1945, Roosevelt spoke candidly. "For two whole years," he said, "I have been terribly worried about Indo-China. I talked to Chiang Kai-shek in Cairo, Stalin in Teheran. They both agreed with me. . . . The first thing I asked Chiang was, 'Do you want Indo-China?' He said, 'It's no help to us. We don't want it. They are not Chinese. They would not assimilate into the Chinese people.' . . . With the Indo-Chinese, there is a feeling they ought to be independent but are not ready for it. . . .'"

Earlier Roosevelt had suggested to Churchill that Britain promise independence to India, Burma, and Ceylon, with the hope that political changes even of such magnitude might be channeled toward limited and peaceful ends. Emerging from the war confident and armed, Asia's new leaders were prepared to exploit anti-colonial emotions to underwrite their final assault on the old political order. Under this new pressure for self-determination the still-existing imperial structures began to disintegrate. Britain, exhausted by war, gave up its wartime struggle for empire. By 1947 London had granted independence to India, Pakistan, Burma, and Ceylon. The Dutch attempted to reestablish their East Indian empire, but faced resistance not only from Indonesian nationalists but also from the new United Nations where Asian and Western spokesmen combined to force an eventual Dutch capitulation.

Meanwhile the French, with British help, had taken control of Saigon while Ho Chi Minh, returning to Indochina in the late spring of 1945 as an agent of the American Office of Strategic Services (OSS), quickly emerged as the primary spokesman for Indochinese independence. As early as 1941 native Vietnamese (Indochinese) leaders, to direct the energies of all nationalists against France, had formed the League for Vietnam Independence, known as the Vietminh. During 1945 this independence movement came under Communist control despite the large number of non-Communist nationalists who gave strength to the movement. "I remember asking Ho if his Vietminh group was Communist," one OSS officer recalled, "and he said the French called all Vietnamese who wanted their independence, Communists." With Japan's surrender Ho, in September 1945, proclaimed the independence of Indochina. Neither

Ho—well established in the North—nor the French would accept a divided country. During 1946 the contest for Indochina degenerated into a bitter civil war. Harold R. Isaacs, in the second reading, analyzes the mood, foundations, and strength of the Asian independence movements of 1946.

Despite his personal preferences for Indochinese independence, Roosevelt had no desire to involve the United States in the burgeoning struggle for power in Southeast Asia. He admitted his hesitancy to act when he addressed the Secretary of State early in 1945: "I still do not want to get mixed up in any Indochinese situation. It is a matter for postwar." What restrained Washington even further was General Charles de Gaulle's warning of March 1945 that the American decision to deny French forces transport to Indochina could succeed in making France "one of the federated states of the Russian aegis." De Gaulle continued: "If the public here comes to realize that you are against us in Indo-China, there will be terrific disappointment and nobody really knows to what that will lead. . . . [W]e do not want to fall into the Russian orbit, but I hope that you do not push us into it." Thereafter Washington pursued two goals—Indochinese independence within the limits of French purpose in Asia, and French support for United States policies in Europe. Key State Department officials argued that American Cold War successes would be measured in Europe, not Asia. For them Indochina's nationalist movement was expendable.

Ho, recently supported in his anti-Japanese activities by the OSS, addressed a series of notes to Washington between October 1945 and April 1946, asking for United States support and recognition. He reminded the Truman administration that the Philippines and India were about to receive their independence; Indochina expected no less. Ignoring Ho's appeal, as well as the advice of the State Department's Division of Southeast Asian Affairs, Secretary George C. Marshall rationalized Washington's support for French policy in Indochina in terms of its overall opposition to Soviet-based communism. In his memorandum of February 3, 1947, to the Embassy in Paris, Marshall explained: "We do not lose sight of the fact that Ho Chi Minh has direct Communist connections and it should be obvious that we are not interested in seeing colonial administrations supplanted by philosophy and political origin emanating and controlled by Kremlin." Abbot Low Moffat describes in the third reading the struggle within the State Department for control of Indochina policy. Marshall later admitted that the State Department had no evidence of a direct link between Ho and Moscow but assumed that it existed.

Yet, in the absence of any clear proof of Ho's independence, United States policy in Indochina became hardened into an anti-Soviet pattern which denied the strength, even the legitimacy, of the Indochinese independence movement. As Secretary of State Dean Acheson explained in May 1949: "Question whether Ho as much nationalist as Commie is irrelevant. All Stalinists in colonial areas are nationalists. With achievement nat(ionalist) aims (independence) their objective necessarily becomes subordination state to commie purposes. . . ." Paris, quite conscious of Washington's willingness to view Ho as a pawn of Moscow, permitted no other view to escape the borders of Indochina. By discrediting Ho's Vietminh as the enemy of the West, the French, with full United States support, managed to transform a local Asian conflict into a massive international struggle.

To such American decisions some Southeast Asian leaders reacted bitterly. Speaking at the University of Chicago in 1949, Philippine Ambassador to the United States Carlos P. Romulo declared:

> There was a fateful moment after the war when America could have made all Asia safe for freedom and democracy. Asia hoped for a new life after the war. Without exception the peoples of Asia looked forward to a new dispensation based on the Four Freedoms and the promise of the Atlantic Charter. The promise was never fulfilled except in the Philippines. Elsewhere America returned to Asia as a liberator and remained–in Asian eyes–as one of the protectors and preservers of the colonial system. American guns helped restore French rule in Indochina against the wishes of the inhabitants. American tanks and planes enabled the Dutch forces to carry out their infamous "police actions." What a difference it might have made in the situation for Asia today if America had stood uncompromisingly for the freedom of Asia. That would have electrified all of Asia's peoples. The consequent disillusionment has had a profound and far-reaching effect in Asia. In lieu of peace the people of Asia found themselves involved in new conflicts. The new life of freedom under justice for which they had fought did not materialize; instead, they were subjected to fresh attempts at domination.

Romulo recognized the problem: the expansion of Europe's Cold War into Asia. "It is a historical misfortune," he observed, "that the renascence of Asia should coincide with the ruthless struggle among the great powers for mastery of the world."

American officials and writers continued to warn the French that they had no chance against Ho's forces unless they separated Ho from the main thrust of Indochinese nationalism, both by promising independence and by supporting a native leader capable of bidding successfully against Ho for the support of the anti-colonial revolution. Ultimately in the Elysee Agreements of March 1949 the French government promised independence to Indochina and named Bao Dai, fromer king of Annam, as spokesman for the new state of Vietnam.

III

Almost from its inception Mao Tse-tung's final rise to power in China divided American officials, politicians, writers and scholars as had no previous external episode in the nation's history. Initially, even as Chiang Kai-shek gave way to the Chinese Communist leadership in 1949, neither the government of the United States nor the American people recognized in this grinding transferal of power any threat of aggression or danger to the United States. Indeed, until 1949 Washington did not reject the possibility of establishing normal and satisfactory relations with the new regime. The United States had not withdrawn its officers from their posts. What determined official attitudes toward the Chinese civil war was the conviction that the Communist success manifested a clear expression of self-determination.

Nothing illustrated better the tendency to view the Communist victory as the legitimate expression of popular approval—and thus no real challenge to American interests or Asian stability—than the noted China White Paper, published in August 1949. In his letter of transmittal, which prefaced the White Paper, Secretary of State Dean Acheson assigned the responsibility for the Nationalist collapse to the failures of that regime. "The Nationalist armies," wrote Acheson, "did not have to be defeated; they disintegrated." The United States, he continued, could have saved Chiang only with a "full-scale intervention in behalf of a Government which had lost the confidence of its own troops and its own people." In eschewing any attempt to control the internal affairs of China, Washington denied that this country had any special security interest in the continuation of Nationalist control of China. Thus at no time did President Harry S. Truman make any effort to extend his burgeoning containment policies to China. The country was too large, the potential financial and military burden too great. There was no possibility, moreover, of building a stable Orient through cooperation with a disunited and warring China. Far more essential after 1948 was the rebuilding of a strong and friendly Japan.

Washington's official response to China's new regime was ambivalent. On September 19, 1949, Acheson reminded a New York audience that recognition did not imply approval. In October a Roundtable Conference of Far Eastern scholars in Washington agreed on recognition as well as aid for the Peking government. Still the President made clear his hesitance to recognize the Communist government. He informed a press conference on October 19, "I hope we will not have to recognize it." At the same time Truman was determined to avoid involvement in the Chinese civil war, perpetuated by the transfer of the Nationalist regime to the island of Formosa. Truman warned Chiang on January 5, 1950: "The United States Government will not pursue a course which will lead to involvement in the civil conflict in China. Similarly, the United States Government will not provide military aid or advice to Chinese forces on Formosa." Already the administration was pushing its fundamental decisions regarding China into some unknown future.

To the extent that numerous Americans and potential critics anticipated the Communist victory in China with deep regret, they regarded the new Chinese leaders as dangerous to Chinese traditions and to China's historic relationship with the United States. They feared above all that Mao might slam shut the Open Door and thus deprive American scholars, missionaries, travelers, officials, and merchants of their former access to a country which was, for them, a region of immense charm. But even for the friends of China and Chiang Kai-shek the closing of the Open Door, and the subsequent mistreatment of American officials in China, was not necessarily evidence of Mao's aggressive intent toward China's neighbors. Communist influence in China might be tragic, but it rode the crest of an indigenous uprising and comprised no threat to American security interests.

Yet there existed in 1949 a marked dichotomy in American at-

titudes toward the impending retreat of Chiang to the island of Formosa. Some Americans could recall Mao's statement of June 1949
that his regime would of necessity ally China with the U.S.S.R. "Not
only in China but throughout the world," he said, "one must lean
either to imperialism or socialism. There is no exception. Neutrality is
merely a camouflage; a third road does not exist." In an era of
continuing imperialism, Mao continued, "it is impossible for a
genuine people's revolution in any country to achieve victory without
various forms of help from the international revolutionary forces.
Even when victory is won, it cannot be made secure without such
help." Washington could not ignore the fact that shortly 900 million
people would be living under Communist-led governments. Indeed,
with the fall of Chiang Kai-shek the nation entered a period of deep
intellectual crisis. What mattered during these critical months of decision was the role which American officials, editors, and political
leaders—the creators of public opinion—chose to assign to the
U.S.S.R. in the triumph of Communist power in China. What had
appeared indigenous suddenly seemed to some in Washington as
possibly the initial triumph of Soviet aggression as it moved into the
Asian sphere. William C. Bullitt develops this thesis in the fourth
reading.

During July 1949, Acheson designated Ambassador at Large Philip
C. Jessup to conduct an objective appraisal of Far Eastern problems
and make recommendations for the formulation of an American
strategy for Asia. Whereas it was quite clear that the administration
would do nothing to save Chiang, Acheson, in a top-secret
memorandum, instructed Jessup as follows: "You will please take as
your assumption that it is a fundamental decision of American policy
that the United States does not intend to permit further extension of
communist domination on the continent of Asia or in the southeast
Asia area." Even in the White Paper Acheson called attention to the
danger of Soviet imperialism in the Far East and reaffirmed United
States opposition "to the subjugation of China by any foreign power,
to any regime acting in the interest of a foreign power, and to the
dismemberment of China by any foreign power, whether by open or
clandestine means." Later that month State Department adviser
George F. Kennan declared over CBS that the new Chinese leadership, whether sincere or not, was committed to unrealistic doctrines
which had induced the Chinese people "to accept a disguised form

of foreign rule." Such statements revealed the extent to which the United States government was prepared to accept the notion that Communist power in China represented Soviet expansion rather than revolution.

Such perceptions of danger in Asia quickly drifted into Congress. In their burgeoning attack on United States policy in China, Senator Kenneth Wherry of Nebraska and other Republicans charged that the State Department's White Paper was "to a large extent a 1,054 page whitewash of a wishful, do-nothing policy which has succeeded only in placing Asia in danger of Soviet conquest with its ultimate threat to the peace of the world and our own national security." Similarly Senator William F. Knowland of California declared in September of 1949 that since communism was global in character, "it did not make sense to try to keep 240 million Europeans from being taken behind the Iron Curtain while we are complacent and unconcerned about 450 million Chinese going the same way, when, if they should go that way, it would probably start an avalanche which would mean that a billion Asiatics would be lined up on the side of Soviet Russia and in the orbit of international communism."

Throughout the autumn months of 1949 the administration continued to search for a definition of the Asian problem, troubled by a lack of evidence. In part the inconclusive discussions of the Roundtable Conference in October revolved around the question of Soviet ambitions in Asia. In November, George C. McGhee, the Assistant Secretary for Middle Eastern, South Asian, and African Affairs, acknowledged again the official fear of Communist aggression in Asia when he declared at Chattanooga, Tennessee, that the rapidity of the Communist advance in China compelled the Soviet Union "to define the nature and extent of its influence over the Chinese Communists, and then to consolidate this vast area within the Soviet orbit." That same month Foreign Service Officer Karl Lott Rankin warned from Hong Kong that Communist China would, through subversion, attempt to extend its influence throughout South and Southeast Asia. "Now that communist control of China proper is all but assured," wrote Rankin, "it may be taken for granted that efforts will be redoubled to place communist regimes in power elsewhere in Asia. . . . China may be considered weak and backward by Western standards, but . . . in Eastern terms, communist China is a great power, economically, militarily, and politically. Supported by com-

munist dynamism, China might well be able to dominate not only
Indochina, Siam, and Burma, but eventually the Philippines, Indonesia, Pakistan, and India itself." To undermine the independence
of the minor countries of Southeast Asia, Rankin warned, China
would employ the techniques of infiltration, sabotage, propaganda,
and support of guerrilla movements.

These two tendencies in official American thought—one accepting
the indigenous, non-Soviet nature of the Chinese revolution, another
detecting Moscow's burgeoning influence in Chinese affairs—
collided in Acheson's noted speech before the National Press Club
on January 12, 1950. Acheson explained the fall of Chiang Kai-shek
in terms of an indigenous revolution. "What has happened," he said,
". . . is that the almost inexhaustible patience of the Chinese people
in their misery ended. They did not bother to overthrow this government. There was really nothing to overthrow. They simply ignored
it. . . . They completely withdrew their support from this government, and when that support was withdrawn, the whole military establishment disintegrated." Within that context, the Secretary argued
logically against any American effort to control the affairs of the new
Asia, especially by military means. Again he assured the nation that
the Communist victory in China did not constitute a threat to the rest
of Asia. He pointedly eliminated South Korea, Formosa, and Southeast Asia from the United States defense perimeter.

But Acheson recognized the danger of Soviet expansion through
the Chinese revolution. "Communism," he said, "is the most subtle
instrument of Soviet foreign policy that has ever been devised, and it
is really the spearhead of Russian imperialism which would, if it
could, take from these people what they have won, what we want
them to keep and develop, which is their own national independence. . . ." Russian ambition toward north China long antedated
communism. "But," Acheson continued, "the Communist regime has
added new methods, new skills, and new concepts to the thrust of
Russian imperialism. These Communistic concepts and techniques
have armed Russian imperialism with a new and most insidious
weapon of penetration." Through these techniques the Soviets possibly had detached Manchuria, Inner and Outer Mongolia, and Sinkiang and added them to the U.S.S.R. "The consequences of this
Russian . . . action in China," warned Acheson, "are perfectly
enormous. They are saddling all those in China who are proclaiming

their loyalty to Moscow, with the most awful responsibility which they must pay for. Furthermore, these actions of the Russians are making plainer than any speech . . . or any legislation can make throughout all of Asia, what the true purposes of the Soviet Union are and what the true function of communism as an agent of Russian imperialism is."

That the Chinese had indeed become puppets of the Moscow Politburo appeared to pass beyond any shadow of doubt when, in February 1950, the world read the terms of the new Sino-Soviet Treaty of Friendship, Alliance and Mutual Assistance. By its terms the Soviets promised China considerable financial and technical aid. Acheson admitted that the Chinese people might welcome such promises, but, he added, "they will not fail, in time, to see where they fall short of China's real needs and desires. And they will wonder about the points upon which the agreements remain silent." The Secretary warned the Chinese that, whatever China's internal development, they would bring grave trouble on themselves and the rest of Asia "if they are led by their new rulers into aggressive or subversive adventures beyond their borders."

Acheson took the lead in defining the new challenge to Asia and in formulating the requirements of American policy. When China appeared to be achieving true national independence, he told the Commonwealth Club of California in March 1950, its leaders were forcing it into the Soviet orbit. "We now face the prospect," he admitted, "that the Communists may attempt to apply another familiar tactic to use China as a base for probing for other weak spots which they can move into and exploit." He warned the people of Asia that they "must face the fact that today the major threat to their freedom and to their social and economic progress is the attempted penetration of Asia by Soviet-Communist imperialism and by the colonialism which it contains." Asia, unfortunately, lay "in the path of a main thrust of Soviet subversion and expansionism." The United States, promised Acheson, would oppose the spread of communism because it comprised the means whereby the Kremlin attempted "to extend its absolute domination over the widest possible areas of the world."

United States officials in Asia joined the Secretary in giving form and unity to this expanding concept of global danger. Ambassador Loy W. Henderson admitted before the Indian Council of World Affairs at New Delhi on March 27 that the United States, with its long tradition of involvement in the Atlantic world, understood better the culture of Europe than that of Asia. Recent events in Asia, however, had given the American people a new and enlarging interest in the region. "It should be borne in mind, in considering various policies of the United States in respect to Asia," he said, "that the United States does not pursue one set of policies with regard to the Americas or Europe and another with regard to Asia. The foreign policies of the United States by force of circumstances have become global in character." Upon his return to the United States, Ambassador Jessup, on April 13, addressed the nation over ABC. Again he cited the requirements for a larger, more pervading policy to stem the tide of aggression in Asia. There was no need, he began, to explain Asia's importance to the United States. "I think most Americans realize that Asia is important," he added, ". . . because Soviet communism is clearly out to capture and colonize the continent. . . ." Everywhere, Jessup informed the nation, Asians relied on the United States to defend their independence. In the fifth reading of this book Hu Shih analyzes political change in China in terms of Stalin's grand strategy for world conquest.

This expanding concept of a single conspiracy, global in its pretensions and centering in Moscow, had not won universal acceptance. Indeed, many American scholars at mid-century rejected the notion completely. Walter Lippmann, speaking before the Chicago Council on Foreign Relations on February 22, 1950, reminded his audience: "While it is true that we have lost our power and for the time being most of our influence in China, it by no means follows that Russia has won control of China or has achieved an enduring alliance with China." Some observers could detect little evidence of Russian dominance in the Sino-Soviet Pact. Indeed, that treaty appeared to serve the Soviet interest so badly that Stalin hesitated to sign it. Years later Mao recalled: "He [Stalin] did not want to sign it, but finally agreed after two months of negotiations." Not until after the Chinese entered the Korean War, believed Mao, did the Russians lose their profound distrust of China's new leadership. John K. Fairbank represented those writers on Far Eastern subjects who analyzed change in China as fundamentally an expression of Chinese nationalism and not Soviet imperialism. His views of China in 1950 appear in the sixth reading. American writers on Far Eastern subjects agreed generally that the United States should not introduce military force into Asia.

But the final Communist victory in China, when added to the official interpretation of the Sino-Soviet Pact, propelled the administration logically toward the extension of the containment principle to the Far East. During 1950 the Chinese revolution itself seemed sufficient to demonstrate Soviet expansionist power in Asia.

IV

In Indochina no less than in China, Washington officials ultimately attributed the pressures of revolution and civil war, not to indigenous conditions, but to Soviet expansionism. The United States resisted the collapse of the French empire in Southeast Asia after mid-century under the clear assumption that Ho Chi Minh was a puppet of the Soviet Union. In January of 1950 both Moscow and Peking recognized Ho's newly established Democratic Republic of Vietnam. Shortly thereafter United States officials announced that they regarded Ho's war against the French, not as a struggle for independence, but as a Soviet-based aggression against the people of Indochina. Secretary of State Acheson declared characteristically that the Soviet recognition of Ho's Democratic Republic revealed him "in his true color as the mortal enemy of national independence in Indochina." The notion that Bao Dai, the Paris-chosen native leader of the new Vietnam state, had better claims to Vietnamese leadership and that he would ultimately triumph over Ho became official doctrine in Washington. Loy Henderson, State Department spokesman, expressed the new American faith when he said, "The United States is convinced that the Bao Dai Government of Vietnam reflects more accurately than any rival claimants to power in Vietnam the nationalist aspirations of the people of that country. It hopes by its policies with regard to Vietnam, to contribute to the peaceful progress of Vietnamese people toward the realization of the fruits of self-government. . . . My government is convinced that any movement headed by a Moscow-recognized Communist such as Ho Chi Minh must be in the direction of subservience to a foreign state, not in that of independence and self-government." And yet it was already clear that Bao Dai had won no defectors from Ho's Vietminh.

When finally, on May 8, 1950, Secretary Acheson negotiated an arrangement with French Foreign Minister Robert Schuman whereby France and the governments of Indochina together would carry the responsibility for Indochinese security, the rationale for United States aid was clear. "The United States Government," declared Acheson, "convinced that neither national independence nor democratic evolution exist in any area dominated by Soviet imperialism, considers the situation to be such as to warrant its according economic aid and military equipment to the Associated States of Indochina and to France in order to assist them in restoring stability and permitting these states to pursue their peaceful and democratic development." With Mao Tse-tung's victory on the Chinese mainland in late 1949, ran the official American analysis, Moscow had captured control of a half billion Chinese people in its cause of world conquest; now through Ho Chi Minh the Kremlin would add Southeast Asia to the widening area under its command. It was against this possibility that Milton Sacks warned in reading seven.

Within the context of this conceptualization of Communist aggression in Asia, the rationale for American involvement in Korea was logical enough. For at stake was more than the independence of South Korea. To Washington the North Korean invasion was another proof of Soviet imperialistic designs on Asia. "The attack upon the Republic of Korea," said President Truman on July 19, "makes it plain beyond all doubt that the international Communist movement is prepared to use armed invasion to conquer independent nations. We must, therefore, recognize the possibility that armed aggression may take place in other areas." Similarly, State Department adviser John Foster Dulles, in a CBS interview, assured the nation that the North Koreans did not attack "purely on their own but as part of the world strategy of international communism."

For Washington the challenge was clear. If the United States failed to repel this invasion, Communist aggression would conquer one nation after another until it would render a third world war inevitable. Thus official American rhetoric quickly elevated the contest for Korea to the level of a preventive war. On its success hinged the territorial status quo throughout Asia. To meet this challenge of Soviet-based aggression the President ordered the United States Seventh Fleet to defend the island of Formosa; he speeded up military assistance to Indochina and the Philippines. In Korea itself, however, the actual

United States response had little relationship to the notion that the Communist threat was overwhelming and global. For the Truman administration assumed that it could, with a limited military commitment, localize the war in Korea and resolve the worldwide contest of power there. Indeed, at the level of strategy it regarded the danger so minimal that it adopted and pursued South Korea's goal of Korean unification under a non-Communist government. From the beginning of the war there was little relationship between the declared ends of policy—to keep all of Asia out of Soviet hands—and the means which the nation intended to employ.

United States officials, in attributing the Korean War to Soviet imperialism, placed enormous faith in China's refusal to become involved. This would demonstrate the actuality of Chinese independence. Acheson revealed his confidence in the good judgment and resistance of the Chinese in a CBS telecast of mid-September of 1950. For the Chinese to enter the war, he said, would be sheer madness. "And since there is nothing in it for them," he added, "I don't see why they should yield to what is undoubtedly pressure from the Communist movement to get into the Korean row." At Wake Island in October, General Douglas MacArthur assured the President that China would not enter the Korean War.

Such expressions of hope, even if backed by logic, proved to be a poor prediction of Chinese action. But they explain why the Chinese advance across the Yalu in November 1950 produced a traumatic reaction in Washington. China's intervention seemed to demonstrate, at last, not only Peking's irrationality but also the absolute control which Moscow had gained over China and China's external policies. "Those who control the Soviet Union and the international Communist movement," Acheson warned the country in a nationwide radio address on November 29, "have made clear their fundamental design." Truman declared on the following day, "We hope that the Chinese people will not continue to be forced or deceived into serving the ends of Russian colonial policy in Asia." Chinese behavior seemed to prove the accuracy of Stanley K. Hornbeck's observation of October: "The conflict in Korea is not a 'civil conflict.' The conflict between China's Communists and China's Nationalists is not a 'civil conflict.' The attacking forces in both cases bear a made-from-by-and-for Moscow stamp." Even *The New York Times* proclaimed on December 8: "The Chinese Communist dictatorship will eventually go down in history as the men who sold out their country to the foreigners, in this case the Russians, rather than as those who rescued China from foreign 'imperialism.' "

Thus Korea perfected the notion of Chinese subservience to Moscow-dominated international communism. Truman reminded the American people in his State of the Union message of January 8, 1951: "Our men are fighting . . . because they know, as we do, that the aggression in Korea is part of the attempt of the Russian communist dictatorship to take over the world, step by step." It was left for Dean Rusk, Assistant Secretary of State for Far Eastern Affairs, and John Foster Dulles, consultant to the Secretary of State, to carry the fears of Soviet aggression in the Far East to their ultimate conceptualization. Both men, as top spokesmen for the State Department, accepted without question the existence of a monolithic Communist enemy, with its center in Moscow. Stalin, from his studies of Leninism, Dulles warned, had seen the possibility of weakening the West mortally through "the revolutionary alliance with the liberation movement of the colonies and dependent countries against imperialism." Rusk, speaking in Philadelphia during February 1951, acknowledged the Soviet assault on Asian nationalism when he declared, "Communism has appeared in Asia not as a Russian preaching the tyranny of the Kremlin but as an Asian preaching nationalism and promising Utopia." Such analyses transformed nationalism as a legitimate quest for self-determination into a fraudulent device for Soviet expansion. That year Dulles carried the notion of Soviet power over China and Chinese behavior to a level of insistence not reached by any previous public statement. His statement is reproduced below in reading eight.

But the pattern of Soviet subversion now appeared equally clear elsewhere in Asia. Disturbances throughout the Pacific and Asian areas, from the war in Korea to the activities of the Communist-controlled United States maritime unions, said Dulles, were "part of a single pattern . . . of violence planned and plotted for 25 years and finally brought to a consummation of fighting and disorder in the whole vast area extending from Korea down through China into Indochina, Malaya, the Philippines, and west in Tibet and the borders of Burma, India, and Pakistan." Rusk noted in February 1951 that the year 1950 marked a new phase in Russia's expansionist policy. "First," he said, "it has clearly shown that it is prepared to wage war by satellites so far as that becomes desirable to further its objective—not only wars by small satellites such as the North Koreans, but full-fledged war by Communist China, a major satellite. Second, the Soviet Union has shown that it is itself prepared to risk a general war and that it is pushing its program to the brink of a general war." Not all agreed. Wilbur W. Hitchcock, in the ninth reading, argued in March 1951 that the decision for the North Korean invasion of South Korea emanated from North Korea and not from the Kremlin. It was an expression of North Korean—not Soviet—ambition.

This concept of a Kremlin-controlled monolith created the ultimate rationale for rejecting Peking from membership in the United Nations and denying it the recognition of the United States. During December 1950 Acheson assured British Prime Minister Clement Attlee, then in Washington, that any compromise with the Peking regime on the matter of U.N. recognition would undermine Formosa and render the Chinese more aggressive. "We should make it a policy," said Acheson, "not to recognize the enemy's gains." Later the President spelled out the administration's position: "If we admitted the Chinese Reds to the U.N., would they be any different from the Russians? I said I expected them to behave just like the other satellites." Truman, through his U.N. ambassador Warren R. Austin, took the first long step toward barring Peking from U.N. membership and thereby isolating it from the main currents of world politics. On January 24, 1951, Austin urged passage of the United States resolution which condemned Peking as an aggressor in Korea. Except for that aggression, said Austin, there would be no fighting in Korea. On February 1 the General Assembly adopted the resolution by a vote of 44 to 7.

Then in a dramatic statement before the China Institute of New York, on May 18, 1951, Rusk announced the United States would not recognize the Peking regime. His reasoning was clear: the rulers of China were the puppets of Moscow. "We do not recognize the authorities in Peiping for what they pretend to be," he said. "The Peiping regime may be a colonial Russian government—a Slavic Manchukuo on a larger scale. It is not the Government of China. It does not pass the first test. It is not Chinese. . . ." Dulles reaffirmed that decision before the same audience: "We should treat the Mao Tse-tung regime for what it is—a puppet regime. The relationship to Moscow is camouflaged more craftily than was the relationship be-

tween the Japanese and the Nanking regime of Wang Ching-
wei. . . . [T]he doctrine and the iron discipline of the Communist
Party binds Mao Tse-tung to the service of Moscow more completely
than was Wang Ching-wei ever bound to the service of Japan.''

Confronted with such perceptions of global danger, the Truman
administration quickly extended its containment efforts to Asia. In
June 1950, Congress, under executive prodding, appropriated $500
million for military assistance in the Far East. In December the United
States signed a special Mutual Defense Assistance Agreement with
France, Vietnam, Cambodia, and Laos for the defense of Southeast
Asia. The Chinese invasion of Korea, Acheson explained in February
1951, made the security of the Pacific area a constant preoccupation
of the United States government. Compelled by this new sense of
urgency, President Truman, in his budget message of 1951, declared
that the military aid program had become an established policy of the
United States. During 1952 military assistance to Asia began to exceed in importance that earmarked for Europe. The bulk of the
military aid channeled into Asia went to four countries regarded
especially vulnerable to Soviet-Chinese aggression: the Republic of
China on Formosa, the Republic of Korea, the Republic of Vietnam,
and Japan.

Korea and Indochina—regions where the principle of containment
was under direct assault—had emerged by 1951 as the keys to the
independence of all Asia. Success in these two areas would establish
the credibility of American policy elsewhere. Late in January Assistant Secretary Rusk explained to the nation over NBC that ''we are in
Korea because we cannot afford to leave Red China and its
neighbors under the impression that the powers of Peiping are ir-
resistible and that Red China's neighbors must now come to terms
with communism at the cost of their freedom. . . .'' By resisting in
Korea, he said, the United Nations had forced the Chinese to commit
their resources of men and material which might otherwise be designated for aggression elsewhere. Much of the official American concern over defense focused on Southeast Asia where, declared Rusk,
the people of Indochina were in danger of being ''absorbed by force
into the new colonialism of a Soviet Communist empire.'' The
French, increasingly hard pressed in Indochina, supported their
claims to greater American financial aid by insisting that they no less
than people of the United States were engaged in fighting interna-

tional communism. Responding to the demands of Asian containment, the United States, after 1951, supported in Korea one of the world's largest non-Communist armies at a cost of almost $1 billion per year. In Indochina the United States eventually underwrote 80 percent of the financial expenditure of the French military effort.

Early in 1951 Washington moved toward a system of military alliances to strengthen its program of containment in Asia. "If the nations of Asia and the Pacific," declared Rusk in February, "conclude that it is time to come closer together in arrangements to safeguard the security and well-being of the area as a whole the United States will take a sympathetic interest in such development." One month later John Foster Dulles returned from the Far East where he had conducted negotiations on the Japanese peace treaty. In his report to the nation Dulles stressed the importance of Japan to any Asian defense structure. The time had come to convert a defeated enemy into a prosperous and stable ally. "It is not merely a matter of liquidating the old war with Japan," he said, "but of building a strong bulwark against the threat of Communist aggression from the East. . . . If Japan should succumb to Communist aggression, there would be a combination of Russian, Japanese, and Chinese power in the East which would be dangerously formidable."

By September of 1951 the Truman administration had negotiated a series of permanent military alliances in the Orient. Japan emerged as the key to the new alliance structure. That Japanese industrial recovery had been slow mattered little until it became clear by 1949 that the political and economic health of Japan was one essential element in the security of the western Pacific. To encourage Japanese economic development, the Japanese treaty imposed no restrictions on Japanese commerce and industry. It stripped Japan of its island possessions, including Okinawa, but it acknowledged Japan's right to self-defense and established the foundation for future Japanese rearmament. At the same time the United States retained the right to land and naval bases on Japanese territory. The Japanese treaty received approval in special ceremonies at San Francisco during September 1951.

Not all accepted the Japanese treaty with equanimity. Some Japanese citizens, recalling the price which Japan had paid for its previous military ventures, resented the thinly disguised American effort to rebuild Japan into another major power. Australian and New

Zealand officials shared that alarm. Remembering their narrow escape from Japanese invasion in 1942, they demanded special security guarantees from the United States before they would sign the Japanese treaty. United States officials joined representatives of Australia and New Zealand in signing the ANZUS pact at San Francisco in September 1951, hours before the Japanese treaty conference opened. Late in August the United States negotiated a similar bilateral defense treaty with the Philippines. The Senate ratified these pacts with Japan, the Philippines, Australia and New Zealand overwhelmingly during the spring of 1952. In these pacts, Dulles reminded Washington, the United States undertook no obligation except to consult in the event of an aggression.

For Washington the American interest in opposing Asian communism had become a "given," rarely if ever explicated internally or externally, rarely if ever questioned by those charged with the conduct of national policy. Early in 1952 the National Security Council issued a statement on "United States Objectives and Courses of Action with Respect to Southeast Asia." It presented the following proposition: "Communist domination, by whatever means, of all Southeast Asia would seriously endanger in the short term, and critically endanger in the longer run, United States security interests." What those security interests were, neither that document nor any which followed defined. Instead the document went on to warn: "In the absence of effective and timely counteraction, the loss of any single country would probably lead to relatively swift submission to or an alignment with communism by the remaining countries of [Southeast Asia]. Furthermore, an alignment with communism of the rest of Southeast Asia and India, and in the longer term, of the Middle East . . . would in all probability progressively follow: Such widespread alignment would endanger the stability and security of Europe." That language of despair created a paranoia, shared by military and civilian officials alike, which overlooked such fundamental determinants as culture, interest, and nationalism.

V

For President Dwight D. Eisenhower and Secretary of State Dulles the world they inherited from Harry S. Truman was scarcely reassuring. Early in 1953 the new President declared that the nation stood in greater peril than at any time in its history. What gave this massive danger its character—and indeed comprised its only sustaining rationale—was the concept of the international Communist monolith. Ambassador Rankin in Taipei saw this clearly when he wrote to Ambassador George V. Allen in India during July 1953. He reminded Allen that the United States could maintain its anti-Peking posture only by denying that Mao enjoyed any independence from Moscow. Whether or not this was true, wrote Rankin, the Chinese Nationalists feared that the United States might accept it as true and thereafter follow the course of Britain and India. "Only so long as they are persuaded that Americans continue to regard Mao simply as a Soviet tool," ran Rankin's warning, "will they feel reasonably assured as to our China policy."

What made the danger of expanding Sino-Soviet penetration into South and Southeast Asia appear so ominous was the theory that Marxism was antithetical to national sovereignty, and that communism would gradually destroy all national entities in Asia and create one vast community under Communist domination. To official Washington, Sino-Soviet imperialism was merely the Asiatic agent for the new universalism. "The Soviet leaders, in mapping their strategy for world conquest," warned Dulles in November 1953, "hit on nationalism as a device for absorbing the colonial peoples." The danger, Dulles noted further, rested in the ability of Communist agitators to aggravate the nationalist aspirations of people so that they would rebel violently against the existing order. Before a new stability could be created, the Communists would gain control of the nation and convey it into the Soviet orbit.

Thus Dulles reversed completely the traditional roles of communism and nationalism as forces impelling Asia toward a new condition. For him communism was not an adjunct of nationalism, giving purpose and direction to a particular program of state-building. Rather, nationalism was an adjunct of communism, to be exploited, not for the cause of national independence, but for the purpose of subjecting Asia to a new foreign rule. Walter P. McConaughy, Director of the Office of Chinese Affairs, stressed this official view in January 1954: "The siren song of communism in Asia, that it is spearheading a pan-Asiatic revolution against white colonialism and imperialism, has beguiled many Asians of good will who would not knowingly play the Communist game."

No spokesman of the Eisenhower administration expressed this thesis more cogently than did Loy W. Henderson at Winfield, Kansas, in May 1959:

> *The distortion of nationalism among many of the peoples of Africa, Asia, and Latin America into feelings of vindictiveness and envy is primarily the result of astute Communist agitation. Nationalism in itself is a noble sentiment. . . . International communism has, however, succeeded in degrading nationalism in certain areas of the world, in using it to nurture and enlarge upon outgrown or fancied wrongs, in transforming it from a constructive force to one of destruction and disintegration. . . . I have seen the trickery to which they have resorted in order to divert the rising tide of nationalism in certain countries into channels hostile to the West, particularly to the United States, which as a leader of the free world is their principal target. We cannot discount the seriousness of their successes in China, in north Korea, and in several Areas of southeastern Asia. . . . It is quite possible that the leaders of international communism will follow a course which, while avoiding the outbreak of war, will nevertheless keep the world in a turmoil for many years to come. They may hope that by making effective use of the highly disciplined masses under their control and by continuing to undermine the unity of the free world they can eventually take it over bit by bit without resort to a total war.*

Washington's verdict was clear: except for Communist agitation Asia would be stable and secure.

For Dulles the Communist threat to Indochina in 1954 was especially dangerous, demanding some form of "united action" to meet it. "Under the conditions of today," he told the Overseas Press Club of New York on March 29, 1954, "the imposition on Southeast Asia of the political system of Communist Russia and its Chinese Communist ally, by whatever means, would be a grave threat to the whole free community." If Indochina's Communist elite, using anti-French slogans to win public support, ever gained a military and political victory, warned Dulles, it would subject the Indochinese people to a cruel dictatorship which would take its orders from Moscow and Peking. But the tragedy would not stop there. "If the Communist forces won uncontested control over Indochina or any substantial part thereof," Dulles declared, "they would surely resume the same pattern of aggression against other free peoples in the area. . . . Communist control of Southeast Asia would carry a grave threat to the Philippines, Australia and New Zealand, with whom we have treaties of mutual assistance. The entire Western Pacific area, including the so-called 'offshore island chain,' would be strategically endangered." Dulles made no effort to explain why any of this would occur.

Several days later President Eisenhower, in a press conference, described as *falling dominoes* this process by which country after country, as if responding to some central force, would allegedly follow one another into the Communist camp. Dulles again warned against this danger at Manila in September when he addressed the members of the new Southeast Asia Treaty Organization (SEATO): "We are united by a common danger, and the danger stems from international communism and its insatiable ambition. We know that wherever it makes gains, as in Indochina, these gains are looked on, not as final solutions, but as bridgeheads for future gains." Despite such broad definitions of danger to Southeast Asia, the administration attributed to China a special role in the Indochinese upheaval. "If China were not Communist," declared Vice President Richard M. Nixon in January 1954, "there would be no war in Indochina. . . ." The Eisenhower administration, no less than that of Harry Truman, denied the existence of any fundamentally indigenous, nationalistic quality in Indochina's struggle for independence.

This concept of falling dominoes was, despite its wide acceptance, a puzzling one, for it assumed that the government and people of one country would carry out the policies of another even at the cost of war and self-destruction. Still it was not clear that the Kremlin could move Communists everywhere, as pawns, into wars of revolution designed to further its influence and authority in a divided world, or that men and women would risk their lives and property in causes that were not their own. The Soviets with a minimum expenditure of words could identify their interests with a revolutionary movement, whether Communist-led or not. They could encourage it with assertions that they were leading a war of national liberation; they might even supply revolutionaries with quantities of arms and equipment. Revolutionary conflicts, under any circumstances, would appear as unsettling devices for achieving change and thus a matter of proper concern to those governments and people of the world who favored the status quo. But Washington never demonstrated that the Soviets could manufacture revolutionary situations or control whatever revolutionary movements they elected to support. Nor did the Kremlin claim such power.

Revolution in itself could scarcely serve the expansionist interests of others. For any successful revolution required both a local base of power and the support of indigenous conditions and issues which might enable its leaders to promise the immediate prospect of better, more effective, government as well as the guarantee of modernization and social change. All revolutionary elites of postwar Asia and Africa, in their emphasis on national performance, were fundamentally nationalistic, whatever the precise programs of economic reconstruction and state-building their ideological preferences might dictate. Such revolutionaries might accept external aid with both hands; they would not accept external control. As the Vietminh moved beyond the immediate goal of removing the French and prepared to restructure the society of North Vietnam along lines consonant with Communist dogma, its purpose embraced a series of domestic "economic leveling" reforms, such as special taxes against the wealthier peasants and businessmen, land rent reduction, and land reform. These "reforms" reinforced the trend toward centralization and socialization, but they served the purpose of no international crusade. In the tenth reading Richard Harris challenges the notion of a monolithic global Communist conspiracy and attempts rather to explain the general absence of a powerful, expansionist communism in Asia.

Washington predicted disaster if containment at the 17th parallel, which after the Geneva Conference of 1954 divided North from United States-supported South Vietnam, should falter, but it never demonstrated why this was true. This mattered little. As long as the regime in Saigon and the new SEATO alliance guaranteed successful containment at little cost, the Eisenhower administration faced no necessity to explain what United States policy was really containing. The intellectual and policy dilemmas of the future were already clear. For the ends of policy assumed a global danger of which Ho's Hanoi regime comprised only a minor segment. Yet the means of policy, as they evolved during the Eisenhower years, did not include even a defense against Hanoi, much less against Moscow and Peking (presumably included in the more abstract phrase, Communist aggression). If the latter two nations comprised the essential danger to American security interests in Asia, policies aimed at the disposal of Ho's ambitions, whatever their success, would not touch, much less resolve, the dangers posed by the two leading Communist powers. If, on the other hand, the challenge to United States security lay in Hanoi, then the rhetoric of a Soviet-based global danger—the initial and continuing rationale for opposing Ho—had no meaning. Whatever the global pressures that demanded successful containment of communism in Asia, the United States would behave as if the danger comprised no more than North Vietnam's determination to unseat the Saigon regime. Washington never contemplated war with China or Russia to settle the question of South Vietnam.

VI

Dulles's Washington never denied the close relationship between Peking and Moscow, although with time it dropped the earlier concept of complete Chinese subservience for that of a Sino-Soviet partnership. The Secretary expressed his view of that relationship in an interview of July 1957: "As far as we can judge, the nations which are within the Sino-Soviet bloc are all dominated by what can fairly be called international communism, a single group which provides a guiding force." The State Department sustained that judgment in its August 1958 memorandum to all United States missions abroad. Attacking the notion that the recognition of Peking might weaken that regime's ties with Moscow, the memorandum declared: "The alliance between Moscow and Peiping is one of long standing; it traces its origin to the very founding of the Chinese Communist Party in 1921, in which representatives of the Comintern played an important role. It is based on a common ideology and on mutually held objectives with respect to the non-Communist world." Even as the Eisenhower administration entered its final months, Under Secretary of State Robert Murphy assured a New York audience: "Some day this might become a most uneasy partnership. However, this day seems far in the future, and in the present in which we must operate there is little doubt but that both Moscow and Peiping regard the continuation of their close alliance as being of overriding importance." This new perception of the Sino-Soviet amalgam elevated China to the status of an aggressor in its own right.

Indeed, during the late fifties, as Nikita Khrushchev managed to establish more reassuring relationships with the United States, China emerged as the dominant threat to Asian stability—the major partner in the Asian Communist monolith. In his noted San Francisco address of June 1957, Dulles reminded his audience that China "fought the United Nations in Korea; it supported the Communist war in Indochina; it took Tibet by force. It fomented the Communist Huk rebellion in the Philippines and the Communists' insurrection in Malaya." Peking did not disguise its expansionist ambitions. It was, said Dulles, bitterly hateful of the United States which it considered the principal obstacle in its path of conquest. Later that year William J. Sebald, Ambassador to Australia, condemned China in what had become standard phraseology. The core of the problem in the Pacific, he said, "is the deadly hostility of the Chinese Communist regime with its unwavering espousal of the principles of Marxism-Leninism. These principles, as we know, envisage the conquest of the non-Communist world and the destruction of free institutions." The subservient China of mid-century, with its aggressiveness dictated by Moscow, had now replaced Russia as the primary source of Asia's turmoil.

By no means had China, in American eyes, achieved full independence from the Kremlin, for the acknowledgment of Chinese independence would have destroyed the major rationale for nonrecognition. However grave the Chinese threat to Asia, nonrecognition carried the chief burden for both the containment and the eventual liberation of the mainland. Even as the perception of China's Asian role changed during the fifties, nonrecognition required a perennial denial that the Peking regime represented the Chinese people. Since a traditional, non-Communist government in Peking would pose no danger to Asia, official American rhetoric could sustain the perennial fear of China only as long as it continued to accuse the mainland leadership of imposing an alien minority rule on an intimidated Chinese populace. As late as March 1959, Walter S. Robertson, Assistant Secretary of State for Far Eastern Affairs, reminded a Canadian audience that the Republic of China on Formosa was the true representative of the Chinese people: "Let no one say that representation is being denied to 600 million mainland Chinese. The fanatical Marxists of Peiping come no closer to representing the will and aspirations of the Chinese people than the puppet regime of Budapest comes to representing the will and aspirations of the Hungarian people or William Z. Foster comes to representing the will and aspirations of the American people."

Still it was apparent even then that the Sino-Soviet relationship after mid-century was never as cordial or mutually reassuring as United States officials insisted. Milovan Djilas, the noted Yugoslav writer on Soviet affairs, observed in 1957 that China no less than Russia had experienced an independent revolution and thus remained independent as a Communist state even when under the most extreme Soviet influence—that is, in a condition of "eternal friendship" with it. Any successful revolution, Djilas wrote, carried a new class to power and control; no such group would willingly surrender its hard-won gains. He continued:

> Where a Communist revolution has won victory independently, a separate, distinct path of development is inevitable. Friction with other Communist countries, especially with the Soviet Union as the most important and most imperialistic state, follows. The ruling national bureaucracy in the country where the victorious revolution took place has already become independent in the course of the armed struggle and has tasted the blessings of authority. . . . Philosophically speaking, it has also grasped and become conscious of its own essence, "its own state," its authority, on the basis of which it claims equality.

That same year Benjamin Schwartz, represented in the eleventh reading, stressed the limits of ideological solidarity in the Sino-Soviet alliance.

Long before 1960 the evidence pouring out of Moscow and Peking dramatized the growing tensions between the two countries over a wide range of historic and ideological issues. Even in the early fifties Sino-Soviet relations did not fit Washington's official description, for throughout the twentieth century Russia and China had sustained a high level of mutual animosity. Ideology could not overcome the conflicting interests which had perpetuated the earlier antagonism. Yet the disagreements which existed after mid-century did not break into open controversy; for a half dozen years the two Communist powers maintained a semblance of cooperation and ideological affinity. Perhaps the years from 1953 to 1958 comprised the Golden Age in Sino-Soviet diplomacy, although before that period ended the cordiality had begun to wear thin. Nikita Khrushchev's attack on Stalin at the Twentieth Congress of 1956 and the resulting clash between the continuing hard-line ideological preferences of the Chinese and the softer revisionism of the Soviets produced a major symbolic and ideological break. Even as Khrushchev stressed the need for coexistence between East and West, Chinese pronouncements, which embraced claims to ideological purity, became more strident and aggressive in tone. Sino-Soviet differences over world strategy became clear during 1960 at both the Bucharest conference of June and the Moscow conference of November. The Chinese refused to abandon Lenin's view, discarded by the Soviets in 1956, that war between capitalism and communism was inevitable.

At the policy level the Quemoy crisis of August 1958 clarified the growing conflict in Sino-Soviet perceptions of danger and the chasm dividing Russian from Chinese interests. Peking coordinated its shelling of the off-shore islands with an effort to invoke its treaty arrangements with Moscow. With the launching of the first Soviet sputniks in the immediate background, the Peking government pressed the Kremlin to support its objectives in the Formosa Strait with some form of nuclear diplomacy. This pressure carried with it an essential test of the character and value of the Sino-Soviet alliance. Soviet abstinence, accompanied by clear warnings that Peking's problems with the Republic of China were and would remain China's own, demonstrated the limited efficacy of any Chinese reliance on Soviet military power. Chinese leaders demanded cooperative policies of opposition to the United States, especially in the Far East. Early in 1960 Peking warned Moscow that the socialist camp would be built only "on a basis of brotherly alliance of equality, mutual respect, mutual assistance, and the common goal of socialism and communism." To China's spokesmen the Russians had abandoned a socialist ally to improve their relations with the imperialists. Even as the Chinese denunciations of Soviet moderation became more open and abusive, they had little effect on actual Chinese behavior. How the Sino-Soviet ideological and policy split affected the Communist parties of Asia Robert A. Scalapino discusses in the twelfth reading.

Despite the universal evidence of the Sino-Soviet rift after 1960, the official American perceptions of the dangers which Asia posed changed little in the transition to John F. Kennedy's Democratic leadership of the early sixties. The new administration accepted the assumptions and postures inherited from the Eisenhower years with little hesitation. In official American language the Moscow-Peking axis remained united on essentials and therefore dangerous. Secretary of State Dean Rusk denied in July 1961 that the prospects of a

Sino-Soviet rift could serve as the basis of sound policy. "I think," he declared, "there is solid evidence of some tensions between Moscow and Peiping, but I would use a little caution in trying to estimate the width of such gap as might be developing between them.. ... [H]ere are two great systems of power which are united in general in a certain doctrinal framework and which together have certain common interests vis-à-vis the rest of the world." Whatever differences separated Peking from Moscow, the disagreements, ran Washington's official view, were over means, not ends. As one administration spokesman remarked in February 1963, "A dispute over how to bury the West is no grounds for Western rejoicing." Shortly thereafter Rusk warned the country in an NBC interview to be "careful about taking premature comfort from arguments within the Communist world as to how best to bury us." Adviser Averell Harriman that year likewise limited the Sino-Soviet quarrel to methods, not objectives. "Both Moscow and Peiping," he said, "are determined that communism shall sweep the world, but there is a deep difference between them concerning the methods to be employed." Indeed, believed Harriman, the deepening conflict between Moscow and Peking would increase the danger from Communist pressures, for the conflict had stimulated both countries to expand their activities, especially in the less-developed areas of the world.

Even more than in the late Eisenhower years China was viewed as the dominant threat to the small countries of Asia. Assistant Secretary Roger W. Hilsman defined the Kennedy administration's standard view of China in an address of June 1963: "In Asia the greatest danger to independent nations comes from Communist China, with its 700 million people forced into the service of an aggressive Communist Party. . . . Communist China lies in direct contact with, or very close to, a whole series of free nations. . . . All these free nations must deal with the facts of Communist China and its ambitions." Kennedy accepted the given assumptions of Chinese responsibility for the instability of Southeast Asia. Without hesitation he claimed validity for the domino theory. "I believe it," he said, "China is so large, looms so high just beyond the frontiers, that if South Vietnam went, it would not only give them an improved geographic position for a guerrilla assault on Malaya, but would also give them the impression that the wave of the future in southeast Asia was China and the Communists. So I believe it."

No less than earlier, the United States government under Kennedy and his successor, Lyndon B. Johnson, saw the specter of international communism in Vietnam. Both presidents and their advisers accepted the orthodox view that American failure in South Vietnam would lead to the extension of Communist despotism through South and Southeast Asia, to India, and eventually to Australia and New Zealand. Secretary of Defense Robert McNamara reported late in 1961 that he, his deputy, and the Joint Chiefs of Staff agreed that the "fall of South Vietnam to Communism would lead to the fairly rapid extension of Communist control, or complete accommodation to Communism, in the rest of mainland Southeast Asia and in Indonesia. The strategic implications worldwide, particularly in the Orient, would be extremely serious." The Secretary made no effort to define the enemy or to suggest the means whereby it would, by capturing Saigon, gain control of the Orient. Again in March 1964, McNamara argued that unless the United States could sustain the Saigon government, "almost all of Southeast Asia will probably fall under Communist dominance (all of Vietnam, Laos and Cambodia), accommodate to Communism so as to remove effective U.S. and anti-Communist influence (Burma) or fall under the domination of forces not now explicitly Communist but likely then to become so (Indonesia taking over Malaysia). . . . Even the Philippines would become shaky, and the threat to India to the west, Australia and New Zealand to the south, and Taiwan, Korea and Japan to the northeast would be greatly increased."

Vietnam acquired its strange importance simply because successive Washington administrations said it was important. Yet none of them ever managed to demonstrate why this small jungle country had come to control Asia's destiny. What aggravated the problem of unwinding the long and costly involvement was the rhetorical escalation employed to cover the nation's elusive stakes in Vietnam. Still, national obligation stops short of massive self-injury. For a dozen years the war tore at the fabric of American society without achieving much promise of victory. If the vast expenditure of American resources—many times that available to the enemy—failed to gain the nation's purposes, the explanation lay outside the American effort. It resided either in the failure of leadership in Saigon or in the nature of the enemy which refused to succumb to American will by negotiating on United States terms.

Washington courted disaster from the beginning when it invariably assured Saigon that American support was both limitless and everlasting. Such policy seldom encourages efficiency or realism in the recipient. But the ultimate failure lay in Washington's perennial refusal to recognize that Hanoi's strength lay in nationalism, not in visions of falling dominoes. The challenge posed by Ho Chi Minh was concrete, not abstract; limited, not universal. The nation's costly experience in Vietnam did not deny that intervention conducted in a vacuum of nationalism might reap momentary, perhaps even permanent, political change. It revealed, however, that intervention, when introduced in opposition to a nationalist movement, arouses such dogged resistance that the price of war eventually exceeds the anticipated gains.

VII

What confirmed Washington's perception of a dangerous and aggressive China was Marshal Lin Piao's doctrinal article which appeared in the Peking press on September 3, 1965. This manifesto of the Chinese Defense Minister proclaimed a worldwide people's war against the West and thereby reaffirmed Peking's commitment to global revolution. For Lin the countryside—the underdeveloped regions of Asia, Africa, and Latin America—would provide the revolutionary bases from which the revolutionaries would go forward to final victory over the cities—the industrialized regions of North America and Western Europe. This revolution, admitted Lin, would be long and costly, but it would triumph. For, he explained:

> However highly developed modern weapons and technical equipment may be, and however complicated the methods of modern warfare, in the final analysis the outcome of a war will be decided by the sustained fighting of the ground forces, by the fighting at close quarters on battlefields, by the political consciousness of the men, by their courage and spirit of sacrifice. The spiritual atom bomb that the revolutionary people possess is a far more powerful and useful weapon than the physical atom bomb.

Lin Piao's manifesto appears in reading thirteen.

United States officials and their supporters in the press accepted Lin's statement with profound seriousness. Here was the ultimate defense for a policy of universal opposition to the Peking regime, for Lin had announced to the world, in concrete terms, both the ends and the means of Chinese expansion. Arthur Goldberg condemned Lin before the U.N. for proclaiming that "the Marxist-Leninists . . . never take a gloomy view of war. . . ." True, the doctrine called for revolution, but by the natives of each country; thus it was largely a "do-it-yourself" program. "But," warned Rusk in April 1966, "Peking is prepared to train and indoctrinate the leaders of these revolutions and to support them with funds, arms, and propaganda, as well as politically. It is even prepared to manufacture these revolutionary movements out of whole cloth." The mainland regime, said Rusk, had encouraged and assisted the aggressions in Vietnam and Laos; it had supported the national liberation forces in Thailand. Malaysia reportedly was next on the list. But the aggressions had gone far beyond Asia; they had penetrated Africa and Latin America as well. Peking's new challenge, warned the Secretary, would lead to catastrophe if not met in a timely fashion. Franz Michael's analysis in reading fourteen provides an evaluation of China as an expansive force in Asia.

Still others insisted that Mao pursued the foreign policies of China, not of communism, and that Chinese support for revolutionary movements in Asia, Africa, and Latin America was marginal and largely inconsequential. Except for the Republic of China on Formosa not one Asian country shared the official United States view of China as a dangerous, expansive state. Every Asian regime capable of independent action had one or more enemies that it regarded more threatening than China. Japan regarded Russia, not China, as the major threat to its security. For Thailand, Laos, South Vietnam, and Cambodia the danger lay in Hanoi, not Peking. Pakistan regarded India its mortal enemy. Pakistani leaders, siding with China, believed that India used its 1962 border dispute with China to obtain military aid from the United States and the U.S.S.R. so that one day it might attack Pakistan more effectively. Indonesia, Malaysia, and the Philippines lay outside the effective range of Chinese action. It was not strange that the United States could never build an effective alliance against China. So limiting was the power of the Soviet Union, India, Indonesia, and even the smaller states of Southeast Asia that China could scarcely appear as a menace to its neighbors. Even

India, in direct conflict with China, refused to regard Peking as dangerous or evil.

No Asian country, including Taiwan, accused the Chinese of aggression in their use of force in Korea, Tibet, the Formosan Strait, and along the Indian border. Asian leaders attributed Chinese action less to expansionism than to nationalism, defense strategy, and traditional Chinese behavior. Every Communist movement in Asia revealed an independence from Moscow and Peking which increased with its success. Neither North Korea nor North Vietnam would accept a position of subordination to either China or Russia. Arguing in 1967 that the small Communist-led nations of East Asia would resist Chinese expansion with greater determination than would China's other Asian neighbors, David P. Mozingo of Cornell University concluded:

> It is by no means clear at this point that China's leaders would prefer to see stable, independent, diverse and highly nationalistic Communist regimes in Southeast Asia in preference to the indefinite existence of the present weak non-Communist regimes led by men who are willing to defer to China's interests as long as China respects the essential sovereignty of their countries. None of the elites of the principal Asian powers, Japan, India, Pakistan and Indonesia, on whose future political and military stance a great deal of China's ultimate position in Asia depends, has shown itself to be anybody's pawn–Russia's, China's or America's.

Oliver M. Lee's 1967 essay, which appears as the fifteenth reading, is an analysis of China as a limited threat to Asia.

A half-decade later the American perception of an aggressive China, meriting every United States effort to isolate it diplomatically, politically, and economically, had succumbed to a revolution in American foreign policy. To President Richard M. Nixon must go the credit or blame for this profound reversal in Washington's official outlook and behavior. Still, if improved United States-Chinese relations demanded new attitudes and perceptions in Washington, it required, as well, conditions elsewhere which would encourage China to identify its deepest interests with that improvement. No American initiatives toward China would have succeeded without the knowledge that they would be received without rancor. China's external relations toward the world generally had fallen on bad times by the mid-sixties. Even then those Far Eastern scholars who argued for the recognition of the Peking regime before the Senate Foreign Relations Committee during March of 1966 agreed that American initiatives would benefit the United States only by casting the blame for China's isolation on Peking. What lay behind the ping-pong diplomacy of the early seventies was the reality of the Sino-Soviet antagonism which official American rhetoric had persistently denied. James C. Thomson, Jr. analyzes, in the sixteenth reading, the changes in China's world outlook that formed the basis of the new détente.

Nixon's new approach to China, which commenced as early as 1969, culminated in his trip to Peking in February 1972, and in the establishment of a permanent United States diplomatic post in China during April 1973. This evolution reflected the President's conviction that peace in Asia required the recognition of China as a major power as well as the possible Chinese contribution to the stability and progress of Asia. By acknowledging the legitimacy of the Chinese government—which four previous administrations had refused to do—Nixon expected Peking to acknowledge the legitimacy of the existing diplomatic order in Asia and the limits of proper political conduct. The new American approach to China assumed, in short, a general equilibrium in Asian affairs and a fundamental desire in Peking to accept the conditions which then prevailed.

That the President's new diplomacy enjoyed almost universal public approval in the United States was not strange. For many Americans the older attitudes and intentions toward mainland China, defended with such flamboyant phraseology, never made much sense. Indeed, they belonged largely to that minority which had a political and emotional stake in the nation's diplomatic and political attachment to the Republic of China. Long before the seventies the charges of Chinese aggression ceased to carry much conviction. Much of the public attitude had moved ahead of policy. As Walter Lippmann observed in October 1971: "The old anti-Communist crusading in which you had to outlaw and blackball anything Chinese had been dead for some time. The reason there was no outcry about the reversal was that it was made under the auspices of a certified anti-Communist like Nixon. There was nothing to object to." Similarly, William Pfaff, writing in *The New Yorker* of June 3, 1972, believed that Nixon's China initiative, while it seemed daring enough, merely capitalized on a suppressed popular impulse for change. "It reversed," wrote Pfaff, "an American China policy that under a succession of previous Administrations had delivered blows, bluster, and grand denunciations in the name of democracy and liberty. That way of conducting ourselves before the world . . . had become so corrupt in recent years, so sterile and thick with hypocrisy, that the country was ready for some Metternichian realism. . . ."

Clearly the Asia of the seventies scarcely resembled the old vision of a continent rent by a dangerous and revolutionary bi-polar struggle. The developments of the early seventies suggested that the lines of major tension in Asia were receding before a realignment of world power. Washington's initiatives toward Moscow and Peking in 1972 encouraged Japan to establish closer relationships with both China and Russia. Japan's influence in Asia expanded with that country's trade and investment around the continent's eastern and southern rim. The powerful bonds between the United States and Japan showed signs of strain. China and the U.S.S.R. were in direct confrontation everywhere across Asia. As early as 1969 Moscow offered defense pacts to defend the countries of Southeast Asia against an aggressive China. Peking retaliated in 1972 by inviting the United States to maintain its bases in Southeast Asia.

Much of the President's new pentagonal world embraced Asia where four powers competed in a fluid relationship. Nothing dramatized more clearly the revolution in the American perception of Asia and the world than the President's assumption of a new balance of power. "We must remember," he declared in January 1972, "the only time in the history of the world that we have had any extended period of peace is when there has been a balance of power. . . . I think it will be a safer world and a better world if we have a strong, healthy United States, Europe, Soviet Union, China, Japan—each balancing the other. . . ."

Late in 1971 the Peking government replaced the Republic of China in the U.N. without producing distress among the American people or bringing disaster to either the U.N. or the free nations of Asia. Whatever the purpose or the necessity of the earlier tensions between the United States and China, those antagonisms never disintegrated into open conflict. Yet the perennial posture of nonrecognition and the words which underwrote it were not without their costs. For they made China the enemy and propelled the country into a wide variety of treaties and guarantees around the eastern fringes of the Pacific with consequences which could require a generation to correct. It was the fear of China especially that sustained the concept of falling dominoes and underwrote the growing United States involvement in Southeast Asia after 1960. As late as 1969 Secretary of State Henry Kissinger based his approach to peace in Vietnam on a presumed Moscow-Peking influence over Hanoi which really never existed. Even as the South Vietnamese armies disintegrated during April 1975, Kissinger warned the country that the collapse of American purpose in Southeast Asia would endanger American interests elsewhere. The Secretary sought thereby to keep alive the assumption that events in Vietnam somehow affected the status of governments and policies throughout Asia and beyond.

In 1972 Fred Branfman, in *Voices from the Plain of Jars*, recounted the massive high- and low-level bombing of Laos's Plain of Jars by United States aircraft through more than five years. Branfman went on to pose questions regarding the American involvement in Southeast Asia: "What does it mean when leaders of the richest and most technologically advanced nation in history use all their weaponry short of nuclear arms against rice farmers who pose the most marginal of challenges to their interests? When they deprive their own citizens of so many billions of dollars in order to wage a secret automated war halfway across the globe, bombing a sparsely populated, rural land of which their own people are but dimly aware?" By September 1975, Laos, like South Vietnam, had fallen into Communist hands. Perhaps it was always true that the rice farmers of Indochina were no threat to American security, but the official United States perceptions of a Soviet-based international conspiracy, which began so imperceptibly in 1947 and thereafter came to dominate American thought and action regarding Asia, transformed the rice farmers into enemies of the United States—the spear-carriers of a Kremlin-directed assault on the free world. Thereafter the United States fought the farmers of Indochina as if they were indeed the willing mercenaries of the Soviets, seeking to conquer in the name and for the purpose of their external masters. As such, ran the official dogma, they merited the death and destruction which they suffered at American hands.

Through the thirty years which began with the end of World War II in 1945 and ended when Ambassador Graham Martin escaped from the roof of the beleagured American embassy in Saigon late in April 1975, the United States played a complex and demanding role in Asia as a "surrogate colonial power." In every country of South and Southeast Asia, except Burma, the United States government was for many years the dominant external factor. Much of the American presence responded to Asia's postwar needs and took the form of political guidance and economic and technical assistance. That which assumed the existence in Asia of a global danger dictated the need for alliances, the positioning of military forces, and ultimately two enervating and divisive wars—in Korea and Vietnam. Much of the American effort failed because Washington miscalculated both the nature of the threat and the capacity of American military and economic power to determine Asia's destiny. Nor was it clear that the continued United States political-military attachment to Taiwan was serving the larger American interest in strengthening its relations with the Chinese mainland.

If the cost of United States policies in Asia had been both physically and emotionally prodigious, not even the ultimate collapse of those policies in Southeast Asia during 1975 produced one official statement which attempted, with some precision, to define the relationship between communism and nationalism in Asia. Richard Holbrooke asked in September 1975: "Aren't we forgetting that the domino theory was simply one small, rhetorical image from the anti-China containment policy that we ourselves had ended, voluntarily, in 1971?" If the American people had escaped the domino trap, it was because of the pain they had suffered as the result of their Asian involvement, not because of increased understanding. Thus the nation emerged from its long, enervating involvement with China and Indochina without receiving that instruction which alone could establish the intellectual foundations for more satisfactory policies in the future and thereby offer some compensation for past expenditures.

I NATIONALISM AND COMMUNISM IN ASIA

G. W. Seabridge

WAR AND NATIONALISM IN SOUTHEAST ASIA

G. W. Seabridge was among those Europeans who evacuated the Far East "with more haste than dignity" with the collapse of the old empires in 1942. In the following essay, an address to the Cape Town Branch of the South African Institute of International Affairs delivered on September 6, 1944, he recalled the circumstances of his escape from Southeast Asia and recognized in those circumstances the fundamental weakness of the Western empires in the face of anti-colonial sentiment. In part the problems of returning would be material–securing sufficient food and supplies for Europeans and natives alike. But for Seabridge the more pervading challenge would be the impact which the Japanese were exerting on the Asian mind, an impact predicted earlier by the varied native behavior during the Japanese conquest of the Philippines, the Netherlands Indies, Malaya, Burma, and Thailand. In Asian eyes the white race had failed; the whites, Seabridge warned, would return in humility or not at all. Certainly for him the only recognizable force for change in Southeast Asia was nationalism.

I have been puzzled for some time past by the persistence with which many of my fellow evacuees from the Far East believe that immediately the Pacific war ends, they will be able to board a ship and disembark in due course at Singapore, Rangoon, Batavia, Manila or Saigon, and straightway pick up the threads of the lives they lived up to 1940. If my reading of the situation is within measurable distance of accuracy, the future holds for us much that is disturbing to contemplate, much that calls for deep thought and careful planning, if we are to fashion firm foundations of which to rebuild in more than the material sense. The manner in which we return to countries from which we departed with more haste than dignity must be conditioned by many factors, some of which can be assessed fairly accurately at the present stage, and others that are quite unpredictable. A single point illustrates the folly of expecting that the gates will be thrown open to all who wish to return within a few weeks of the cessation of the fighting. We know that food is scarce in the occupied countries; public amenities have been subordinated to the enemy's needs. At

Reprinted by permission from "Some Problems of the White Man's Return to South-East Asia," *International Affairs* 21 (April 1945):196–205.

the time of the re-occupation, health services may be bad, or they may be very bad. They will certainly be far below the standards that were considered to be an absolute minimum before capitulation. There will be a great deal of hard pioneering to be done all over again, much of it in difficult climatic conditions. To allow any large-scale influx of Europeans before that work is far advanced, before food shortages have been rectified and essential services restored to something approaching normal, would constitute an invitation to disaster. And it must be remembered that demands for labor, supplies and expert guidance will come simultaneously from many directions. No doubt we can all make some sort of case for the grant of priority to a particular country in which we are personally interested. Nevertheless, there must be delays somewhere, and it will not be for the individual to decide how far a special locality is to be favored.

But those are essentially material problems, problems of supply to meet measurable needs. If nothing more difficult lay ahead, we should have little cause for apprehension. But the material considerations are of relatively minor importance, if we are to plan successfully for the distant future.

The manner of the return of the white man to the Far East must be governed to a large extent by the manner of his departure therefrom. It must be governed in some measure by the political atmosphere prevailing at the time of his departure. Those are ponderables, although they vary acutely as between the many smaller territories of the Pacific area. The return must also be influenced by several factors that are at present imponderable. They include the behavior of the Japanese now, and in the closing days of their occupancy; the effect produced on the Asiatic mind by a long period of intensive and undisputed propanganda by the enemy; the manner in which the local peoples react to the experience of seeing the white man only as a captive in the hands of a fellow-Asiatic. Again, countries which have to be fought over once more are not likely to be well served by plans prepared on the assumption that they will be re-occupied without further violence. And who can say where the Japanese will fight, and where he will not fight? No plan providing for anything approaching uniform treatment of the whole Pacific area has the smallest chance of success. Conditions differed markedly at the time of surrender, and they will differ still more markedly when the Japanese are expelled. It is impossible, for example, to group the whole of the smaller territories of the Pacific and define a level of political advancement applicable to them all. It is impossible to set a level of loyalty to the white man that would cover all peoples when they were last subject to white rule, or nominally under the protection of the white races. Unfortunately the nearest we can approach to uniformity is the failure of the white man to fulfill his undertakings to provide for these many countries and peoples adequate protection against aggression. We know the reasons for that failure. We were the victims of circumstances. Far Eastern territories had to be relinquished temporarily in the wider interest. We can explain the occurrence quite simply, and to our own complete satisfaction. But it is impossible to suppress all doubt in any attempt to assess the degree of conviction which the explanation will convey to the Asiatic mind, particularly the mind of the Asiatic whose loyalty to the white man was an uncertain quantity before his abandonment. In this connection, we would do well to remember that that amiable weakness of attaching paramount importance to our own particular experience is not a monopoly of the white man.

Just as there was a lack of uniformity in the political advancement and loyalty of the various communities, so was there lack of uniformity in the measure and character of the resistance offered to the enemy in the different countries that he overran. In the Philippines a Filipino army fought with the utmost gallantry and on terms of almost complete equality with the American garrison. In Netherlands India there were regular forces of Asiatics officered by Europeans. Their status was not so near to complete equality with the white man as that of the Filipino, but those Javanese soldiers and sailors also fought magnificently. Their experience in that fighting, coupled with the unhappy outcome of a campaign that was directed by white men, may be expected to have a pronounced effect on their political outlook in the future. Before the war there was in Netherlands India a Nationalist movement that was sturdy but fairly amenable. I predict that it will be much less amenable when the next Dutch Governor General takes up residence in Batavia.

Malaya had one infantry regiment comprised of Malays, plus a handful of Malays, Indians, locally born Chinese and Eurasians serving in the Royal Artillery, the Royal Engineers and the various Volunteer units. For the rest, the effect of the indigenous population was confined to the work of passive defense. Whatever the people of that country were called upon to do, they did with the utmost enthusiasm and courage. I have lived among those Malays and Malayan Chinese in good days and bad. In the good days they were delightful friends and colleagues; in the bad days they were magnificent fellow-citizens. At the end, disappointment and sorrow were writ large on their faces, but very, very few words were said to carry the smallest hint of reproach. I offer grateful tribute to those people, not as a mere formality, but in complete sincerity, as one who is deeply conscious of his own security at a time when others are left to bear the consequences of inability to implement promises, given in the name of the people of a protecting Power that failed to protect. The complaint of the Malayan peoples when disaster overtook them was not that they had been called upon to do too much, not that they were inadequately defended, but that they had not been allowed to do enough in their own defense. They had accepted the assurance of protection; they had sought no independence. By a great majority they favored retention of a system of benevolent autocracy in which they held faith to the end. Will there be any cause for surprise if they show indications of a belief that they could have done less badly for themselves than was done for them? By what right can we expect complete survival, or even the ultimate revival, of unbounded confidence in ourselves and our system? We may be fortunate in that respect, but only if we show an immense amount of tact, and not a little unaccustomed humility.

Burma provides further evidence of a lack of uniformity prevailing before the war and which must be regarded as inevitable after it. In Burma there was a powerful anti-British element which seized upon the Japanese invasion as an opportunity for settling old scores. Many of the leaders of the revolutionary movement now occupy positions of power under the Japanese. They may be expected to fight for the retention of that power, and to do everything possible to prevent restoration of a form of rule to which they were bitterly opposed.

Indo-China presents problems of a different character. Her rulers were placed in a quandary by Japanese threats and demands. Even so, the weakness of their attitude, the very half-hearted nature of the resistance offered and the final system of collaboration agreed to were disastrous from the point of view of European prestige. I need not stress the importance of "face" in the estimation of the Asiatic peoples. Nor, unhappily, is it necessary to quote chapter and verse in support of a statement that in 1942 the face of the white man was very dirty indeed—and nowhere dirtier than in Indo-China.

Siam is a case apart. She was a fully independent State, weak in every particular, yet occupying a position of vital strategic importance, with frontiers adjoining Indo-China, Burma and Malaya. She is recovering from the aftermath of an almost bloodless revolution, and her people were intoxicated by an illusion of new-found power when the position in the Pacific began to worsen. She was ruled by opportunists, some of whom were concerned with increasing the status of their country by any means that came to hand, while others acted from motives of personal gain. They did not scruple to betray. They played off one Power against another with what must have appeared to them to be marked success, until the Japanese threw off the cloak of pretense and insisted on receiving full payment for favors granted. Siamese political maneuvers from 1939 to 1941, and their culmination, were such as to make the white man appear excessively stupid in the eyes of the Siamese people. To what extent that opinion will be changed by experience of life under Japanese protection, coupled with the knowledge that all the treachery and the subtlety led only to the backing of the wrong horse, remains to be seen. But I cannot understand, in view of Siam's record of double dealing and the vital importance of her geographical position, how the future of that particular small nation can be allowed to conform to the assurances that this war is being fought to ensure the absolute freedom of all small nations. A free Siam was as potent a factor in the precipitation of the Pacific disaster as the vacillation of the administration of Indo-China. The resurgence of France will reduce to negligible proportions, if not eliminate entirely, the possibility of a recurrence of a situation that was a direct outcome of the collapse of metropolitan France in 1940. But the crux of the Siamese problem is Siamese freedom. If complete independence is to be restored to that country, it will not be many years before Bangkok is again a hotbed of intrigue, of bidding and counter-bidding by persons intent upon securing the key points for further acts of aggression. . . .

It must be remembered that in each of the smaller countries of South-East Asia there is a substantial Chinese population. Many of those people are locally-born and they have played prominent parts in local affairs. They have been among the most loyal subjects of

Great Britain, the United States, France or the Netherlands. But their greatest loyalty is to China. He who slights the land of their ancestors is their enemy, whoever he may be, wherever he may be. Those overseas Chinese will exert a tremendous influence on the future of the Pacific areas, and their conduct as collaborators or opponents of the systems we seek to restore or establish in the countries of their domicile will depend to a large extent on the attitude adopted by us in our dealings with their homeland. The Chinese contributed greatly to the prewar development of the many Pacific lands to which they had emigrated; they lost much by the white man's failure to hold those lands against Japanese aggression. They will have it in their power to do a great deal to make or mar the work of reconstruction, and it is vitally necessary, not only that we should keep faith with China as a nation, but that we should destroy, wherever we find it, any remaining belief that the Chinese people are born to subservience. They are a proud race and an ambitious one. They are industrious and they possess marked creative ability. They are adaptable and their country possesses great natural resources. They are fully conscious of their assets and their qualities, and determined to make the most of them.

For some years after the war, China will need immense quantities of manufactured goods and services. During that period she will again offer great scope for the British and American merchant and technician. But industrial development is likely to be swift, and in many categories, China will pass from the stage of competing for the products and services of the white man and become herself a competitor for markets held by the white man. The days of privileged position in China are ended. Henceforth, the non-Chinese, of whatever nationality, must stand or fall on the merits of his wares, his service or his professional skill. And he must do so in competition with an intensely patriotic people, who will be striving not only for personal gain, but for the greater glory of their country and their race.

Japanese propaganda, to the Western mind, is crude in the extreme. We would be very foolish indeed, however, if we dismissed it as unworthy of serious attention, because to our way of thinking it is comic when it is not disgusting. The essential point to be borne in mind in regard to it is that it is propaganda designed for Asiatics by

Asiatics. It may well be that the Japanese is not a good judge of the mentality of his neighbors, but in this business of propaganda he has some very good talking points. The cry of "Asia for the Asiatics" for example. Asia, with its immense wealth, houses more poverty than all the other continents put together. Many educated Indians, Chinese, Javanese, Malays and others recognize that poverty and disease decreased with the coming of the white man, and that in the process of realization of the wealth, there have accrued to the indigenous populations such benefits as shatter entirely the extremists' lurid picture of soulless exploitation. In the Japanese occupied territories there are Asiatics of great wealth, whose great-grandfathers, grandfathers or even fathers, labored in field, forest or mine for the white man. A few of those prosperous men may feel that they would have been even more wealthy and powerful if they had been freed of all white influence. On the whole, however, if the motive is put at its lowest, those people are fully alive to the material advantages they owe to the white man's coming and I see little cause for apprehension as to the effect of Japanese propaganda on the well-to-do sections, or on the great majority of the educated classes of the Asiatic peoples. But there were still, in 1941, illiterates by the million, living at or near the subsistence level. Their lot had improved greatly in the years immediately preceding the outbreak of war, and it was still improving, surely and not very slowly. But the rate of improvement was slower than the growth of the powers of understanding. Those masses are the people to whom the "Asia for the Asiatics" cry has been directed. They are the people for whom that which we regard as crude has been specially designed, and they are the people whose attitude to the returning white man is a very important and a very uncertain quantity.

The problem, again, requires piecemeal examination. Although the systems of government in American, British, Dutch and French Asiatic territories had a great deal in common theoretically, it would be idle to pretend that there was, in 1941, a general level of kindliness and forbearance on the part of those in authority, and uniform appreciation of those who governed by those who were governed. The cry of "Asia for the Asiatics" will have evoked no enthusiasm for Japanese tutelage in the Philippines, where complete independence was so near at the time of invasion that some of those who had cried loudest for it were showing signs of nervousness at the project of its early arrival. The cry will have little effect in Malaya, where the indigenous population enjoyed a standard of living and a measure of content unequaled in any other Asiatic country. What will be the effect of it in Netherlands India, Burma, Siam and Indo-China will depend largely on another unpredictable factor. There is little reliable information as to how the Japanese are behaving toward the people of the occupied territories. There is some evidence of cruelty in Hong Kong in the first few months following capitulation, and there have been a number of ugly reports from the Philippines. It is significant, however, that the Japanese General who was in command at the time of the capture of Hong Kong and was later transferred to Manila is notorious for his ruthlessness. Elsewhere, so far as it is possible to judge, the Japanese have refrained from any undue harshness toward the Asiatic populations of former colonial territories, except, of course, in cases where there has been active opposition to their administration. Will they maintain the same degree of moderation to the end? If the answer to that question were known, it would be possible to be much more definite in assessing the problems which will confront the white man on his return to the Far East. At present, of course, the Japanese need the manpower of the occupied countries; there is strong inducement to try to establish friendly relations. Whether, when the time for withdrawal approaches, and the local peoples have ceased to be of use, the Japanese will go berserk and vent their wrath on everything and everyone in sight cannot be foretold. The tragedy of the situation is that the more shockingly the Japanese behave toward their Asiatic captives, the better are the prospects that the white man will be welcomed on his return. If, on the other hand, a reasonable attitude is maintained throughout, and people are subjected to a renewal of the horrors of war in the form of further battles for their countries, they may well find it difficult to understand how their best interests have been served by additional devastation and slaughter.

There are, then, many uncertain factors to complicate the business of planning a return to the Far East, and in the face of them the scope for constructive suggestion is severely limited. There is, however, one certainty which must form the basis of all our preparation. It is not a pleasant thing to contemplate, but if we thrust it behind us because it happens to be distasteful, we shall pile up a mountain of trouble for ourselves. When we are able to set foot once more in the countries from which we were driven by the Japanese, our compatriots will have won victory in the greatest of all wars. In that hour of triumph, there will be a great temptation to show a little of the bearing of the conquering hero, but that is a temptation to be resisted at all costs. In its early stages, the situation of the returning white man will call for much more humility than pride.

Let me try to picture for you what the Asiatic will see when we return to his shores. However abjectly Japan may have surrendered, however tremendous Allied achievements in the West may be, the Asiatic will see the return of one of several races that were driven out of the Pacific by a single Asiatic nation. He will see men who were kept out of the Pacific for three years or more by that one Asiatic Power. He will see fellows of the white men and women who have been herded behind barbed wire and kept in utter subjection by people for whom they professed the utmost contempt. He will know that Japan has been beaten, but he will know that the task has required the combined might of Great Britain, the United States, China and a host of smaller nations. He will be primed with Japanese propaganda, designed to convince him of the magnitude of the Japanese triumph in standing out so long against overwhelming odds. Those considerations in themselves will hardly provide an atmosphere conducive to wild enthusiasm for the return of a triumphant warrior. But there is more, much more. The European will return to Asia as a man who failed in a mission on which the very lives of his charges depended. He failed to give the protection that he promised. The whys and the wherefores of the failure are unimportant in this connection. The essential fact is that he did fail, and an undertaking solemnly given and frequently reiterated, went unfulfilled. Those of us who go back will be in a position to do so because we escaped from the Japanese. We ran away from an Asiatic foe. How late we ran, and in what circumstances, may mitigate individual feelings of failure. Many of us were helped to freedom by Asiatics who knew they had to stay behind. But when all that is said, there remains the unalterable fact that we failed as a race.

I suggest, then, that the keynote of plans for the re-occupation of Eastern territories must be humility. I would not have the word interpreted in the sense of groveling for opportunity to make good losses, or of truckling to extremist elements when and where they may be found. I do not mean a cringing defeatism. I mean the true humility of the man who has made grievous errors and has the courage to acknowledge them; the man who has betrayed a trust, however unwillingly, however helplessly, and is determined to make restitution in the fullest possible measure. We have much to redeem in the Far East, and almost all of it is wrapped up in that one word "face." Where faith in our promises remains unimpaired, we shall have to restore faith in our ability to fulfill our undertakings. We shall have to establish faith in our ability to recognize that we are neither infallible nor invulnerable, faith in our readiness to profit by past mistakes. And we shall have to establish confidence in the sincerity of our condemnation of any theory of racial superiority.

Those things will require very special qualities, such as are possessed by few men at the present time and cannot be speedily acquired. They will require an intimate knowledge of the peoples concerned and a high place in the esteem of those peoples. The white man who can do most to restore the prestige of his race is he who feels respect and affection for the Asiatic, and enjoys the respect and affection of the Asiatic. For the most part, men who are still free and meet those requirements are in late middle age and had retired, or were about to retire, from the Far East when they were forced out by the Japanese. They have spent thirty or forty years controlling large labor forces and, unofficially, ruling great areas with no other authority than that derived from the affection of the local population. I know several such men, and I know they would willingly give a few more years of their lives, or all if needed, to the service of countries and people that are the source of many happy memories. Unfortunately, I do not know of a single case in which an unofficial of the older generation has been asked to take part in the delicate task of restoring the good name of the white man. I know I am out of accord with the spirit of the times in urging the claims of age and long experience, but the men I have in mind would do invaluable work without any great physical, or even mental, effort. They could do an immense amount of good, merely by going back and being themselves, by renewing old associations and by giving a sense of reality to the assurances that the nightmare has ended. The educated minorities will be adequately cared for by the formal administrative structure. It is the peasantry and the labor forces, numerically an overwhelming majority, that will require the gentleness and understanding born of many years of close association.

Already, the vanguards of the organizations that will follow the armies into the re-won territories of the Pacific are assembling. They consist almost entirely of men in early middle age or younger. There are brilliant administrators among them—but many of them were administering when disaster came. The last that the Asiatic saw of them was not impressive. . . . Those men are now preparing for the future, and part of the preparation consists of fitting them out with nice uniforms and giving them military rank. That, to my mind, is the ultimate in folly. Uniforms were not exactly popular in the countries concerned at the time of capitulation, with the possible exception of police uniforms, and it is unlikely that they will have become more popular in the meantime. The advent of a youthful, bustling crowd of uniformed enthusiasts, determined to get things going again at top speed, is not calculated to create an impression of peace in the minds of the local populace. The technicians and the forces of law and order will be wanted, but let them go in unobtrusively. Keep regimentation to an absolute minimum. Remember that an air of quiet will be a prime need after years of strain. Let the human factor receive the consideration that it deserves. A few additional weeks or months devoted to the work of restoring faith among the people may mean the difference between success and failure of all the scheming.

I feel there is too much insistence upon material considerations in the planning that is now in progress, and too little regard for the things of the mind and the heart. Organization, efficiency, speed, vigor—those are the watchwords. Sentiment, emotion, affection: where do they find place in the calculations of the efficiency expert? And yet sentiment, emotion and affection have always been powerful factors in the creation and maintenance of happy relations between the white man and the Asiatic, and I hope most earnestly, though not very confidently, that they may yet find their rightful place in the thoughts of those who will be at the heels of the soldiers on the road back.

I would feel I had well served a country and a people for whom I have what I am not ashamed to describe as deep affection, if I could persuade those who have the ordering of such things to send to Malaya an advance guard of men of the older generation. If a small band of unofficials could go back to districts wherein they were respected but not feared, they would do more than is likely to be done by any other agency to wipe out the tragic memories of the recent past. Such men represent to the Asiatic more than anything or anybody else can do, the days which are dead, days which we must pray the Asiatic will be as eager to see re-born as we are eager to take part in their re-birth. For if we cannot so conduct ourselves that we are accepted in a willing spirit on our return to the countries of the Pacific, then most of the fruits of the victory won in that theater, by the courage and sacrifice of our sailors, soldiers and airmen, will be dead and bitter.

Harold R. Isaacs

THE PATTERN OF REVOLT IN ASIA

In the preceding reading G. W. Seabridge warned his fellow Europeans in 1944 that they would return to the Far East with difficulty. With Japan's defeat in 1945, Harold R. Isaacs, then a correspondent for Newsweek, *observed the war's aftermath in India, Korea, Japan, Indochina, and Java. The Asia which he saw seemed to demonstrate the validity of what Seabridge had predicted—that Asians everywhere were determined to prevent the reestablishment of the prewar empires in the Orient. World War II had unleashed the demand for independence which some observers had seen as early as 1942. That experience, Isaacs noted, convinced Asians that the Western powers were no more fit to rule them than they themselves. Nowhere, Isaacs discovered, was the movement for independence more determined than in Ho Chi Minh's Indochina, but the desire for freedom was clearly in evidence in India, Korea, and Indonesia as well. What disturbed Isaacs was the general inclination of the Western powers in 1946—the United States included— to oppose the independence movements in Indochina and, to a lesser degree, in Indonesia.*

Across Asia, with anger and bitterness and in defiance of great odds, subject peoples are again struggling for independence. And they mean independence. Not trusteeship or self-government or dominion status but independence. Not in five years or ten years or in some indefinite future but now.

For Indians, Burmese, Annamites, Koreans, Indonesians, the basic issue is simple: to submit no longer to any foreign rulers. They are intent upon becoming their own masters. Their determination cuts across all the arguments and counter-arguments, all the ifs and buts and howevers. Whatever the real or fancied perils of freedom, they insist upon being free. After the spectacle the world has presented in the past decade, it is difficult for subject colonials anywhere to agree any longer that anybody is more fit to rule them than they are themselves.

"I'm sick of being told that we're not 'ripe' for self-rule and that we'll only make a mess of things," a young Annamite told me in Hanoi. "Are the French, of all people in the world, 'ripe' enough to rule even themselves? Can we possibly make more of a mess of things than all the rulers of the world have already made? We agree it's a mess. You can explain our cause very easily: we are fighting for the right to make our mess for ourselves."

The mood cuts deep, extends far. Conditions vary and backgrounds vary and the struggle goes on at many levels. The sullen and devitalized Indian can flare all at once into blind anger. In open challenge to the British Raj on the streets of Calcutta or Bombay he suddenly confounds his tried leaders and surprises himself. In India nothing is clear, nothing moves along a straight line. Only a great mass convulses within its bonds. Yet, amid all the division and confusion, the pressure on Britain grows. Always present, the explosive force which took the form of open insurrection in August of 1942 plays upon the nerves and calculations of the British masters and the Nationalists, of Congress men and Moslems. India groans under the accumulated corruption of too long a history, with its castes, its races, its deep social and religious cleavages. So its politics can be shaped now by the mysticism of a Gandhi and the fanaticism of a Jinnah. Still there is a kind of half-recognized common ground on which all are forced to express themselves. None of the compromises or offers of compromise ever settle anything. The pressures always tend to concentrate on independence, as if all in common somehow realize that the starting point is there, that throwing off the hated rule of the British is the first and inescapable step in the task of throwing off the whole dead weight of the past.

Everywhere the impulse is the same. Backward and ignorant people, remote from the educational refinements of politics, the unconsulted ones who are not supposed to know any better, these suddenly have plain answers to plain questions. I remember a day I spent in the Korean countryside talking to farmers and small village shopkeepers. There was a tall farmer named Yoon who held his round-faced, black-eyed son in his arms against his spotless white jacket. "What do you want?" I asked. He smiled. "Better living" was the way the interpreter phrased his answer. I asked him what that meant. "It means good crops and good prices," he said. "It means getting our young men back from the Japanese forced labor gangs. It means getting a government of our own."

Farmer Yoon knew exactly what he wanted. He and all his people in those first days of the American occupation of southern Korea believed that the end of enslavement to Japan meant the coming of Korean freedom. That was why farmers straightened up in the fields and raised their arms in greeting and children shouted and cheered and one ancient old lady danced nimbly in the road grinning toothlessly, her tired old eyes brimming. But Korea was partitioned and the divided country placed under Soviet and American military occupation and Military Government. The gloss wore off and when the Moscow conference offered nothing more than continued partition and a five-year "trusteeship," Koreans erupted in anger. They still do not understand why, if the Japanese emperor may still sit on his throne, Koreans may not resume their ancient freedom. A young Korean woman doctor said to me wearily: "We spent long years learning Japanese. Now we must learn Russian and English. When shall we be able to concentrate on learning Korean?" The Koreans want to concentrate on being Korean and they believe the way to start learning how to rule themselves is to start ruling themselves.

II

Down in Indo-China the Annamites have carried the same determination to the battlefield. The French took their country by conquest eighty years ago, ruled it by force, then bowed supinely to the superior force of the Japanese. When the Japanese collapsed under American blows, the French moved to regain their power. The British, using Indian and Japanese troops, helped the French win a foothold on the Saigon peninsula. The Annamites, who had proclaimed their independence and set up their own government as the Republic of Viet Nam, resisted with a sprinkling of modern weapons, with ingeniously devised bows and arrows and muzzle-loading rifles and incendiary torches and homemade grenades. Little reported now, this war goes on, the Annamite war for independence and the French war for reconquest.

In Hanoi—which lies in the zone, north of the sixteenth parallel, which was marked for Chinese occupation—the Annamites enjoy uneasy tenure; here they maintain their government and organize their resistance to the French. Ho Chi-minh, for forty-four years a persistent and almost legendary leader of the people, heads the movement with an honesty of purpose and absence of illusion that keep strength in his frail body. "It is clear we must depend on ourselves," he said. "We will keep on fighting and our children, if necessary, will keep on fighting. Independence is the thing. What will follow will follow, but independence must come first if anything is to follow at all."

The Annamites offer the French everything but trust in French promises of future freedom. They want independence now but will compromise on everything else, including grant of economic priority for the French in the country. Short of that they will fight with all their might. Shaggy-haired Dran van Giau, thirty-four-year-old veteran guerrilla organizer and graduate of France's penal colony prison system, spoke with a calm that gave peculiar fire to his words: "The French have launched a war to reconquer our country. If they want war, we will make war. They will fight by their means. We will fight by our means. They will advance along the roads and railways, the rivers and canals, razing our villages, killing our people. We will make war our way. We will be everywhere. We will destroy everything the French own. We will destroy their factories, their plantations, their railroads. We will blow up their bridges and tear up the rails. We will make Indo-China uninhabitable for the French. We certainly do not want this war but if we have to have it we'll destroy everything there is in order to build a new life for ourselves, even if the French force us to start from the veriest beginning."

Among these Annamites, more impressively than almost anywhere else, there is a quality of exaltation, of moral force and devotion, of indifference to odds and obstacles, of profound hatred and scorn for their foe. I think of the teen-age boy who stood alone on the stage of the hideous old empire-style theater in Hanoi and spoke to an intent audience of more than 3,000 young men and women. He spoke of the fighting in the south, of clashes and devoted heroism wherever Annamites fought with British or French or Japanese troops. He clothed his comrades and their cause in that richly shining inspiration which comes only when men see things by their own inner light. "Yes," said this youth, "we are inferior to the French in the matter of arms." He paused. "Also in the matter of cowardice." The houseful of young people cheered until they were hoarse.

When men mean what they say, the most abused phrases and raveled clichés suddenly acquire a fresh relevance. Both in Indo-China and in Java I heard nationalists say in substance: "Maybe to the Powers words like freedom and justice and self-determination are empty and brittle and meaningless conveniences. For our part they are a matter of life and death. We mean to translate them into reality the best way we can. We talk about freedom and we mean being free; and being free, to begin with, means to have no foreign masters to govern our lives. We talk about self-determination and we mean determining ourselves, for better or worse. We're ready to cooperate with the whole world for peace, but to begin with we have to stand on our feet, speak with our own voice, have a hand in our fate."

Across Batavia's walls and houses and public buildings, the Indonesians had scrawled slogans to greet the arriving occupation troops. They had expected these to be American and they drew their phrases from the American lexicon: "Government for, by, and of the people . . ." Or: "We fight for our inalienable right to life, liberty, and the pursuit of happiness." Or: "Give us freedom or give us death!" The occupying forces turned out to be British but the effect was not wasted. "Your damned American revolution is still giving us trouble," one weary British officer said to me.

In Batavia sat the British, harried and defensively righteous; the Dutch, sullen and uncertain and bolstered only by their violent and savage Eurasian and Amboinese mercenaries; and the Indonesian cabinet, made up of moderate politicians, pushed forward to see what, if anything, could be gained by negotiation. In the hinterland, while evacuating internees, British forces were clashing constantly with the hated and feared "extremists." Repeatedly Japanese troops, operating under British command, were thrown into the local battles. After one action at Semarang in the late fall, the British brigadier commanding in the area said in his report, "The Japanese were magnificent." But across Java, the "extremists" held the mountains and the valleys, hating all foreigners and suspicious even of their own politician-leaders. The Dutch, unhinged by outrageous fortune, seriously argued that the docile Javanese had suddenly gone mad. Most Dutchmen angrily rejected the counsel of the few soberer minds who grasped the fact that a whole people was aroused and that the old days were gone forever. Queen Wilhelmina was offering confederation. But the Indonesians did not want to confederate. *Merdeka* was the word now, *independence*. Not even the most moderate Indonesian politicians dared suggest they might settle for less.

III

The British fell heir to these problems when a Big Three deal placed all of Southeast Asia within their sphere. Many Britons, embarrassed by the role they are playing, argue defensively that American troops would have had to carry out the same policy had they been assigned these areas to occupy. This is presumably true, for the United States is fully party to the Allied policy of restoring the imperial *status quo ante* in the colonies as a prerequisite to any "reforms." Until January, the United States was formally associated with all operations conducted by Lord Louis Mountbatten, and in these actions the United States was represented by great stores of lend-lease weapons and equipment freely used by French and British and Dutch against colonial insurgents. Nor is Russia any less engaged in the responsibility for the guiding top Allied policy in which it shared. Not until it suited its maneuvers at London late in January did Russia abruptly raise the issue of Indonesia while remaining notably silent on the subject of Indo-China, because it is more interested in detaching France from British influence than it is in the fate of the Annamites. In Korea, reactionary American policies in the south have been fully matched by Russian totalitarian strong-arm policies in the north. By commission or by omission, all the Powers are joined in the effort to dam up somehow the nationalist flood in Asia rising in the wake of this war just as it rose in the wake of the last.

There is a sobering and terrifying symmetry in this pattern. For after 1918, too, the subject peoples rose from long simmering to a boil. There was a titanic surge toward a new dispensation in backward and subjected Asia. The peoples rose, in layer after layer, to change the face of their world, to end imperialist rivalries in the East by taking their destinies in their own hands. One after another they were put down or led up blind alleys by the British in the Middle East and India, by the French in Africa and Indo-China, by the Dutch in Indonesia, and by the Japanese in Korea. In China in 1925–27 occurred the greatest national revolution of them all. It broke on the rock of internal class conflict, producing a foreign-supported Kuomintang tyranny which sapped China's meager strength instead of revitalizing it. Prisons were choked with rebels and execution grounds ran red. Britain filled its penal colonies in the Andamans, and the French theirs at Poulu Condor, and the Dutch their prison camps in the remoter Indies. There was more than a decade of strife and failure and frustration. It was against such an Asia, weakly held by foreign rulers or their native puppets, that Japan was able to launch its final drive for hemispheric control. . . .

Japan was fundamentally too weak to succeed. It came too late onto the scene and brought too little to sustain its claim to power. It had too narrow a base of its own at home to be able to maintain its military effort or to afford political wisdom or patience. Yet the Japanese came very close to pulling it off. In ninety days they wrested a vast empire from the British, Americans, and Dutch. For France's territory they did not even have to fight. They exposed the weakness of the Westerners and demonstrated their own apparent invincibility. But they had neither the time nor the ability to reap the political rewards of their victories.

Their slogan "Asia for the Asiatics" struck a deep note; but they meant Asia for the Japanese and it did not take long for all the other Asiatics to find that out. Instead of fostering real national independence and cashing in on the support they could win thereby, the Japanese had only puppet roles to offer to the nationalists and everywhere practiced brutal terrorism and systematic looting. The conquered countries were stripped of food, raw materials, and machinery and thrust into an economic morass from which they will not emerge for a long time to come. The Japanese used stooges and tools among the colonial peoples but many a genuine nationalist also turned to them, either out of hope or cynicism, and quickly turned away. The Japanese could not avoid being conquerors and thus insured the loss of their empire.

But if in victory the Japanese could offer nothing durable to subject Asiatics, in defeat Japan presented many of them with a rich and unprecedented opportunity. Japan was defeated in the Philippines and the northwest Pacific by American arms. In Southeast Asia, except in Burma, its armies had not even been engaged. The British, French, and Dutch, so ignominiously expelled or subjugated at the war's outset, were given no chance to recapture prestige by military victories. And the manner of their regaining their territory cost them even more face than the manner of losing it. There were neither Dutch nor French troops available, and by the time the British made their delayed arrival, the nationalists in Indo-China and Indonesia seized the advantage. They proclaimed their independence, promulgated constitutions, and set up their governments. They refused to admit any restoration of Dutch or French sovereignty and offered their collaboration to the British only in the limited task of rounding up and disarming the Japanese. The British instead interpreted restoration of "order" to mean in effect the displacement of nationalist power. The result in both countries was war.

In Indo-China the British openly connived at a coup by the French which overthrew the Annamite government in Saigon. They armed French troops and attempted to disarm the Annamites. They ordered the Japanese forces to hold their garrison points against the Annamites. The result was bloody war on the Saigon peninsula. More French troops kept arriving, in American ships and with American equipment, and when the French seemed strong enough to carry on alone, the British pulled out.

In Java no fighting occurred until a small force of Dutch troops came in behind the British. The Indonesians showed strength, more strength than the British had thought possible, and the Dutch, to their own angry chagrin, were restrained from sending in more troops too soon. In Surabaya fighting did not start until the Indonesians were given the impression that the British would attempt to disarm them, and after that it took the British five weeks to subdue the city. In December the Allied high command in Singapore took a decision to apply more force to "pacify" the island of Java, but London put the brakes on and called in the Dutch to see whether better terms could not be arranged. Yet British policy, as announced by Attlee and Bevin both, stands for restoration of Dutch sovereignty in the Indies and this is precisely what the Indonesians will not willingly accept. Across their banners the Javanese write "*merdeka* or death" and there are hundreds of thousands of them who mean this quite literally. They are people who, to borrow another forgotten phrase, have nothing to lose but their chains.

IV

The nationalists in these countries had hoped for a different outcome. There was a certain amount of naive belief in the Atlantic Charter and the pledges of self-determination so freely bandied about during the war. But this belief was by no means based wholly on illusions. The war itself was a gigantic and costly demonstration of the futility and waste and indefensibility of the old imperial system. Since the old dispensation had led the Powers so close to the edge of total disaster, many nationalists believed that out of sheer self-interest the victors would agree to a drastic change. They did not believe this seriously of the old masters, the British, the French, the Dutch. But they did believe it of the United States. Political independence of their old masters seemed to them the minimum guarantee they could accept because they no longer would believe in half-promises or be content with half-measures.

They looked to the United States for moral and political and practical support of this position. They have not received any such support. American official statements have offered verbal sympathy with the ultimate goals of the nationalists but American action has consisted of practical support for the immediate aims of the imperialists. The result is a growing defection from the great hope in America. A crucial political fact in Asia today is the crumbling of American prestige in the eyes of subject peoples. For with this faith may be passing the last hope of a less painful transition toward a new and more hopeful order of things.

So there is no peace in Asia, nor any prospect of peace in the foreseeable future. The great Pacific war settled nothing but Japan's attempt to master the continent. Wearily we must now face reiteration of the old pattern of blood and agony drawn by the continued rivalry of Great Powers in the East. With periodic eliminations and comebacks, this rivalry feeds on all the unresolved issues of Asiatic nationalism and monotonously explodes into wars. It has been going for a long time and it seems, must go on still.

The wars of 1895 (Japan against China) and 1905 (Japan against Russia)—to go no further back—brought Japan into the Great Power picture and eliminated Russia. The war of 1914–18 eliminated Germany from the Far East. The resultant contest for hegemony among the United States, Britain, and Japan led up to the war of 1941–45. This war eliminated Japan—but brought back Russia. And already in China civil war, or the constant threat of civil war, or the efforts to prevent civil war, involve thinly masked conflict between the two new principal protagonists for mastery. Asia remains a battleground on which power, not peace, is the stake. Thus we start again, at the end of a half-century cycle during which nothing has really relieved the misery and subjection of Asia's billion people or the insecurity thus imposed on the rest of the world.

There is the final paradox. The fight for national independence in the colonies will be fought by these peoples with desperate determination. But national independence, even won, is scarcely the beginning of a solution. Should they succeed in emerging now as new national states, they would suffer—as China has suffered—the fate of all the small or weak nations of the world: to be pawns or victims in the interplay of intercontinental power politics. . . .

Abbot Low Moffat

NATIONALISM AND COMMUNISM IN POSTWAR INDOCHINA

Both Franklin D. Roosevelt and his Secretary of State, Cordell Hull, adopted the principle that the Atlantic Charter, with its emphasis on self-determination, should triumph in Asia as well as in Europe with the defeat of the Axis powers. But one issue divided the government by 1947–that of Indochina. Abbot Low Moffat, Chief, Division of Southeast Asian Affairs, recalled in the following statement the sharp disagreement which developed that year between the pro-French European Division of the State Department and the new pro-Indochinese (and thus pro-Ho Chi Minh) Division of Southeast Asian Affairs. Ultimately the conflict in Washington centered on the critical question: What was the nature and significance of Communist leadership in Asia? For the European experts Ho represented a Soviet presence in Asia; for Moffat and his associates Ho was fundamentally a nationalist, seeking independence and a socialist state for Indochina. Such men, at a critical moment in United States-Asian relations, lost control of both policy and the language needed to defend it with consequences quite beyond calculation.

It is not possible to understand some of the developments in 1945 without knowledge of what happened before. Until the spring of 1944 the Office of Far Eastern Affairs had no jurisdiction over those areas of the Far East which were colonies of European countries, important though those colonies might be in Far Eastern policy questions. The British Commonwealth desk and the Western European desk in the Office of European Affairs handled the problems and policies concerning all British, French, Dutch, and Portuguese colonies as integral parts of relations with the mother countries. In the spring of 1944, however, there was established in the Office of Far Eastern Affairs a new Division of Southwest Pacific Affairs, the name of which was later changed to Division of Southeast Asian Affairs as our major activities clearly related to Southeast Asia other than the Philippines. To this Division was given primary jurisdiction of matters relating to Thailand and concurrent jurisdiction with the appropriate European

"Causes, Origins, and Lessons of the Vietnam War," *Hearings Before the Committee on Foreign Relations, United States Senate, May 9, 10, and 11, 1972,* 92d Congress, 2d Session (Washington: U.S. Government Printing Office, 1973), pp. 172–179. (Reproduced with minor typographical alterations.)

desk of matters relating to the European colonies in Southeast Asia and in the Pacific Ocean. The significant word in that statement is "concurrent." . . .

There had been many hopes and generalities uttered about the postwar world including not least the Atlantic Charter, and the colonial powers from time to time spoke vaguely of more self-government for their colonies after the war. As we considered the prewar nationalist movements in Southeast Asia and studied such reports as we then had from the area, we reached the conclusion that nationalist sentiment was becoming an important force in Southeast Asia. We felt that not only to accomplish self-government which traditional American policy has always favored, but also to capture the nationalist movements in behalf of the war effort, our allies should be urged to be specific in what they proposed to do after the war. Our division prepared, therefore, a briefing paper for the President's use at the Second Quebec Conference in September, 1944, which was initialed by all the appropriate Divisions and Offices and was signed by the Secretary of State, Mr. Hull, on September 8. I would like to quote from that memorandum as it appears in Mr. Hull's Memoirs because it states our government's goal at that time and because of its reference to trusteeships.

> In this [memorandum] we suggested the value of "early, dramatic, and concerted announcements by the nations concerned making definite commitments as to the future of the regions of Southeast Asia." We added:
> "It would be especially helpful if such concerted announcements could include (1) specific dates when independence of complete (dominion) self-government will be accorded, (2) specific steps to be taken to develop native capacity for self-rule, and (3) a pledge of economic autonomy and equality of economic treatment toward other nations. . . ."

So far as I know no effort was made to seek such concerted announcements presumably because of the implacable opposition of Mr. Churchill to the trusteeship principle and to any discussion of British territories. Yet as Mr. Hull explains,

> It might be thought that we were presumptuous in seeking to present our ideas to the British, French, and Dutch Governments as to what they should do with their own Pacific possessions. We had, however, two rights to take such action. One was the fact that the liberation of those

possessions would not have been achieved—and possibly never could have been achieved—except by the United States forces. The other was our interest in seeing that peace in the Pacific, restored by our forces, should continue. And we could not help believing that the indefinite continuance of the British, Dutch, and French possessions in the Orient in a state of dependence provided a number of foci or future trouble and perhaps war. Permanent peace could not be assured unless these possessions were started on the road to independence, after the example of the Philippines. We believed that we were taking the long-range view, and that a lasting peace in the Pacific was of greater ultimate benefit to Britain, France, and the Netherlands—as well as to the whole world—than the possible immediate benefits of holding on to colonies.

While the European Divisions had installed the memorandum because, I believe, of its importance in psychological warfare, I did not feel that they were entirely happy with the more basic objective. From then on and as more and more information was received, one of our major tasks, during the whole time that I was with the Division of Southeast Asian Affairs, was to try to convince the European Divisions of the mounting groundswell of nationalism which was engulfing all Southeast Asia and indeed, before I left the Division, Southern Asia as well.

Their concern, of course, focused on our relations with the major European powers; rather naturally they tended to consider the colonial problems in Southeast Asia as of relatively minor importance. I well recall one senior officer asking me one day, "Why are you concerning yourself with Indonesia? It's only a Dutch colony." There seemed to be little understanding of what was happening in Southeast Asia. Time and again the nationalist movements were characterized as simply the effect of Japanese propaganda. There was also, I felt, little concept of the effect on the people of Southeast Asia of seeing the Europeans driven from the area by the Japanese, and no thought seemed to be given to the effect of the massive, indeed total dislocation of the economic and social life of these people under the impact of the changes wrought by the war. We felt strongly that the colonial powers could not pick up where they had been forced to leave off or even with an allowance for four years of political development. We became convinced that during the four years of war nationalist sentiment had progressed faster and farther than it would have evolved during twenty or more years of peace. . .

As the war approached its climax, the French, through the British, pressed harder for American help in the recovery of Indochina from the Japanese and for an active part in such operation, and also for a formal civil affairs agreement between the United States and France relating to the military administration to be established as the Japanese were driven out. As late as January, 1945, the President was adamant that he did not want the United States to be mixed up in any decisions affecting the future of Indochina; those were for postwar. And he did not want to get mixed up in any military effort to liberate Indochina from the Japanese. But the French did not give up. When in March Japan ousted the collaborationist regime in Indochina and took over direct control, several thousand French troops briefly opposed the Japanese before crossing into China and the French asked for supplies and assistance from the 14th Air Force in China. Although the President disapproved the release of a statement suggested by the Department explaining that the United States would give such help as it could consistent with the operations and plans to which it was committed, the Department and the Joint Chiefs authorized the 14th Air Force, in aid of the French, to undertake operations against the Japanese in Indochina provided such action did not interfere with other planned operations.

During this period we had increasingly the impression that the European Office favored the outright return of Indochina to France and had little real concern about autonomy or self-rule or even of increased native participation in the government. An indication of this arose when a briefing memorandum should, we felt, be prepared for the President for the Yalta Conference. We knew we could not get concurrence in a statement about Indochina that would meet our views, so we circulated again the memorandum signed by Mr. Hull on September 8. This time the European Divisions declined to initial the document they had initiated less than six months before. No briefing paper concerning Southeast Asia accompanied the President to Yalta so far as I know.

The net result of all this was that as the war in Europe ended the Department had no agreed policy regarding the future of Indochina. The European Office and the Western Europe Division, confronted with the major problems relating to a hoped-for resurgence of France in Europe, believed that our relations with France were of paramount interest to the United States; that we should not risk jeopardizing them in any way over a French colony which in any event was no business of ours; and in all good faith thought it was not in our best interests even to press for reform in Indochina because it might embarrass our relations with the French. Indeed, a senior officer in the European Office told me some two years later, when war between the French and Vietnamese had begun, that if he could have had his way American troops would have been used to restore the French to power in Indochina.

On the other hand, we in the Division of Southeast Asian Affairs felt that the United States had definite responsibilities with regard to Indochina. It was our military power that would liberate Indochina from Japan; the French in Indochina had collaborated with the Japanese; they had not even attempted to honor their protectorate responsibilities; there was a strong nationalist movement among the Vietnamese who had for centuries comprised a proud and independent country; and future peace and stability in the area depended, we felt, on a recognition of the natural aspirations of the peoples of the area. My personal hope was that the French would grant independence to the peoples of Indochina, but I did not feel we should carry our support of the Indochinese to the point of a break with our ally. France, weak as she then was, was still a stronger and more valuable ally to us than Indochina would be if we had to make a choice between the two, and France, which was striving to rebuild its strength and regain its soul, needed our help, not a fracturing of relations. But I disagreed totally with the European Office in its opposition to putting pressure on the French to do what I felt was not only in our interest but also actually in the interest of France.

This conflict of viewpoints came to a head a week after President Roosevelt's death when a memorandum for President Truman was prepared in the European Office and sent to the Far Eastern Office for concurrence. As I recall the occasion, I was handed a copy of this memorandum about 5 o'clock on a Friday afternoon with the request that our approval or comments be ready for a meeting of the top level Staff Committee the next morning at 11. We did succeed in having our comments and an alternative draft memorandum for the President ready next day but not in time for the meeting, and more than a month elapsed before in fact the Staff Committee considered the issue. Then Mr. [Joseph C.] Grew, who was Acting Secretary in the absence of Mr. [Edward R.] Stettinius in San Francisco, told the group that he had two papers concerning Indochina, one from EUR;

one from FE; that he had read both; and that he concurred in the paper from FE. . . .

The EUR viewpoint was expressed by Mr. [James C.] Dunn, who on reading our paper said he believed it would be better to let the matter drift rather than base United States policy on the FE version of the Indochina paper. He believed that we should draw close to Great Britain and France, the two strongest Western European countries; we should attempt to remove sources of friction between France and the United States and try to allay her apprehensions that we were going to propose that territory be taken from her. "We should use our influence to improve the government of Indochina," he said, "but should not interfere." He wanted wholehearted cooperation with France and indicated that he shared Bidault's fear for Western civilization as a result of the dominance of Russia in Europe.

In our view pressures for specific reforms would not, of course, be liked by the French, but they would not cause a break in our friendship or fundamental support. We felt that what we were seeking was actually in the French interest as well as our own: self-government would release the French from the heavy economic drain which Indochina had been for years to everyone but the Banque de l'Indochine; and with her long association with the Indochinese, France would easily conserve her cultural influence and would clearly be a favored country in international economic relations. Admittedly, the inferiority complex from which France was suffering as a result of the war was turning French thoughts to dreams of a restored imperial glory rather than to more prosaic problems of substantive economic and practical power, but I thought this obstacle not so great as to preclude us from pressing for what seemed to us both right and sensible. . . .

A few weeks later Japan surrendered and the situation in Indochina changed rapidly. The Vietnamese tried to take over all Vietnamese territory and disarm the Japanese before the Allies should arrive in Indochina. They were successful in establishing a working administration in the two northern provinces of Tonkin and Annam, but factional dissension among various independence groups in Cochin China minimized the effectiveness of their administration in that province. Nevertheless for twenty days the Provisional Vietnam Government ruled all the territory inhabited by Vietnamese. Then the British placed the French back in power in the area they controlled south of the 16th parallel. In the north the Vietnamese remained in power by arrangement with the Nationalist Chinese who were there to secure the disarming of the Japanese north of the 16th parallel.

With French forces back in Indochina and with all potential leverage gone, there was little that the United States could do to alter the outcome. We watched the negotiations between French and Vietnamese from the sidelines, encouraged when at times it seemed as if a liberal arrangement would be worked out, sorrowfully when both sides would breach agreements that had been made and when it gradually became apparent that as the French brought more military forces into the country their willingness to concede self-rule correspondingly decreased. I think both EUR and FE hoped that the French would reach an effective agreement with the Vietnam Provisional Government, but late in 1946 a concern about Communist expansion began to be evident in the Department.

We are reaping today, in my opinion, and so are all Vietnamese, Laotians, and Cambodians, the tragedy of our fixation on the theory of monolithic aggressive communism that began to develop at this time and to affect our objective analyses of certain problems. I have always been convinced that if the French had worked sincerely with Ho Chi Minh, Vietnam would have evolved with a Communist regime, but a regime that followed the interests of Vietnam first. There would have been no domination by China after China became Communist, and cooperation with the Soviet Union would have been primarily as an instrument to offset Chinese pressures.

I have never met an American, be he military, OSS, diplomat, or journalist, who had met Ho Chi Minh who did not reach the same belief: that Ho Chi Minh was first and foremost a Vietnamese nationalist. He was also a Communist and believed that communism offered the best hope for the Vietnamese people. But his loyalty was to his people. When I was in Indochina it was striking how the top echelon of competent French officials held almost unanimously the same view.

Actually there was no alternative to an agreement with Ho Chi Minh or to a crushing of the nationalist groundswell which my own observations convinced me could not be done. Any other government recognized by the French would of necessity be puppets of the French and incapable of holding the loyalty of the Vietnamese people.

As Department concern about the Communist domination of the Vietnam Government became more apparent and more uncritical, we began, I felt, to allow fears of such domination to overrule better judgment; we let the nationalist feelings of the country recede in importance and we ignored the father figure that Ho Chi Minh was becoming for most Vietnamese. The French seemed not averse to taking advantage of our increasing preoccupation with communism.

A telegram from our able consul at Hanoi, James O'Sullivan, at the end of December, offered some sound cautionary advice. He thought it "peculiar" that the French should only now become concerned about the Communists in Hanoi. To his certain knowledge, they had known for years that Nguyen Ai Quoc and Ho Chi Minh were one and the same person and that he stood high in the Third International, and for over a year they had suspected that Ho Chi Minh might be receiving instructions from Moscow. He further thought it was "very peculiar" that French concern should be brought to the Department's attention at the very moment they were apparently beginning to shift their program in Tonkin and when they might be preparing to force the Vietnam Government to collaborate on French terms or to establish a puppet government in its place. "French concern over Communism," he concluded, "may well be devised to divert Department's attention from French policy in Indochina."

I always felt that we could see the situation in Southeast Asia more objectively than the British, the French, and the Dutch because we could, until the fear of communism affected objectivity, analyze problems without the handicap of self-interest, prejudice, pride, or domestic politics. I struggled to preserve Siam from excessive British pressures at the conclusion of the war and was convinced that we were serving not only the Siamese interest but also the British interest, a view they have, I believe, long since accepted. As to Indochina and the Netherlands East Indies, I felt it essential that these countries be granted the political independence they longed for; that by making such a grant France, for instance, would in fact develop close ties with Vietnam because the Vietnamese had always great respect and liking for French culture, and many, including Ho Chi Minh, would have liked to maintain warm ties with France and to have French advisers in posts where foreign expert help was needed. Voluntary elimination of hated foreign control would have permitted happy and mutually beneficial relations to develop between the two countries. This was in fact the policy France successfully followed later in West Africa, but the French people felt a deep affront to their pride at the thought of giving up any sovereignty or control over Indochina, just as later they suffered similar imagined loss of face over Algeria.

I still believe that had the French been willing to grant independence to Vietnam in 1946 they could have worked out arrangements with the Vietnam Government that would have protected their cultural influence and left them with an obvious advantage over all other nations in economic dealings with Vietnam. It would have taken a greatness they did not then possess, and it would have taken a breadth of vision to see beyond the spiritual ashes from which they were rising, as Jean Monnet later had vision for Europe; but the failure to see their own true interest, misplaced ideas of prestige and glory, pressures from the Banque de l'Indochine, pressures from petty officials and those French who had settled in Indochina (not the best type of Frenchman generally), domestic politics, and the indecision arising from unstable governments at home—all these conspired to make the French intransigent at the time. Whether if the concern about the extension of a monolithic communism had not arisen at that particular moment of history the story would have ended differently, I do not know. . . .

On my return to the Department in mid-February I found that a telegram had been sent to Paris earlier that month in an effort to exert influence towards securing a settlement with the Vietnamese. That telegram had, however, spoken sharply against the danger of Ho Chi Minh's "direct Communist connection" and our opposition to seeing a colonial administration supplanted by an administration controlled by the Kremlin. This was impeccable theory with which one could not quarrel, but it was a prejudgment of the facts for which I could find no support. So far as I was aware no evidence to support the assumption of a direct tie to the Kremlin had ever been received, and it completely disregarded Ho Chi Minh's intense nationalism.

The French presently indicated that they were seeking "true representatives" of the Vietnamese with whom they could negotiate. We were deeply concerned in my Division because we felt that would be futile and any resulting government would be a puppet of the French. We determined to make one final try, and in a telegram that was sent on May 13, 1947, we spoke of the seven new nations that were in the process of achieving or struggling to achieve independence or autonomy in southern and southeastern Asia, and that in view of the great strides towards autonomy made by other people in this area it could be dangerous if the French-Vietnamese arrangements accorded less autonomy.

We said that we felt the best safeguard against Communist control or anti-Western, pan-Asiatic tendencies would be close association between the newly autonomous peoples and the countries with which they had long been associated, but such association had to be voluntary if it was to be lasting and achieve positive results. A protraction of the situation then existing in Indochina could only destroy the basis for voluntary cooperation and leave a legacy of bitterness that would irrevocably alienate the Vietnamese from France and those values represented by France and other Western democracies. We were inescapably concerned with the situation in the Far East generally and with those developments in Indochina which could have a profound effect on that situation. We hoped that the French would be generous in their attempt to find an early solution which, by recognizing the legitimate desires of the Vietnamese, would restore peace and deprive anti-democratic forces of a powerful weapon. . . .

II CHINA: CREATION OF THE MONOLITH

William C. Bullitt

SOVIET EXPANSION AND CHINA

After 1947 the Sino-Soviet relationship became the perennial test of the relative strength of nationalism and communism (as an international force) in Asia. It was not strange that William C. Bullitt, whose The Great Globe Itself *(1946) had defined the Soviet danger in global, ideological terms, would be among the first Americans to warn that Mao's coming victory in China would be a triumph for Soviet expansionism. Bullitt no more than others could suggest precisely how the Kremlin would control a Communist-led China. But his assertion that the Chinese Communists were tools of the U.S.S.R. denied that they possessed an authority and purpose separate from Soviet influence. Bullitt's views, because they satisfied the presumed political and intellectual needs of the day, quickly became commonplace; within two years even United States officials would repeat them with such an absence of restraint that most Americans would accept them as self-evident truths. Those who regarded the Chinese revolution as an expression of an indigenous Chinese nationalism found themselves at a serious emotional and intellectual disadvantage.*

To prevent the domination of China by any nation which might eventually mobilize the 450 million Chinese for war against us is a vital interest of the U.S.

Only two great powers have threatened to dominate China—Russia and Japan—and the U.S. has opposed whichever of those powers has been momentarily the more dangerous aggressor. Today Japan is no longer a great power. But Soviet imperialism, following in the footsteps of Czarist imperialism, and using the Chinese Communists as instruments of Soviet power politics, is striving to reduce China to the status of a satellite of the Soviet Union. Not merely the territorial integrity of China but her very independence is at stake. In our own self-defense, therefore, we must act to prevent Soviet domination of China and the eventual mobilization of Chinese manpower for war against us.

Can China be kept out of the hands of Stalin? Certainly—and at a cost to ourselves which will be small compared to the magnitude of our vital interest in the independence of China. . . .

From "A Report to the American People on China," by William C. Bullitt for *Life*, October 13, 1947, pp. 35–37, 139–154. Copyright © 1947 by Time, Inc. Reprinted by permission.

As all Americans now know, President Roosevelt after our entry into World War II based his foreign policy and his hopes of world peace on the gamble that he could convert Stalin from Soviet imperialism to democratic collaboration. Although on Feb. 10, 1940 the President had stated, "The Soviet Union, as everybody who has the courage to face the fact knows, is run by a dictatorship as absolute as any other dictatorship in the world," he began to have the Soviet Union referred to in official communication as a "peace-loving democracy." Until Truman's speech of March 12 this year the official doctrine of the U.S. government remained the farce that the Soviet Union was a peace-loving democracy and that the Chinese Communists were mere agrarian reformers who did not take orders from Moscow. . . .

After the failure of General Marshall's mission American policy toward China fell into a tired apathy, marked by a weary and petulant inclination to "let China stew in her own juice." In order to bring pressure on the Chinese government to compel it to accept our erroneous thinking that the Soviet Union was a "peace-loving democracy" we cut off all aid to the Chinese government. The $500 million loan earmarked for China was withheld. The "Eight and One Third Air Group Program"—by which we agreed to equip and provide maintenance parts for eight and one-third groups of the Chinese air force—was stopped by our unilateral action in September 1946.

Most serious of all, having equipped some Chinese divisions entirely with American artillery, machine guns and rifles, and others partially, and promised to help maintain this armament, we had held up export licenses for munitions. In consequence Chinese divisions without ammunition and with worn-out American equipment were facing Communist troops newly equipped in Manchuria by the Soviet Union with abundant supplies of Japanese rifles, maching guns and cannon. . . .

Today the Chinese government holds firmly all China as far north as the Yangtze River. Small bands of bandits, some of whom call themselves Communists, hold remote areas south of the Yangtze; but the Shanghai fashion of calling the area south of the Yangtze "the zone of peace and reconstruction" is justified. The area from the Yangtze north to the borders of the Soviet Union is definitely a war zone. . . . Whatever the issue of battle may be, the Chinese government cannot withdraw from Manchuria and must attempt to reenforce its troops in Manchuria at any cost. If Manchuria should be abandoned to the Communists or should fall into their hands by conquest, a course of events fatal to China would follow.

It is not difficult to foresee that the Communists would at once proclaim the "independence" of a "People's Republic of Manchuria," or that this "republic" would soon be recognized by the "Independent People's Republic of Outer Mongolia," which is entirely controlled by the Soviet government, and that the two "independent republics" would then enter into a mutual-assistance pact. And it is not difficult to imagine that the Chinese ambassador in Moscow would then be summoned by Molotov and politely reminded that the Soviet Union has a mutual-assistance pact with the "People's Republic of Outer Mongolia." Therefore if the Chinese government should attempt by arms to regain its province of Manchuria, and Outer Mongolia should go to the assistance of the "People's Republic of Manchuria," the Soviet Union under its pact with Outer Mongolia regretfully would be obliged to use force to prevent the Chinese government from inflicting injury on the forces of Outer Mongolia. Under penalty of Soviet intervention the Chinese government would be forbidden to attempt to recover its province of Manchuria—and Stalin's work at Yalta would be crowned with final success.

He would have all Manchuria firmly in his hands. And Manchuria is the finest piece of territory in Asia. As large as France and Germany combined, containing in its valleys agricultural land as rich as any in the world, where wheat, corn, soya beans and all our northern crops grow superbly; holding great deposits of coal and iron, and even gold; having immense wealth in forests and in waterpower both developed and undeveloped; containing before the war 70 percent of Chinese industry but populated by only 40 million people and offering immense possibilities for further settlement of overcrowded Chinese farmers, Manchuria is vital for the future development of China. . . .

By acting in time we can keep Manchuria out of the hands of the U.S.S.R. and thus insure China's territorial integrity. But essential as this is, it is not enough. China must not only be preserved as a free national entity but made a healthy and strong one—a power of such stature that in time she can serve as a real counterweight to the

Soviet empire in the Far East. To become strong she must have internal stability, and to achieve this she must above all have financial stability.

China today is caught in the sort of vicious circle that has become familiar to Europeans since World War I. She has been at war since 1937. The Japanese occupied nearly all her great cities, banking centers and industrial regions. The sources of such wealth as she had were in Japanese hands. Therefore she could not finance her war against the invader by sales of bonds, and she could cover only a small portion of the cost of the war by taxation. In consequence she covered her war costs by the only method open to her—the issuance of paper currency. . . .

Most of [the Chinese officials] graft to live, and there is no possible way to stop this sort of graft until all government employees, military and civilian, receive a living wage. But raising of government salaries will increase the inflation, inflation will raise the cost of living, the rising cost of living will quickly absorb the raises in salaries, graft will start again—nobody will be better off. How can China break this vicious circle?

There is only one ultimate answer to that question: finish the war. But how can victory be achieved if the vicious circle in which China is caught prevents the war from being fought effectively?

This is where the U.S. comes in. We can break the vicious circle at several points and at a cost to ourselves which will be small compared to the advantages to be gained for our own security.

The most astonishing facts to be found in China today are not in the realms of war or politics but in the field of finance. Chinese government expenditures, when translated into U.S. dollars at the prevailing rate of exchange, are on a Lilliputian scale. To govern the 450 million Chinese in a territory one-third larger than the U.S. and to carry all the expenses of the war, the Chinese government now spends approximately the same sum annually as the municipal government of New York City.

It is a fact that the total government expenditures for the year 1947, at the present rate of exchange, will amount to approximately one billion dollars. It is a fact that all the trillions of Chinese government currency outstanding could theoretically be bought, at the present rate of exchange, for only $250 million.

These figures are of the first importance for only one reason—they prove that the problem of giving effective aid to China is within dimensions that we can handle. We can break the vicious circle of Chinese inflation without coming anywhere near breaking ourselves. . . .

Today the tired Chinese people, who expected peace, have war, heavy taxes, rising costs of living and death. They want peace. And they blame the government because they do not have peace. It is the habit of all peoples after great wars to turn in disillusionment against their war leaders—the ejection of Winston Churchill and Charles de Gaulle are recent cases in point. And it is obvious that no Chinese government could be popular under present circumstances. Graft and inefficiency in the administrative services increase the government's unpopularity. But aside from the Communists and fellow travelers, even the Chinese who are most critical of the government do not speak ill of Generalissimo Chiang Kai-shek personally. They admit that his services to China have been greater than those of any man in modern times except Dr. Sun Yat-sen. They admit his complete personal honesty and devotion to his country's welfare. But they say that he is no longer well informed and does not know what is going on in the country, that he listens too much to old friends who helped him 20 years ago, that he has held supreme power so long that no one any longer dares to talk frankly to him, that he is too set in his ways to change either his policies or his intimate advisers, that he cannot, therefore, meet the terrible new problems which confront China today. But to the question, "By whom should he be replaced?" the answer invariably is, "There is no one to replace him." . . .

Let us now turn to the military side of the problem, remembering that it is absolutely essential that the President should release immediately certain stocks of munitions and have them rushed to the government troops in Manchuria. This cannot be delayed, or by next spring we shall find Manchuria a Soviet satellite.

According to the estimates of the ablest American and Chinese military men, to drive out of Manchuria the 350,000 Communists will require the training and equipment in the American manner of 10 new divisions. Furthermore, an efficient service of supply from the point of origin of the supplies to the front is essential. The great Manchurian port of Dairen cannot be used because by the Yalta Agreement it is now occupied by Soviet forces. Port improvements in

Hulutao and Chinwangtao and the rehabilitation of at least one railroad will therefore be necessary. Until all graft shall have been eliminated from the Chinese army, it would be wasteful to turn over American supplies to a Chinese service of supply. No American can take responsibility for commanding the Chinese army, but American military men can and should run the service of supply in Manchuria. . . .

But all this aid will be ineffective unless the Chinese can revitalize their political life, arouse a new spirit in the country and raise morale in the army. Can we help them to do that, or will suggestions from us be considered impertinent? They will not be considered impertinent if they are made by the right man in the right way. Too many Americans, clothed with a little brief authority, when they go to China confuse the might, majesty, power and dominion of the U.S. with their own personalities and talk down to Chinese who, in turn as men, are their superiors. In the pages of history Generalissimo Chiang Kai-shek bulks larger than any living American. He and Winston Churchill will be remembered together as leaders who had the courage and will to rally their countries in their darkest hours. To protect a vital interest of the U.S. and to defend the very life of China, the closest cooperation between Americans and Chinese is essential. What American has the military knowledge, political skill and personal magnitude to organize such cooperation?

We have in the Far East today a general of supreme stature who possesses all those qualities. If President Truman were to ask General MacArthur to add to his present duties and powers the title of Personal Representative of the President with the rank of Ambassador and to fly to China to organize with the Generalissimo a joint plan to prevent subjugation of China by the Soviet Union, the whole Far Eastern horizon would brighten with hope. The general would not have to abandon his work in Japan. He could divide his time between Tokyo and Nanking. His military, economic and political proposals might well be those outlined in this report. He could establish rapidly with the Generalissimo the relations of two comrades in a front-line trench. They would work together as brothers for their common cause.

The cause is a common cause. If China falls into the hands of Stalin, all Asia, including Japan, sooner or later will fall into his hands. The manpower and resources of Asia will be mobilized against us. The independence of the U.S. will not live a generation longer than the independence of China.

Hu Shih

CHINA IN STALIN'S GRAND STRATEGY

A noted Chinese citizen and diplomat—prewar ambassador to the United States—Hu Shih suffered the exile and disillusionment of all officials of Chiang Kai-shek's Nationalist government. He no less than his associates rejected the notion that the Nationalists, in their neglect of China's needs, were responsible for their own failure. The Nationalists, supported by powerful elements within the United States, preferred to attribute Chiang's fall in 1949 either to subversion in the American government or to Soviet influence in Chinese affairs. Either of the two explanations would relieve the Nationalists of guilt for what occurred, and by attributing the Communist victory to external causes they could also assume that it would be short-lived. In the following essay Hu Shih built the Nationalist case for the conclusion that Russia, by 1950, had gained control of China through its command of world communism. Hu Shih made no distinction between Soviet control of the Slavic states of Europe and Soviet control of China. He denied completely the special force of nationalism in China and of Soviet arms in Eastern Europe. He assumed that a powerful Red Chinese army and a Communist-led China would serve the interests of the U.S.S.R.

In the following pages I propose to study Stalin's grand strategy of world conquest as it can be discerned in China—its stages of experimentation and modification, of successes and failures, and its victories after long failures. The story covers 25 years, from 1924 to 1949, and culminates in the recent and, I trust, temporary conquest of continental China by the overwhelming military power of world Communism. I propose to use the history of the long and bitter struggle between Nationalist China and world Communism, between Chiang Kai-shek and Stalin, as source material for a new examination of that almost unbelievably successful strategy which has enabled world Communism to place under its domination immense areas of the earth and 800 million of its population. . . .

How did Stalin annex the Baltic States? How did he twice conquer Poland? How did Vyshinsky take over Rumania in February 1945? How did Communism take over Yugoslavia, Bulgaria and Hungary? What were the steps leading to the coup d'état in Czechoslovakia in February 1948? What was Stalin's strategy in his conquest of Man-

Excerpted by permission from *Foreign Affairs* 29 (October 1950): 11–40. Copyright 1950 by Council on Foreign Relations, Inc.

churia? And how did Stalin direct the campaign for the conquest of China and how did he finally succeed after 25 years of stubborn resistance by Nationalist China? Can we discern some similarity in the pattern of conquest? Can we reconstruct the strategical lines of the great Stalin from the fruits of these successful campaigns of conquest? . . .

I believe that from the historical standpoint, what has happened in Eastern Europe from 1945 to this day, just as what has happened in China from 1924 to this day, gives us the authentic subject matter for studying the real strategy and tactics of Stalinist Communism for the conquest of the world. . . .

All the strategical elements . . . are present in the Eastern European conquests just as they are present in the Asiatic conquests. There is always the Communist Party in full strength; there is always the maximum aid including armed force from the "base of Socialist revolution"; and there is, above all, the objective condition of revolution, namely, the greatest war in human history.

But there seem to be other equally important elements not revealed in a documentary research which can be clearly seen in a comparative study of the many Communist conquests extending from the Baltic Sea to China and Korea. First, it is not enough to have the conscious leadership of the Communist Party. To be an effective instrumentality of conquest, the Party must be fully armed: it must have a strong army of its own. Second, it is not enough to use Soviet Russia as a base for revolution. It is necessary first to make Soviet Russia the greatest military Power in the entire world, and then to achieve "revolutionary" conquests of adjacent and contiguous territories by sheer overwhelming superiority of military strength. Third, to avoid the appearance of "overt violence" or "revolutionary violence," it is necessary to bring about a "coalition government" with all the "democratic" and "anti-Fascist" parties or groups in a country. And lastly—and above all—there is the strategy of deceit which has been best expressed by the great Lenin: "We must be ready to employ trickery, deceit, lawbreaking, withholding and concealing truth." . . .

In short, the whole strategy is no more and no less than a strategy of naked militarism aided from time to time by the most unscrupulous use of all possible forms of trickery and deceit. Such a strategy could never have succeeded in a world of peace and orderly international life. Its success has depended upon "the objective condition" of an unprecedented world war—a condition which the author of the strategy has sought by all available means to prolong and perpetuate.

II

There is one historical fact which differentiates the Chinese Communist Party from the Communist movements in any other country outside of Soviet Russia—a fact which is essential to a clear understanding of what has been happening in China during the last quarter of a century. It is that the Chinese Communist Party, partly by design and partly by extraordinary historical circumstances, has possessed a formidable army of its own almost from the very early years of its founding. Mr. Edgar Snow, sizing up the Chinese Communist Party at the end of 1937, said: "It is the strongest Communist Party in the world, outside Russia, and the only one, with the same exception, that can boast a mighty army of its own." This unique feature of the Chinese Communist Party has been the most important source of its strength, which Stalin, the masterful strategist of world Communism, has been able to nurture, support, and in the course of 25 years develop into a most powerful instrumentality for subjugating China and thereby dominating the whole Asiatic continent.

Last year, on August 1, a special commemorative postage stamp was issued to mark the 22nd anniversary of the Red Army. Chinese Communist leaders proudly announced to the world that the Red Army, now renamed the "People's Liberation Army," had a regular strength of 4 million men. A year later, August 1, 1950, the newspapers report that Communist China is celebrating the 23rd anniversary of the founding of the Red Army in China. A *New York Times* dispatch from Hong Kong says: "Preparing to mark their Red Army Day tomorrow, the Chinese Communists today described their 5 million-men force as 'one yet destined to play a significant rôle in defending the peace of East Asia and the world.' " This Red Army of 5 million men, supported by a Russian-trained and Russian-supplied Air Force, is the ever-growing Asiatic arm of the militaristic power of world Communism today.

There seems no doubt that the organization of a Communist armed force in every country occupies a very important place in the grand strategy of Stalin and the Comintern for the ultimate success of the world proletarian dictatorship. In the program of the Communist International adopted by the Sixth World Congress on September 1, 1928, one of the eight most important special tasks that the Communist Party in every country must seek to accomplish is specified as "the organization of revolutionary workers' and peasants' armies." In the same program, there is a section devoted to "The Fundamental Tasks of Communist Strategy and Tactics." One of these "fundamental tasks" is for the Communist Party to lead the masses to a direct attack upon the bourgeois state whenever the time is considered ripe for this final step of revolution. "This it does by organizing mass action. . . . This mass action includes: a combination of strikes and demonstrations, a combination of strikes and armed demonstrations, and finally the general strike conjointly with armed insurrection against the State power of the bourgeoisie. The latter form of struggle, which is the supreme form . . . presupposes a plan of campaign, offensive fighting operations and unbounded devotion and heroism on the part of the proletariat. An absolutely essential condition precedent for this form of action is the organization of the broad masses into militant units . . . and intensified revolutionary work in the army and the navy."

Among the 21 "Conditions of Admission to the Communist International," adopted at the Second World Congress of the Comintern, July–August 1920, the fourth condition reads: "Persistent and systematic propaganda and agitation must be carried on in the army, where Communist groups should be formed in every military organization. Wherever, owing to repressive legislation, agitation becomes impossible, it is necessary to carry on such agitation illegally. *But refusal to carry on or participate in such work should be considered equal to treason to the revolutionary cause,* and incompatible with affiliation to the Third International."

Since no country under normal conditions will permit either revolutionary propaganda and agitation in its army or the organization of an armed force by a revolutionary party, it was a most extraordinary opportunity for the Third International to be requested in 1923–1924 by Dr. Sun Yat-sen, leader of a revolutionary party and many times head of an independent regional government, to send political and military experts to China, not only to help reorganize his own party, but actually to organize a new army for a new revolution. It was equally extraordinary for Dr. Sun Yat-sen, in his sincere desire to "bolster the strength of revolutionary elements in the country," to admit Communists as regular members of his own Nationalist Party, thereby making it possible for Communists to influence the policy of the Nationalist Party and even to carry on revolutionary propaganda and agitation in the new army.

The Chinese Communist Party, founded in 1921, had already affiliated itself with the Communist International. The three years of collaboration between the Kuomintang and the Chinese Communist Party (1924–1927) formed the period when the Comintern was making full use of a most unusual opportunity to try out its strategy of world revolution on a large scale in one of the most important strategical areas of the world—China.

This was the time when Stalin was formulating his thesis of the consolidation of Soviet Russia as the base for world revolution, a thesis which never meant abandonment of the cause of world revolution in favor of "Socialism in one country" but only emphasized the importance of effective aid that could come from a strong base. A political struggle for power was then going on in Russia between Stalin and Trotsky, but Stalin was already in full control of the policies of the Comintern. There is little doubt that Stalin was directing the Comintern's China adventure throughout those years of Nationalist-Communist collaboration. . . .

The Communist International went all-out in giving aid to the Nationalist-Communist collaboration. Aid came largely in the form of matériel and expert advisers. The Comintern was able to send to China a remarkable group of political and military advisers, headed by Mikhail Borodin, one of the most brilliant and astute revolutionary organizers, and General Galen, who years later came to be better known as Marshal Blucher. Borodin soon became the dictator of the Chinese Communist Party and at the same time the most influential man in the new government, directing the policy and the strategy of the Revolution. The Whampoa Military Academy was established in Canton in June 1924, with General Chiang Kai-shek as its Director. The Russian military mission under Blucher was helping Chiang to train large numbers of new officers who were to be the nucleus of a new revolutionary army.

Chiang Kai-shek's future Army of Nationalist Revolution was organized on the model of the Russian Red Army and was under the political discipline and indoctrination of the political commissars, many of whom were trained Communists. In that way, Communists and Communism were able to exert much influence over the officers and men of the Nationalist Army. Important Communist leaders of the future, such as Mao Tse-tung, Chou En-lai, Lin Tsu-han (Lin Po-ch'u), etc., played important rôles in the government and in the army. These Communists helped to organize the masses, conduct propaganda and indoctrinate the officers and men of the army. The training centers in Moscow—the Lenin University, the University of the Toilers of the East, and later, the Sun Yat-sen University—were sending back well-trained young men for work in the Party and in the Army.

Dr. Sun Yat-sen died in March 1925. In June 1926, the Army of National Revolution, led by Chiang Kai-shek as Commander-in-Chief, launched the Northward Expedition from Canton. The progress of the revolutionary armies was almost an uninterrupted series of victories. The northern armies were incapable of effectively resisting an inspired army supported by powerful propaganda and organized masses. Changsha was taken in July, Hankow in October, Kiukiang and Nanchang in November. Early in 1927, the Revolutionary forces had reached the Yangtze Delta. The Chinese city of Shanghai was taken in March, and only strong forces of foreign marines protected the foreign settlement from the Nationalists.

Then came the great crisis of the revolution. On March 24, 1927, Nationalist troops entered the city of Nanking after the flight of the northern forces, savagely attacked foreigners in the city, looted and defiled foreign dwellings and consulates, and killed a few of the foreign residents, including the vice-president of the American missionary University of Nanking. Foreign gunboats stationed in the river were forced to fire a barrage to warn against further violence and to guide the fleeing foreigners to escape to the boats.

"The (Nanking) incident," says Professor Latourette, "so aroused the ire of foreigners that for a time extensive intervention seemed imminent." . . .

As we now look back, the Nanking incident seems to be the last of a series of deliberate anti-foreign moves designed to force the foreign Powers to resort to armed intervention and thereby to create a situation of a real "imperialist war"—which, we must remember, Stalin and the Comintern regard as the necessary "objective condition" for the victory of the revolution. The commanding general of the offending army in the Nanking incident was General Ch'en Ch'ien who is now with the Chinese Communist régime. And the man who was considered by the United States Government as being responsible for the whole affair was Mr. Lin Tsu-han, the chief political commissar of the Army. Mr. Lin is one of the most prominent Communist leaders today.

During this period of collaboration, the Chinese Communist Party was functioning efficiently, and the work of infiltration into the Government and especially into the Army was going on smoothly and successfully. What was lacking was a real war, a great imperialist war, without which, according to the Stalinist line of thinking, it was difficult to capture the whole of the Russian-influenced Nationalist Army and convert the Nationalist Revolution into another glorious "October Revolution." All the gigantic anti-British strikes and boycotts throughout 1925–1926 had been directed toward breaking British power in China and forcing Britain to armed intervention. But Britain chose not to fight back. Even after the British Concession at Hankow had been seized by force on January 4, 1927, the British Government persisted in its policy, and ordered its Peking Legation to send a mission to Hankow to negotiate a settlement with the Hankow régime which was under the domination of the Communists. The British Concessions at Hankow and Kiukiang were officially returned to China as a result of these negotiations. But this non-resistant attitude of the British defeated the Communist strategy, which was to start an international conflagration in China by pushing the British to the wall. It is quite probable that the Nanking affair of March 24 was a deliberate strategical move to involve many foreign Powers in armed intervention, which, as I have shown, almost became a reality.

This danger of foreign intervention and a Communist Revolution was averted by the decision of Chiang Kai-shek and the moderate leaders of the Kuomintang to "split" with the Communists, end the collaboration, and "purge" the Nationalist Party of the Communists and their sympathizers. The "purge" began on April 12, 1927, in Shanghai and later in Canton. On April 18, Chiang, with the support of the Elder Statesmen of the Party, set up the National Government in Nanking.

III

Mr. Edgar Snow reports that as early as 1926 Trotsky began urging the formation of Chinese soviets and an independent Chinese Red Army. Such advice from Stalin's opposition at least indicated a line of thought fairly current in Communist circles at that time.

After the moderate wing of the Kuomintang had brought about the "split" and the "purge" in the lower Yangtze Valley, and had set up the National Government at Nanking, the Kremlin sent a secret message to Borodin in Hankow ordering the Chinese Communists to demand majority control of the Kuomintang, confiscation of land of the landowners and the formation of a separate Workers' and Peasants' Army. Borodin did not want to present these demands, but Roy, the Indian representative of the Comintern, gave the message to Wang Ching-wei, chairman of the Left Wing Kuomintang Government at Hankow. Even the Left Wing Kuomintang could not tolerate such open violation of the terms of the collaboration. Borodin and the other Russian advisers were expelled from the Party and ordered to leave China. Eventually the Hankow régime collapsed and was merged with the Government at Nanking.

It is significant that the organization of a Chinese Workers' and Peasants' Red Army was actually ordered by the Kremlin and therefore constituted a part of the strategy of Stalin. And the order was carried out by those Communist leaders and army commanders—Chu Teh, Ho Lung, Yeh T'ing, Mao Tse-tung, Li Lisan and others—who wanted to carry on the Chinese Communist Party but who realized that, after the 1927 coup d'état, the Party must have an armed force of its own. It was these men who started the Nanchang Uprising on August 1, 1927, and the Autumn Crop Uprising in Hunan in September, and who after their defeat and retreat into the mountains, pooled their remnant forces to form the first Red Army. . . .

Toward the end of 1927, the first "soviet" was set up in Chaling, in Hunan. The soviet form was extended to larger areas and early in 1930 a Provisional Soviet Government of Southern Kiangsi was proclaimed. In August 1931, the Executive Committee of the Communist International advised the Chinese Communist Party to establish in some secure region a full-fledged "central Soviet Government" and to carry out a "Bolshevik national policy." Such a "Central Soviet Government of the Soviet Republic òf China" was set up in December 1931, with its capital at Juichin, Kiangsi, near the border of Fukien. Mao Tse-tung was elected Chairman of the Central Soviet Government, and Chu Teh, Commander of the Red Army.

There is no authentic record regarding the highest numerical strength attained by the Red Army in those years of the Kiangsi Soviets. At the 13th Plenary Session of the Executive Committee of the Comintern held in December 1933, Wang Ming (Ch'en Shao-yu), the Chinese delegate, reported that in the territory of the Chinese Soviet Republic, "the regular formations of the Red Army numbered 350,000 men; the irregular forces, 600,000." . . .

This Red Army was essentially a guerrilla force, having terroristic control of the rural area which is the source of food supply and manpower. It was a fighting force of great mobility. Snow has made famous these slogans of Red Army tactics:

1. When the enemy advances, we retreat!
2. When the enemy halts and encamps, we trouble them!
3. When the enemy seeks to avoid a battle, we attack!
4. When the enemy retreats, we pursue!

The declared object of the Army at that time was "to overthrow the Kuomintang régime and destroy its military power." Even the outbreak of Japanese aggression in Manchuria in September 1931 and its rapid expansion into North China and Shanghai did not stop or even diminish this fierce antinationalist insurrection. The National Government issued an appeal for unity against Japan. But the Communists responded with the manifesto of September 30, 1931, in which they vehemently condemned the talk about "a united front against the external enemy" as "ridiculous, absurd, and lying inventions." They declared: "The Communist Party of China is and remains the irreconcilable enemy of the imperialists and the Kuomintang." And in Moscow the Executive Committee of the Comintern adopted a resolution in September 1932, emphasizing that "the Communist Party of China must fight for the overthrow of the Kuomintang, the agent of imperialism."

The Communists in the Red areas of Kiangsi did in February 1932 send out a circular telegram "declaring war" against Japan in the name of the Provisional Central Government of the Soviet Republic of China. Yet in the same month, when a part of the Fifth Army of the Nationalist Government was ordered from Kiangsi to fight the

Japanese in the "First War of Shanghai," the withdrawing troops were attacked at Kan Hsien, Kiangsi, by the Communist armies from the rear and suffered heavy losses. . . .

From 1930 to 1934, the National Government forces under Generalissimo Chiang Kai-shek carried out a number of military expeditions against the Communist armies. By the fall of 1933 the Red districts were being narrowed down to a relatively small area in the border regions between Kiangsi and Fukien. To counteract the mobility of the partisan warfare, the 1933–34 campaign (which is often termed the Fifth or Last Campaign) relied mainly on a combination of military encirclement and economic blockade. This campaign lasted over a year and is said to have involved the mobilization of nearly 1 million men. By means of a network of military roads and thousands of small fortifications, Generalissimo Chiang Kai-shek's strategy was designed to build around the Soviet districts a kind of Great Wall "which gradually moved inward. Its ultimate aim was to encompass and crush the Red Army in a stone vise."

The encirclement and the economic blockade proved so effective that the Red Army and Government were forced to adopt the bold strategy of retreat—to escape annihilation by retreating westward, then southwestward, then northward, and then northeastward, finally reaching their destination in northern Shensi. This retreat has been called "the Long March," which lasted for a whole year and covered about 6,000 miles. . . .

How great were the casualties suffered by the Red Army in the battles and in the Long March? Mr. Snow tells us that Chou En-lai admits that "the Red Army itself suffered over 60,000 casualties in this one siege" (*i.e.*, the long blockade of 1933–34). Mr. Snow also records that "the main forces of the Red Army" at the start of the retreat from Kiangsi, October 1934, were "estimated at about 90,000 men," and that in October 1935, at the end of the trek, they numbered "less than 20,000 survivors."

But the most significant fact is that the Red Army had survived the great extermination campaign of 1933–34, had survived the one-year-long heroic march, and was now joined by the Communist forces that had already established a small Soviet base in Shensi in 1933. Here, in northern Shensi, just below the Great Wall, the survivors of the Red Army and the leaders of the Chinese Communist

Party now settled down to build up their new base as close as possible to the borders of Soviet Russia—the base of revolution. . . .

IV

But the remnant Red Army settling in northern Shensi—one of the poorest areas in the whole of China—was still facing the danger of being once more surrounded and destroyed by the superior military power of the National Government, which had become increasingly strong in the years 1934–36. One of the unexpected results of the Long March of the Communists was the fact that the National Government, in following the trail of the Red Army, was able to consolidate its political control over such southwestern provinces as Kweichow, Yunnan and Szechuan, which had previously succeeded in maintaining a degree of regional autonomy. The rich and economically self-sufficient inland province of Szechuan, for example, when it was invaded by the Red Army in 1935, sent a representative delegation to Nanking to request the Government for adequate military aid to help the provincial armies combat the Red forces. It was, therefore, the Red Army's Long March which enabled Chiang Kai-shek to consolidate the great southwest as the future base in the long war against Japan. And the Generalissimo was determined to exterminate the military power of Chinese Communism before he had to face the greater war of resistance to Japan.

Stalin and the Communist International were then to play another and even more important rôle in protecting and preserving the Red Army strength and providing it with ample opportunities for growth and expansion. The new strategical line was to be the "united front."

Even when the Red Army was fighting its way to the northwest, the policy of the Communist International underwent an important change. The Seventh World Congress, held in Moscow from July to August 1935, officially proclaimed the policy of a "united front" against the rising dangers of aggression by the "Fascist" Powers. The Congress called upon Communist Parties in all countries to cooperate or seek coalition with bourgeois governments and political parties willing to fight Fascism. Special attention was paid to China and the Chinese Communist Party. . . .

Under this new party line, the Chinese Communist Party was or-

ganizing all kinds of front organizations such as "The Association for
National Salvation and Resistance to Japan," "The People's United
Association against Japan," and so on. These associations were carrying on antigovernmental agitation under the cloak of anti-Japanism.
They demanded immediate war against Japan and immediate cessation of the civil war against the Communists. In the summer and
autumn of 1936, seven well-known leaders of the National Salvation
Societies were arrested, and that, of course, gave cause for more
agitation against the Government. Throughout the winter of 1935–36,
student strikes and student demonstrations broke out in Peiping and
other metropolitan centers of education. Hundreds and even
thousands of young students, boys and girls, would often block
railway transportation by lying down on railroad tracks and demanding free passage to Nanking to petition the Government to fight
Japan.

These anti-Japanese demonstrations and the popular demands for
a united front against Japan could not fail to affect the psychology of
the Government troops who were sent to Shensi to fight the remnant
Red Army. This was particularly true of the Tungpei (Northeast) Armies, which had retreated from Manchuria after the Japanese invasion and were now under the command of their former leader, the
"Young Marshal" Chang Hsueh-liang, Deputy Commander-in-Chief of
the campaign against the Red Army in Shensi, with his headquarters
at Sian, the capital of Shensi Province. The propaganda slogans
against these armies were especially effective: "Go back to Your Old
Home and Fight the Japanese Devils!"

Before long, the "Bandit-Suppression Army Officers" were beginning to fraternize with the "bandits." By the summer of 1936, some
kind of secret understanding was reached between the Communist
leaders in Northern Shensi and Chang Hsueh-liang and his Sian
colleague, General Yang Hu-ch'eng, Pacification Commissioner of
Shensi Province. The war against the Reds was slowing down,
thereby giving the Red Army a much-needed opportunity to rest and
recuperate.

Chang Hsueh-liang, the Young Marshal, then in his middle thirties,
was a spoiled child who never matured intellectually. Born to wealth
and power, he was ambitious and vainglorious. Being patriotic and
intensely anti-Japanese, he was easily persuaded to lend his support
to the work of anti-Japanese agitation and demonstration by the

National Salvation Societies and student bodies. The Nanking Government began to hear reports that the Deputy Commander-in-Chief of the Bandit-Suppression Campaign, second only to Chiang Kai-shek in command, was financing the antigovernment front organizations. He was drifting into a position where he could imagine himself at the head of the anti-Japan and anti-Chiang "United Front."

It was against such a background that the "arrest" of Chiang Kai-shek by Chang Hsueh-liang took place in Sian on the morning of December 12, 1936. Because of the almost complete absence of authentic records, the story of the Sian affair has never been, and may never be, fully told. But the following facts seem to be of importance.

First, Chiang Kai-shek went to Sian with the full knowledge that he was going into the territory of the conspirators. Dr. Wong Wen-hao, my geologist friend who was serving as Secretary-General of the Executive Yuan, told me in Nanking at least five days before the coup that the Generalissimo was fully aware that the Young Marshal was plotting a revolt against the Government. Then why did Chiang go? The answer has to be a conjecture. Chiang was a prodigal son turned Puritan Christian at a mature age, and the world must try to understand him in that light. He probably wanted to win back his wayward "younger brother," Chang Hsueh-liang, by convincing him that he still had complete trust in him. He not only went to Sian practically unguarded; he actually called a military conference to meet at Sian to which all his highest ranking generals were summoned. The conference began on December 7. So what actually happened on the morning of December 12 was the arrest of Chiang Kai-shek and of practically all the best-known generals of Nationalist China, the only notable exceptions being Ho Ying-ch'in and Ku Chu-t'ung.

Why did he call the military conference? Chiang probably wanted to convince the conspirators how futile it would be for them to attempt any revolt in face of the overwhelmingly strong position of Government forces in Loyang and along the Lunghai railway. He probably also wanted them to see how the Government could carry on the anti-Red campaign even without their help. In short, it was possible that the military conference was called at Sian for the purpose of convincing the conspirators that the Government had nothing to hide from them.

Second, Chang Hsueh-liang must have planned the whole affair by himself. He was fully capable of quick decision and cold-blooded murder, as he had shown in his killing of two of his father's ablest and most trusted generals—Generals Yang Yu-t'ing and Ch'ang Yin-huai, when the victims were dinner guests in his own home. And he must have planned it as a part of a rebellion under the banner of "the Anti-Japan and Anti-Chiang United Front." This is shown by the announcement on December 14 of the formation of the United Anti-Japanese Army, to consist of the armed forces of the Red Army, the Northwest Army of Yang Hu-ch'eng and the Northeast Army of Chang Hsueh-liang. And the Young Marshal was "elected" chairman of the United Anti-Japanese Military Council. . . .

And, lastly, the all-important question: Why was Chiang Kai-shek able to fly back to Nanking on Christmas Day? What had happened to make that possible? Miss Agnes Smedley, who was in Sian at the time, reported that after Chiang's party had left Sian a group of young Northeast officers and National Salvation leaders said to her: "We have been betrayed! The Red Army induced the Young Marshal to release Chiang." Edgar Snow believes that the Communist delegates (Chou En-lai, Yeh Chien-ying and Po Ku) whom Marshal Chang summoned to Sian were "most effective" in bringing about Chiang's release.

The United States Department of State and David J. Dallin seem to agree that the release of the Generalissimo was apparently ordered by Moscow. "The Chinese Communist Party . . ." says the Department of State, "at first favored the execution of the Generalissimo, but, apparently on orders from Moscow, shifted to a policy of saving his life. The Chinese Communist concept, inspired from Moscow, became one of promoting a 'united front' with the Generalissimo and the National Government against the Japanese; this concept seems to have played a considerable rôle in saving the life of the Generalissimo."

Mr. Dallin, however, points out that, before the Sian incident, Moscow and Nanking had already made progress in negotiating "a new nonaggression pact of momentous importance." This new pact (not signed until August 1937) was to serve as the basis for future Russian aid to China in the early years of the Sino-Japanese war. So Dallin believes that "Moscow . . . valued a pact with Chiang more highly than one with the irregular forces of the insurrectionists," and that this probably explains why Moscow "adopted an unequivocally hostile attitude toward the Sian rebellion." As evidence of this "hostile attitude," Dallin quotes the editorial from *Izvestia* of December 14, the very first day that the news of the Sian rebellion was published in Moscow. "Under whatever slogans and program the Sian insurrection be conducted," says the *Izvestia* editorial, "this move . . . represents a danger not only to the Nanking government, but to all of China. It is clear that despite Chang Hsueh-liang's anti-Japanese banner, his move can benefit only Japanese imperialism. *So long as the Nanking government conducts a policy of resistance to the Japanese aggressors, the united popular front against Japan is understood by all its participants to mean not a front against Nanking, but a front together with Nanking.*" Mr. Dallin's conclusion, therefore, is that "there is no doubt that the position taken in Moscow had a decisive influence on the course of events in Sian and perhaps did save Chiang's life." But, Dallin adds, "in the last analysis Chiang owed his rescue to Japan's vigorous offensive on the Asiatic continent, and to the reality of the Japanese menace to both Russia and China." . . .

While the above conclusions may be correct in general, I am inclined to think that, in the light of the future trend of events, Stalin's strategy was probably greatly influenced by his solicitude for the future of the Chinese Red Army, which, we must remember, was one of his own creations. My friend, the late Agnes Smedley, may be more revealing than she meant to be when she quoted a young Army officer as saying, one hour after Chiang Kai-shek and Chang Hsueh-liang had left Sian by air: "The Red Army induced the young Marshal to release Chiang." The Reds knew that the newly-formed "United Anti-Japanese Army" could not stand the furious attacks of the advancing Nationalist armies that were already surrounding Shensi on all sides. And they knew what opportunities for expansion there would be if their Army were to become a part of the National Army. . . .

The Generalissimo returned to Nanking amidst the really spontaneous rejoicings of the Chinese people. He left Sian without having to sign any terms. But this Puritan Christian was won over, probably for the first time in his life, by a masterful stroke of strategy. Of all the things Stalin has ever done, that act came closest to statesmanship. The Generalissimo felt reassured that he could take in the Chinese Communists as partners in the common fight against the

Japanese aggressor. The war for the extermination of the Red Army was ended. The Red Army was saved.

Seven months later, in July and August 1937, China took up the fight against Japan. The Second World War, which had actually started on September 18, 1931, in Manchuria, and which Chiang Kai-shek had for six years tried to avoid, often under most humiliating circumstances, was now in full swing.

Another month later, in September 1937, the Red Army was incorporated as the Eighth Route Army of the National Army. It was now sent to the war front in Shansi, where it looked forward to a future of unlimited growth and expansion.

V

When the Red Army was first incorporated in the National Army in September 1937, its numerical strength was officially estimated at 25,000 men. Seven years later, in September 1944, Lin Tsu-han, a member of the Central Committee of the Chinese Communist Party, reported to the People's Political Council that "In the course of more than seven years of war, the Communist military force has developed along the right tracks and consists now of an army of 475,000 men and a people's militia force of 2.2 million men." And a few months later, in April 1945, Mao Tse-tung presented a 50,000-word report to the Seventh Congress of the Communist Party, held at Yenan, in which he said: "As I am preparing this report, our regular army has already expanded to 910,000 men and our people's militia force has increased beyond 2.2 million men." . . .

From 1935 to 1937, the Communists on the Shensi-Kansu border area occupied only 21 or 22 counties. According to their own estimate, the population was about 1.5 million. But in April 1945, Mao Tse-tung claimed that "the Liberated Area now extends from Inner Mongolia in the north to the Hainan Island in the south, extending into 19 provinces and containing 95.5 million people." "In most of the territories occupied by the Japanese enemy," said Mao, "there will be found the Eighth Route Army, or the New Fourth Army, or some other people's armies carrying on partisan activities." The 19 provinces mentioned by Mao include Liaoning, Jehol, Chahar, Suiyuan, Shensi, Kansu, Ninghsia, Shansi, Hopei, Honan, Shantung, Kiangsu, Chekiang, Anhui, Kiangsi, Hupei, Hunan, Kwantung and Fukien.

The Chinese Government has expressed doubts about the figures of Red Army strength. According to its estimate, Communist forces of 25,000 in 1937 were increased at the end of the war to 310,000. Mr. Dallin also considers Mao Tse-tung's figure of 910,000 men as much exaggerated. Dallin thinks that the real strength of the Chinese Communist armies in 1945 probably amounted to from 300,000 to 350,000.

That was a small army scattered over 19 provinces. And it was poorly armed and poorly supplied. After 1941 it had practically ceased to receive monetary subsidy or allotment of ammunition from the National Government. Soviet Russia tried to act properly during the years of the war: the military supplies under the Sino-Soviet barter arrangement were delivered to the Central Government. The amount of ammunition that could come through from Soviet territory to the Communist area in the northwest must have been very small.

American aid and arms for the Communists in China never materialized. Even President Roosevelt's attempt in 1944 to place General Joseph W. Stilwell in command, under Chiang Kai-shek, of all Chinese forces, "including the Communist forces," did not succeed. The President had said to Chiang Kai-shek: "When the enemy is pressing us toward possible disaster, it appears unsound to reject the aid of anyone who will kill Japanese." But Chiang Kai-shek was opposed to it. His position was supported by the American Ambassador, Patrick J. Hurley. So General Stilwell was recalled. The Chinese Red Army remained poorly armed and ill-equipped. It remained a guerrilla force of great mobility and skill, but as late as the last year of the war, it had not attained the stature of an established army that could face the Japanese enemy or the Government forces in open battles.

Then came the sudden end of the Pacific war in August 1945. On August 9, Soviet Russia declared war on Japan. On the same day, the Soviet Army began to move into Manchuria. On August 14, Japan surrendered. Air landings of Soviet troops were made at Mukden, at Kirin, and at Changchun. Before the end of August, Soviet Russian troops were in complete control of Manchuria—of its railroads, of the great naval base of Port Arthur, of the great port of Dairen, and of all the other ports and cities.

On August 11, General Chu Teh, commander-in-chief of all Communist forces, issued an order to four Communist Army Groups to

march on to the northeast into the provinces of Chahar, Jehol, Liaoning and Kirin.

Within two or three months large numbers of Chinese Communist
troops were in control of many important sections of Manchuria.
Many of these Communist soldiers came into Manchuria
camouflaged as unarmed "civilians" and uniformed "Nationalists,"
who upon their arrival inside Manchuria, were quickly and fully
armed and equipped from the huge military stocks left over by the
surrendered Japanese Kwantung army.

With the invading Soviet armies there also came the Chinese Army
that had been organized on Soviet soil out of different Chinese
detachments which had left Manchuria in the 1930s. "A considerable
number of Chinese Communists who had spent years in Russia came
with them. This force . . . brought with it technical and administrative skill, discipline, and loyalty to Russia; it was to play a primary
rôle in the future of Manchuria."

The Soviet Army did not withdraw until the end of April 1946.
During the nine months of occupation in Manchuria, every facility
was given to the Chinese Communists, while serious obstacles were
placed in the way of Nationalist troops that were being slowly trans-
ported into Manchuria with the logistical support of the United States
Government.

In October 1945, Vice-Admiral Daniel E. Barbey's fleet was ordered
to escort Chinese Government troops to Manchuria. But all the seaports on the Manchuria coast were closed to them. At Hulutao,
Communists on shore fired upon a launch from Admiral Barbey's
flagship. The American task force and transports turned away. On
October 29, Marshal Malinovsky, the Commander-in-Chief of Soviet
forces in Manchuria, agreed that Chinese Nationalist troops could
land at the port of Yingkow, and that Soviet troops would leave the
port by November 10. But on November 6, Admiral Barbey learned
that the Russians had deliberately evacuated five days ahead of
schedule and left the port in the hands of the Chinese Communists
who threatened to open fire on the American convoy. Once more
Admiral Barbey's flotilla turned away. The Chinese Government
troops were eventually landed at the port of Chinwangtao, inside the
Great Wall—from which point they commenced the long march over-
land into Manchuria, which the outside world considered already lost
to world Communism.

In June 1946, the Chinese Communist broadcast announced to the world that the People's Liberation Army now numbered 1.2 million, in its regular formations. In a speech broadcast on December 25, 1947, Mao Tse-tung said that "from 1937 to 1947, in 11 years, the Chinese Communist Party has developed a Party membership of 2.7 million and a People's Liberation Army of 2 million men." A Communist broadcast dated October 14, 1948, placed the Red Army's strength at 3 million. On August 1, 1949, it was 4 million. On August 1, 1950, it was 5 million.

In December 1947, Mao Tse-tung presented a report to the Central Committee of the Party under the title, "The Present Situation and Our Duties." In this lengthy report, he painted a glowing picture of the military successes of the Red Army:

> The Chinese People's Revolutionary War has now come to a turning point. The People's Liberation Army has smashed the offensive war of Chiang Kai-shek's reactionary armies, and has now started its own offensives. In the first year (July 1946–June 1947), our Armies defeated Chiang's offensive attacks on several fronts, and forced him to take a defensive position. In the first quarter of the second year (July–September 1947) our Armies have turned to offensive attacks on a nation-wide scale.

Out of Manchuria, Communist armies, newly equipped and reconditioned, were pouring into Shantung across the sea, and into North China by land. By September 1948 Shantung was lost. By November, Manchuria was lost. By early 1949, North China was lost. Through a most astute and wicked stroke of strategy, Stalin had taken Manchuria and made it the contiguous base for the new military strength of Chinese Communism, behind which lay the unlimited support of Soviet Russia, now the mightiest military Power in the whole world.

A conference of the Big Three had been held at Yalta in February 1945. The conference lasted seven days. At one of the very last sessions, Prime Minister Churchill was not present, and President Roosevelt, according to Harry Hopkins' record, "was tired and anxious to avoid further argument." At this meeting, Stalin proposed the conditions for Soviet Russia's entry into the Pacific war. The resulting agreement was kept secret from China until June 14 when Ambassador Hurley informed Generalissimo Chiang Kai-shek in Chungking that on February 11, 1945, Roosevelt, Churchill and Stalin, on behalf of their Governments, signed at Yalta a secret agreement. The following is the text:

The leaders of the three Great Powers—the Soviet Union, the United States of America and Great Britain—have agreed that in two or three months after Germany has surrendered and the war in Europe has terminated, the Soviet Union shall enter into the war against Japan on the side of the Allies on condition that:

(1) The status quo in Outer-Mongolia (the Mongolian People's Republic) shall be preserved.

(2) The former rights of Russia violated by the treacherous attack of Japan in 1904 shall be restored, viz.:

(a) The southern part of Sakhalin as well as all the islands adjacent to it shall be returned to the Soviet Union.

(b) The commercial port of Dairen shall be internationalized, the preeminent interests of the Soviet Union in the port being safeguarded and the lease of Port Arthur as a naval base of the U.S.S.R. restored.

(c) The Chinese Eastern Railroad and the South-Manchurian Railroad which provides an outlet to Dairen shall be jointly operated by the establishment of a joint Soviet-Chinese Company, it being understood that the preeminent interests of the Soviet Union shall be safeguarded and that China shall retain full sovereignty in Manchuria.

(3) The Kurile Islands shall be handed over to the Soviet Union.

It is understood that the agreement concerning Outer-Mongolia and the ports and railroads referred to above will require concurrence of Generalissimo Chiang Kai-shek. The President will take measures in order to obtain this concurrence on advice from Marshal Stalin.

The Heads of the three Great Powers have agreed that these claims of the Soviet Union shall be unquestionably fulfilled after Japan has been defeated.

For its part the Soviet Union expresses its readiness to conclude with the National Government of China a pact of friendship and alliance between the U.S.S.R. and China in order to render assistance to China with its armed forces for the purpose of liberating China from the Japanese yoke.

By these very loosely worded articles, the fate of Manchuria, and of China as a whole, and of Korea (although she is not mentioned here) and very possibly of the whole continent of Asia, was sealed and history was set back 40 years. Of the three signatories, apparently Stalin alone had remembered his history well. For on Japan's surrender, Stalin issued a proclamation in which he depicted his four-day war with Japan as Russia's revenge for her defeat in 1904–05 at the hands of Japan. "The defeat of Russian troops in 1904, . . .'' said the proclamation, ''left bitter memories in the minds of the people. It lay like a black spot on our country. Our people believed and hoped that a day would come when Japan would be smashed and that blot effaced. Forty years have we, the people of the old generation, waited for this day."

That is the historical meaning of the principal clause in the secret agreement that "the former rights of Russia violated by the treacherous attack of Japan in 1904 shall be restored." It was in this historical light of Russia's revenge that Stalin appealed for the support of Roosevelt. According to Hopkins' record, "Stalin said to Roosevelt that if his conditions were not met, it would be very difficult to explain to the Russian people why they must go to war against Japan. . . . However, Stalin said, if the required political conditions were met, then it would not be difficult for him to explain to the Supreme Soviet and the people just what was their stake in the Far Eastern war."

The whole affair was a strategy of deceit. China was not a participant, but the President was to take measures in order to obtain China's concurrence. Even this undertaking by the President was not enough. Stalin insisted that this agreement must be put in writing and must contain the statement: "The Heads of the three Great Powers have agreed that these claims of the Soviet Union shall be unquestionably fulfilled after Japan has been defeated." That is to say, Soviet Russia must have these claims fulfilled even if China refuses to give the concurrence!

That Stalin was deliberately deceiving and blackmailing Roosevelt, I have not the slightest doubt. For years past, Stalin and Molotov had taken every occasion to impress on the American leaders that Soviet Russia had no interest in supporting Chinese Communists, because they were not Communists at all. The Soviet leaders had insisted that Chiang Kai-shek was a great man and deserved support, and that the United States must take a leading part in giving aid to China. Molotov in August 1944 even told Ambassador Hurley and Mr. Donald Nelson the "inside" story about the Generalissimo's imprisonment at Sian in December 1936, and assured them that it was "the political and moral support of the Soviet Government" that saved Chiang's life and returned him to the seat of his government.

Henry Wallace, Hurley and Hopkins had all told President Roosevelt of this friendly concern and political and moral support which Soviet Russia and Stalin had for Chiang Kai-shek. In the Department of State version of the Yalta Agreement on the Far East, there is a very revealing footnote which quotes Ambassador Harriman's comment on the clause relating to the "lease of Port Arthur as a naval base of the U.S.S.R." Mr. Harriman says: "I believe President Roosevelt looked upon the lease of Port Arthur for a naval base *as an arrangement similar to privileges which the United States has negotiated with other countries for the mutual security of two friendly nations.*" . . .

VI

Such, in brief, is the story of the unfolding of Stalin's strategy of conquest in China. The heart of this strategy has been the creation, preservation and nurturing to full strength of the Chinese Red Army. It has taken nearly a quarter of a century for the Red Army to achieve sufficient power for the conquest of continental China. This Red Army was many times defeated, broken up and nearly annihilated by Chiang Kai-shek's armies; and Stalin and world Communism might never have succeeded in China if the greatest war in human history had not intervened.

Stalin himself has summed up the China situation in one sentence: "The special characteristic of the Chinese revolution lies in the fact that it is an armed people fighting an armed counter-revolution." In plain language, this formulation meant that the Communist conquest of China by armed force had up to then been successfully resisted by the armed force of Nationalist China. Because of this successful resistance by the Government, the whole Chinese Communist movement came to be conceived by Mao Tse-tung and his fellow militarists as essentially an armed struggle for power. "In China," said Mao in a 1939 speech, "there is no place for the proletariat without armed struggle; there is no place for the people without armed struggle; there is no place for the Communist Party without armed struggle; and there is no victory of the revolution without armed struggle."

The pattern of conquest is therefore the same in China as in Poland, Bulgaria, Hungary, Rumania, Yugoslavia and Czechoslovakia. It is the pattern of conquest by force and violence projected from the contiguous Russian base. What seems to differentiate China from the seemingly much easier conquests in Central and Eastern Europe has been the much greater complexity and difficulty of the conquest, which made it necessary for Stalin to resort to the most cunning forms of secret diplomacy in order to overcome the resistance that Nationalist China had been able to summon for over two decades.

John K. Fairbank

REFORM AND REVOLUTION IN CHINA

Reacting to the rise of Mao Tse-tung to power in China late in 1949, John K. Fairbank, the distinguished Harvard scholar, sought to explain the political upheaval, not in Stalinist, but in Chinese terms. Those who viewed the Communist triumph in China as a Russian plot, he advised, overlooked its all-Chinese cast. Fairbank, who spent seven years in China before, during, and after the war, condemned the notion that the explanation for the Nationalist collapse lay in United States leadership which allegedly favored a Communist victory. Regarding this a form of self-flattery, he continued: "It assumes that we Americans can really call the tune if we want to, even among 475 million people in the inaccessible rice paddies of a subcontinent ten thousand miles away." If the United States could not control events in China, it seemed equally certain that the U.S.S.R. could not do so either. Fairbank attributed the Chinese upheaval largely to a great national reform urge which found its ultimate expression in the leadership of Mao Tse-tung. He agreed that Russia and China were deeply influenced by Stalinist dogma, but he noted that the Sino-Soviet relationship had its flaws which would become evident with the passage of time.

There are many interpretations of the Chinese Communist rise to power and most of them go to extremes. Some regard it as simply a Russian plot, overlooking its all-Chinese cast. Others see it as an unavoidable act of nature like an earthquake, neglecting the very human nature of history. Some say we helped Chiang Kai-shek too little, and some—rather few—protest that our error lay in helping him too much.

    Amid all these confusing claims and considerations, military, economic, and political, we have neglected the realm of ethics. I believe

From "China," *The Atlantic* 186 (November 1950): 21–25. Copyright © 1950, by The Atlantic Monthly Company, Boston, Mass. Reprinted with permission.

our chief failure in dealing with the Communist revolution in China has been to underestimate the vigor of Chinese moral sentiment as the basis of patriotic effort and to pay too little attention to the morality of our own position in the eyes of the Chinese. . . . We find ourselves most violently condemned in China, not only by the Communists but also by patriotic Chinese who have been close to our way of life. This is an unhappy denouement to a century of Sino-American friendship. How shall we account for it?

The quick and easy explanation is Communist propaganda and indoctrination. Communist lies are so big that they really constitute an entire realm of thought, beginning with Lenin's great half-truth that imperialism is the final phase of capitalism. In China the Malik view of the world now holds sway. The Chinese people are at present a "captive audience." If Mao Tse-tung can feed them the "facts," he can control the judgments they reach. This still does not explain, however, how so many Chinese have come to put their trust in Mao. What is the explanation of his rise to power?

On this point our counsels are discordant; yet it is plain that if the American public cannot agree on why we failed in China, we have little prospect of constructing an effective policy either toward China or for the rest of Asia.

The popular explanation among Republican political aspirants is to blame it on the Democrats. This is reminiscent of the old Chinese ritual which made the Emperor in Peking responsible for drought, flood, famine, or other acts of nature anywhere in the empire. As used today by people who ought to know better, there is a slick element of self-flattery in blaming the revolution in China on the administration in Washington. It assumes that we Americans can really call the tune if we want to, even among 475 million people in the inaccessible rice paddies of a subcontinent ten thousand miles away.

This theory that Mao Tse-tung's rise to power in China is some-how our fault in America appeals both to the Puritan conscience and to our view of ourselves as world arbiters, but it leaves Chiang Kai-shek out of account. After all, he came to power in Nanking during the Coolidge administration. Since then the leadership of Japan, Korea, the Philippines, Indonesia, Burma, India, and Pakistan has seen cataclysmic changes amid two decades of violence and disaster. Hoover, Roosevelt, and Truman have occupied the White

House. Chiang Kai-shek sat on top of the Chinese revolution as long as he could, fighting it with arms rather than reforms, but no amount of American aid could have kept him there forever, nor could even a nation of MacArthurs put him back today.

The final word on the Generalissimo as a recipient of American aid and advice has long since been written, by several score American specialists who were not political appointees and who included General George C. Marshall. Six hundred pages of their sober reports and appraisals were published as appendices to the White Paper on China in August, 1949, and may still be obtained from the Superintendent of Documents for three dollars. Among them General Wedemeyer in his famous report of September, 1947, concluded that "the only working basis on which national Chinese resistance to Soviet aims can be revitalized is through the present corrupt, reactionary, and inefficient Chinese National Government." Wedemeyer recommended military aid "under the supervision of American advisers." Secretary of State Marshall, who had sought vainly for a year to advise Chiang Kai-shek, refused to take the risk involved in trying to save him with American military power. This was fortunate, indeed, for by 1947 Chiang was beyond saving. The explanation of his collapse, like the explanation of Chinese anti-Americanism today, must be found within the Chinese scene, in the realm of Chinese public opinion and its moral and ethical sentiments.

II

An ancient Chinese military maxim runs: "Know your own side. Know the other side. In a hundred battles you will win a hundred victories." With our European background, we know little of Asia or its ethical values. Today our greatest danger is that the Russians may capitalize on our ignorance.

The conditions of Chinese life are far outside our experience or even imagination; rice or millet without meat, shoes without leather, a board to sleep on, worms in the belly, and an age-old dislike of landlords and foreign invaders—all this has been the stuff of everyday experience among an intelligent people crowded in a hundred thousand villages across the face of the world's oldest country. In a modern world where there is hope of betterment, these conditions have been inevitably the wherewithal for revolution. When our missionaries and traders first stimulated the revolutionary process in the old Chinese empire by importing subversive Western ways a century ago, they represented a dominant Western society which had no need to understand the effete East. Today it is different. The spread of industry and nationalism, science and democracy, has turned the tables on us. Asia is changing faster than we are.

The Communist success-story in China is now well known in outline: the methods of indoctrinating students who can mobilize peasants, the techniques of rent reduction and land redistribution, of village "liberation" and class reorganization, of personal conversion and guidance by self-criticism. Not many serious observers fell for the line that the Chinese Communists were "mere agrarian reformers." They take pride in being Communists, but they use agrarian reform as a basis for power, just as they use Chinese patriotism. As yet no signs of Titoism have appeared. Nor should they be expected as long as the Stalinist dogma retains its appeal to Chinese idealism, and its moral respectability in Chinese public opinion.

This peculiar Chinese public opinion is a pervasive force which we have neglected to our own disaster. It is not expressed in editorials, in a country where the press is controlled and the people largely illiterate. But it led Chiang's armies to surrender, taking with them the American weapons that Mao's armies now can use against us. This Chinese public opinion is the force that bestows the traditional Mandate of Heaven upon the successful rebel in Chinese politics. It goes back to the beginning of Chinese history and is intimately bound up with the Chinese moral sense. It includes a healthy respect for military and police power, but not for them alone. In political life this force of opinion is seen in the acquiescence of the people in the government of the day. One might call it part of the "unwritten constitution" of the Chinese polity; and let us remember that the Chinese body politic is the oldest in the world. In short, in the crowded life of China the attitude of the populace, their cooperation or avoidance of cooperation with the regime in power, has been the index of that regime's longevity. This attitude has not been expressed through political institutions like the elections and parliaments of the West, but it has been made evident through many centuries in the daily conduct of the people. Bad government, for example, invites corruption, which produces worse government. A regime whose leaders have lost public respect is soon knifed by its own bureaucracy, in which bad men drive out good. Community noncooperation, well known to us in Chinese shopkeepers' boycotts, can spread to the whole nation.

The Russians or the Nazis may have been able to get results from a slave-and-police state, but the Chinese Communists are taking no chances. They rose to power by establishing within China greater moral prestige than the Kuomintang, and thus far they have worked hard to keep it—long hours, ascetic living, incorruptibility, and devotion to their cause. Their Communism, though genuine Marxism-Leninism of the Moscow orthodoxy, is operating in the shadow of twenty centuries of Confucianism. While no one expects China's dead past to reassert itself, one must still acknowledge that the Chinese way of life is distinctive and persistent. In dealing with the Chinese people neither we nor the Communists can disregard it.

III

It may seem paradoxical that a Communist system which uses slave labor and terror in East Europe and Russia can maintain a genuine moral prestige in China. Of course many millions in China oppose the new order. Newly "liberated" peasants find themselves taxed as never before. But let us remember that our own revolution of 1776 was carried through by the active one-third among us. The inner core of the Chinese Communist Party, which now claims five million members, has been knit together and battle-tested over a generation. It is operating a coalition in which non-Communists actively participate. The broad extent of this active non-Communist collaboration among China's small literate elite is the index of Communism's ideological success and of our failure. These non-Communist intellectuals include scholars and administrators of international repute, men of integrity who defied Japan, spent the war years in the shanty towns of Free China's universities, and refused to be intimidated by Kuomintang police. They are not men easily bought or coerced. Their active collaboration seems due to several factors.

First, China is in a period of hope; the promises of the new order are still untarnished, as in the first years of Soviet Russia. Second, the period of Nationalist collapse is still fresh in memory—the inexorable inflation, the Kuomintang terror against intellectuals, the insecurity. Today the inflation has been suppressed, albeit by Draconian methods, and civil war is over. Third, what one expects of any government in China is not what we would expect in America. Incorrupt officials are a blessing even if public services are few. Young Communist administrators can shine against a background of warlordism. Fourth, while the Peking regime is far from thoroughly established over large areas of the South, where disaffection and unrest are reported on a large scale, the fact remains that for the patriot who wants to save his country there is no rival channel for his effort, no competitor to Mao as a leader, no one else with his prestige.

What is this moral prestige? Mao has it not merely because he fought for thirty years and won. It springs rather from his apparent "sincerity" (in the sense in which Chinese and Japanese diplomats used to accuse each other of lacking it), his purity of intention. By his pronouncements and conduct, Mao and his party have established the general belief that they mean well toward the Chinese masses, that they know China's basic problems and have the means and determination to solve them. If he and his party lead China only to disaster in the end, it will not be the first time that self-appointed saviors have believed themselves utterly sincere.

This sincerity can be understood only in the old Chinese context, where the ideal government is not "the rule of law," but "the rule of men and virtue"—that is, government by superior men whose decisions are guided by their enlightened moral sense. This was the essence of the Confucian tradition. The rigorous training in the classics, the ancient examination system, the inculcation of orthodox Confucian morality, all aimed at administration by superior men who could rule benevolently and justly by applying the moral precepts of the sages, not by following the letter of the law. The opportunity for Marxism-Leninism to exploit this Chinese tradition is obvious.

The inveterate evil in the grand moral concept of sage-government has been that Chinese officials often mouthed virtue but grew corrupt. Personal despotism has been the twin brother of Confucian morality. The pluralism of our society, which requires no One Man at the top and which gives us variety and strength, stems from the rule of law as opposed to the rule of men. It is on this ground that we line up against Marxism-Leninism and also against the Confucian tradition. But in the Chinese context, a Marxist-Leninist regime which is distinctly below the level of political life which we would tolerate in our own country seems to hold the promise of being an improvement over the old order. It is judged by the professed intentions and the conduct of its leaders. Can their promise be realized?

If we also judge by the aims set forth by Mao and the Chinese Communist Party, it seems possible; judged by the Russian record, it seems entirely improbable. Russian manipulation of the Chinese revolution, so badly bungled in the 1920s, has achieved a new high point. The Marxist-Leninst ideology of the Chinese revolution, which commends itself by promising increased production and welfare at home, is the same ideology that proclaims the Kremlin's international crusade against "capitalist-imperialist aggression" in foreign relations. The Communist thought-control system which mobilizes great production drives and efforts at national reconstruction within China is the same system that feeds the Chinese people Moscow's lies about American "aggression" in Korea or Formosa. Russia contrives to get the Chinese people to do her dirty work. Militarism is likely to eat up China's small productive surplus and impoverish her people; Mao is likely to lose his moral prestige and find himself head of another Communist police-state. But this is still for the future.

IV

Our first step in the necessary long-term job of appealing to Chinese moral sentiment and enlisting it against the Russian system is to recognize our own past errors. When we supported Chiang Kai-shek, both he and we fell into a trap. Relying on our support, his shaky Nationalist regime was under less pressure to carry through reforms which would compete with Communist reforms; with our arms, it was the more inclined to use force against the Communists, which quickly proved disastrous. On our part, having committed ourselves to approach China only through Chiang as the legitimate channel during our war against Japan, we were less able to bargain with him for postwar land reform and other reconstruction programs which might have headed off collapse. The White Paper documents our long frustration in this quagmire, unable either to influence the Nationalist regime effectively or to dissociate ourselves from it, impotent either to reform Chiang Kai-shek or to disillusion his political backers in America.

First, we must recall that Chiang, like other Asian leaders in contact with the West, had to have two faces: toward us abroad he was a true patriot and a Christian, incorrupt and unflinching; toward the world of Chinese politics, he functioned as a power-holder and political manipulator, head of the government, party, and army, but not a reformer. While chief of state, he had to be his own Boss Hague, enmeshed in political deals with the conservative landlord-warlord forces of the countryside. This made him the natural target of complaint and moral indignation.

Second, the Chinese Communists used against us the well-tried tactic of polarization, which operates in two phases. In phase one they espoused all things good and desirable, all the reforms and freedoms dear to the liberal heart, and denounced all Nationalist evils. This made the liberals regard the Communists as almost liberal, and made the Nationalist right wing regard the liberals as almost Communist. Phase two followed when the Communists proclaimed, "There is no middle road; who is not for us is against us," while the Nationalist right wing, being themselves totalitarian-minded, attacked the liberals who tried to stay on a middle ground. Examples abound of this pulverizing of the center by both extremes. Thus in June, 1946, a non-Communist liberal peace delegation from Shanghai came to Nanking to protest against civil war. Nationalist thugs surrounded them at the station for several hours and finally gave them a professional beating up—no one was killed but all were hospitalized. Several of these genuine would-be liberals are now collaborating at Peking. In incident after incident the Communists, with an assist from Nationalist goon squads, won over the liberals of China.

Third, it has not been difficult for the Communists by ceaseless repetition and illustration to identify the United States with the hated Nationalist regime, especially when the Nationalists themselves and their ardent American backers have constantly asserted this identification. Our asserted identity with Chiang has been the Communists' trump card, the big gun used against us. Thus the good name earned by three generations of our missionaries and educators has been all but smothered, and China is being steadily mobilized against American influence.

V

What is the remedy for our disaster? In general I think we must bring the moral factor more fully into our political-economic-military thinking. We must distinguish in our own minds between the Communist reform program within China, which has both good and bad points, and the Chinese Communist integration in the Russian system of imperialism, which menaces both world peace and the welfare of the Chinese people. We must abandon any hope of engineering a Chinese Titoism by some tactic of wooing or bargaining; yet we must never forget that China and Russia are two different countries with different ways of life and different group interests, which may not be forever controllable by Stalinist dogma. It seems apparent to us that the best interest of the Chinese people conflicts with the ulterior interest of the Kremlin; within the wall of Moscow propaganda, however, the Chinese people may have great difficulty in seeing this. We should make it possible for them to do so. This calls for a more vigorous American information program, but primarily it calls for an American determination to avoid the Russian trap of polarization.

This tactic has given the Russian and Chinese Communists their greatest success. When Mao says, "We lean to one side," we play his game by saying, "China is in the Russian camp." Actually, Mao is engaged in trying to drag the Chinese people into the Russian camp, but we give a push, too, by refusing recognition. It now seems plain that the Stalin-Mao axis never wanted us to recognize Communist China: the British recognition has not been accepted in practical terms, nor would ours have been. But to the Chinese people we, not the Communists, now bear the onus of preventing friendly relations between the United States and the new China. By neglecting the struggle for moral prestige within China, we have let the Communists consolidate their position as defenders of China's welfare and national interest. In actual fact, we are convinced that Chinese Communism is selling out China's true interest to that of Moscow. But we cannot demonstrate this so long as we are successfully pictured by Moscow as acting out the role of "imperialist aggressor" which Moscow ascribes to us, and which keeps us in an immoral and suspect position in Chinese eyes.

This Russian success has two bases, one domestic and one

foreign. In domestic affairs the Chiang Kai-shek regime, as the record is compiled and reiterated against it, has no way to regain its shattered moral prestige: the Communist tactic is therefore to keep us identified with it. This is done much more effectively than the American people realize. As long as the Chinese Communist effort to solve China's domestic problems keeps its momentum, as long as the Chinese people are brought by persuasion and coercion to acquiesce in Communist leadership, and as long as we seem to threaten the Communist-led effort at China's national upbuilding by our apparent support of Chiang, this tactic will work. Our big news and picture magazines help it week by week.

In foreign affairs, the Russian effort in China is like the Russian effort elsewhere, to pin the evils of aggression upon us. Since this concerns events outside the direct experience of the Chinese people it can be accomplished by the Moscow lie-machinery, and we can combat it only by getting our own information into China, as into other parts of the Soviet orbit.

This suggests two essential lines of approach to China. First, it is absolutely essential that our information program become effective. The Voice of America is hardly a whisper in China, and must be greatly enlarged, but it may prove to be less important than other channels of information that we might develop. The overseas Chinese communities of Southeast Asia are closely connected with South China. The traditional grapevine, by word of mouth, still operates in every village if we can only reach it with the facts.

Second, we must make every effort to avoid taking *unnecessary* positions where the Chinese Communists can force us into conflict with the Chinese nation. Either diplomatic or military conflict with us helps them to consolidate their control in China and to wipe out our moral and practical influence among the Chinese people. In such conflicts, Chinese Communism stands to build up further support for its polarized anti-American position in China, while Russia stands to involve us in an enormous side show which cannot be decisive but can weaken us. Our strategic problem is therefore to decide what positions we must hold at all cost, even at the cost of fighting Chinese, and what positions are not necessary to us.

. . . A majority decision to seat China in the U.N., by which we have promised to abide, might help the Chinese people view the world more independently. Meanwhile Formosa is of marginal military value to us and less distinct than Korea as an issue of principle. As General MacArthur's famous letter made clear, it could be neutralized by whichever side had air superiority in a war. Thus with superior air power on Formosa we could dominate the air over the coast; but with superior air power on the continent, an enemy could dominate the air over Formosa. Meanwhile Sino-American hostilities over Formosa can waste the military strength of both parties and make Stalin that much stronger. In the long term Formosa is less valuable to us than peace with China. We must try to settle its disposition through the United Nations.

In summary, we will get nowhere in China either by further support of Chiang or by appeasement of Mao. We can, if we try hard on all levels, build up our prestige by helping other, accessible parts of Asia solve their problems. We can try to get this story into China; we must get the facts before the Chinese people. Although under Communist control, it will be many years before they can be thoroughly "communized." In the meantime we have a bare chance to rebuild our moral position in their eyes and to combat the prostitution of China for purposes of Russian imperialism. But this requires a recognition among patriotic anti-Communist Americans that our failure in China has only partly been due to the knavish tricks of Communism and was partly our own grievous fault, for giving our aid too carelessly to a regime which had grown incapable of representing its own best aspirations or our moral position. It is on the score of domestic reform in China that we parted company with Chinese public opinion, for we (thinking of ourselves first?) considered that the evil of Russian imperialism would outweigh the benefit of the reforms promised by Chinese Communism; and too many of the Chinese people did not agree with us. It is never too late in history for great peoples to change their minds. But there is no hope of friendly relations with the Chinese people until we take ourselves out of their purely domestic politics, take China out of American party politics, and concentrate upon the paramount menace of the Russian totalitarian imperialism which we both face.

III MOMENTUM: INDOCHINA AND KOREA

Milton Sacks

COMMUNIST STRATEGY IN SOUTHEAST ASIA

Milton Sacks, a well-known student of Asian communism, found the cause of the upheaval in Southeast Asia in the Communist parties of the region and their association with international communism. For Sacks communism in Southeast Asia in 1950 was no longer tied to nationalism but had become an international force. Even in the thirties, he added, the Communist parties of Asia had revealed "a remarkable ability to veer and tack with each gust of wind from the Kremlin." After the war the Communists had sought to use the rival nationalists in their effort to achieve power. Such Communists as Ho Chi Minh were not, to Sacks, in pursuit of independence for its own sake, but to expand the power of international communism in Asia. He assumed that Ho's government was in the camp of Moscow and Peking. Communism in Southeast Asia, to Sacks a coordinated movement, had the objective of eliminating all Western influence from the region. As such it was dangerous to the security of the non-Communist world.

. . . The agencies of international Communism concerned with Southeast Asia are manifold. They include the Soviet, Chinese and Korean Communist radio networks, whose fulminations against "American imperialism and colonialism" are echoed by the clandestine stations of Communist Ho Chi Minh's Vietnamese government. They embrace the international "front" organizations and their local affiliates, such as branches of the World Federation of Democratic Youth, Women's International Democratic Federation, and World Federation of Trade Unions, whose conferences in the Far East provide opportunity for liaison and planning as well as for unfolding the new tactical line to be followed. They include the various "friendship" organizations with ostensibly cultural and educational aims which advertise the benefits of Soviet and Chinese Communist society for the edification, and in the vernacular, of the nationals of the country in which they have been set up. Among the Chinese minorities, which constitute significant economic and political elements within the various Southeast Asian communities, functions the

From "The Strategy of Communism in Southeast Asia," *Pacific Affairs* 23 (September 1950): 227–247. Reprinted by permission of *Pacific Affairs*, University of British Columbia.

China Democratic League for those who do not wish to affiliate directly with the overseas branches of the Chinese Communist Party or with the most important agencies of international Communism, the various national communist parties. It is through this vast apparatus that the Communists carry on their revolutionary activities throughout Southeast Asia.

Before considering the strategic objectives and tactical operations involved, some general historical observations are in order, in view of the misconception in some quarters regarding the "nationalist" character of Communism in South Asia, which bears a striking similarity to the "agrarian reformer" label given the Chinese Communists prior to their accession to power. In reaction to the dislocations produced by World War II and to the practices of the colonial metropolitan powers, Southeast Asia is undergoing a vast nationalist upheaval. The indigenous peoples desire political independence. Both Communist and nationalist leaders in this struggle have been drawn from the small urbanized populations that had been shaped by concepts derived from Western civilization. Nevertheless, there is a basic distinction between nationalism and Communism, although they may tap the same social reservoirs in pursuance of their aims. Nationalism is primarily an indigenous force responding to local community needs and aspirations and translating international pressures into these terms, while the Communists have always subordinated the achievement of independence to the wider aims of the international movement which they represent. The Communist movement in Southeast Asia, as elsewhere, has lost its "nationalist" character and become an extra-national force.

The evolution of the Communist movement in Southeast Asia has been similar to that of the other sections of the Communist International. Many nationalists were attracted to Communism because of the success of the Russian revolutionists in 1917 and their avowed intention of promoting world revolution and the liberation of colonial peoples. From among these nationalists were recruited the first cadres of Southeast Asian Communists. Small though they were, the resulting Communist organizations were torn by the same factional struggles that marked Stalin's rise to power within the Russian Communist Party and the Third International. Long before World War II, the Communist parties in Southeast Asia had become disciplined organizations showing a remarkable ability to veer and tack with each gust of wind from the Kremlin. In various areas, expelled dissidents attempted with little success to build rival "revolutionary" parties.

Since the Sixth World Congress of the Communist International in 1928, the policies pursued by the Communists of Southeast Asia and their European counterparts have coincided exactly. Up to the era of the Popular Front, inaugurated in France in 1935, Southeast Asian Communists denounced their nationalist rivals with the venom reserved elsewhere for the Communists' social-democratic competitors. When the Soviet Union found it necessary to conclude the Franco-Soviet pact and to advocate collective security, the Southeast Asian Communist parties suspended their struggles for national independence of colonial areas and sought to join with moderate nationalists in a "united struggle against the menace of German and Japanese Fascism." They likewise discovered the "imperialist nature" of the war between Hitler and the Western Powers during the period of the Stalin-Hitler pact. After the German attack on Russia, they became devoted partisans of the United Nations coalition and denounced as collaborators with German and Japanese reaction those nationalists who pressed any demands which they believed might hinder the Allied war effort.

World War II provided the Communists in Southeast Asia with an unprecedented opportunity. They had successfully survived years of police suppression and had perfected underground organizations that were now transformed into agencies of a broad anti-Japanese guerrilla movement to which the Allies supplied arms and training facilities for espionage and partisan warfare. Their skill and training won the Communists positions of leadership within these movements. New nationalist fighters joined in an increasing stream as the imminent victory of Allied arms promised liberation from the Japanese and, possibly, from all foreign control. When the Japanese war effort collapsed in 1945, the Communists were in positions to influence the course of events in Vietnam, Malaya, Burma and Indonesia.

At this time international Communist policy sought to achieve its objectives by utilizing Great Power cooperation under United Nations auspices. The Soviet Union attempted, by negotiation and collective agreement, to gain world approval for far-reaching alterations in the balance of power. Similarly, the national Communist leaderships worked for the creation of coalition governments behind whose façade they could consolidate their own power. Throughout Southeast Asia the Communists joined with nationalists in demanding that the provisions of the Atlantic Charter be implemented. Instead of opposing the landing of Allied occupation forces, they attempted to negotiate agreements that would grant recognition to the "front" organizations and their armed forces. In general, they followed a policy of compromise, even indicating a willingness to establish a new basis for union with the colonial powers.

When, as a result of changed relationships among the Great Powers, the Soviet Union adopted a policy of opposing the "capitalist stabilization" of Europe, the strategy applied in Southeast Asia underwent similar alteration. A. Zhdanov, in his speech outlining the new Communist estimate of the international situation at the founding conference of the Communist Information Bureau in September 1947, referred significantly to the "rise of a powerful movement for national liberation in the colonies" that "has placed the rear of the capitalist system in jeopardy." In December 1947, E. Zhukov amplified the official Soviet view on the changed character of the "liberation struggle" in the colonial areas in a magazine article. The new course involved a decisive break with former moderate nationalist allies in Southeast Asia and a direct Communist bid for power through armed struggle wherever possible. This new line was made public in Southeast Asia at the regional meeting of the World Federation of Democratic Youth at Calcutta in February 1948. Within a short time, after maneuvering to create the most favorable environment locally in which to begin military operations, the Stalinist Communists in Malaya, Burma and Indonesia promoted armed insurrections. . . .

Any possible doubt concerning the integrated nature of past Communist operations and the coordinated structure of their organization in Southeast Asia must have been dispelled by the Asian and Australasian Trade Union Conference at Peking, November 16-December 3, 1949, which approved the previously-determined course of action and gave programmatic unity to the Communist-led struggles throughout Southeast Asia and to the objectives of the Soviet and Chinese Communists. The importance attached to this regional meeting of the World Federation of Trade Unions is apparent in the speeches of the participants, in the decisions adopted and in the treatment it received from the Chinese and Soviet radios. The meeting was designed to capitalize on the shift in the Asian balance of power brought about by the victories of the Chinese Communists, and to recognize the new preeminent position of the Chinese by honoring them with a major policy conference in their capital city. The special nature of the Conference becomes clear when its threefold task is compared with the actual content of the reports made; its ostensible "trade-union" character gave way to a detailed statement of Communist aims and reports of Communist success in the leadership of the various "working-class liberation movements" represented.

The opening speech was delivered by Liu Shao-chi, vice-president of the World Federation of Trade Unions and honorary president of the All-China Federation of Labor. Liu is recognized as an outstanding theoretician of the Chinese Communist Party. Certain of his remarks demonstrated that the Communists regard the expulsion of all "imperialist" influence as their major aim in Southeast Asia, and pointed the road by which they believe this objective can be accomplished.

> *Nourished by rich spoils of colonies and semi-colonies in the East as well as in other parts of the world, the imperialists became strong enough to oppress the working peoples of their own countries, throwing them also into unemployment, starvation and oppression. . . .*
>
> *The colonies and the semi-colonies are the rear bases of world imperialism, on which it relies for its existence. . . .*
>
> *The war of national liberation in Vietnam has liberated 90 percent of her territory; the war of national liberation in Burma and Indonesia is now developing; the partisan warfare against imperialism and its lackeys in Malaya and the Philippines has been carried on over a long period; and armed struggles for emancipation have also taken place in India. . . .*
>
> *The national liberation movement and the people's democratic movement in the colonies and the semi-colonies will never stop short of complete victory. Their struggles are entirely righteous. They should, and will, win victory. The great victory of the Chinese people has set them the best example. . . .*

Luu Duc Pho, Secretary of the General Federation of Vietnamese Workers, stated that "the path of the 475 millions of Chinese people is the path to be taken. . . . The essential principles . . . defined . . . by Comrade Liu Shao-chi in his opening speech . . . must serve as the compass for all the workers of Southeast Asia. . . ." In another speech, he acknowledged Communist leadership of the Vietnamese nationalists: "From 1930 onward, with the birth of the Indochinese Communist Party, the leadership of the movement for national independence was assumed by the working class. . . ." The Malayan delegate, Lu Cheng, "emphasized that no repression, shooting or execution could break the resistance of the working people in Malaya and make them yield to the monstrous regime of exploitation and oppression by the British Imperialists in Malaya." Aung Win, as the representative from the All-Burma Trade Union Congress, told the assembled delegates that "The new Government of Burma was created by the British Imperialists after reducing the country to a state of financial bankruptcy and insuring complete political, economic, and military dependence on Anglo-American Imperialism. . . . The Burmese working class has raised the victorious standard of revolution against the colonial exploiters. They are fighting for the cause of proletarian internationalism. . . . The program . . . includes the complete destruction of the Thakin Nu Government. . . ." S.A. Wickremasinghe, President of the Ceylon Trade Union Federation, noted that "The working class, led by the Ceylon Trade Union Federation, is not only unifying the working class movement but is also assuming the leadership of the anti-imperialist struggle of the broad masses. . . . The workers and peasants of Ceylon in their anti-imperialist struggle now raise the slogan 'China today, Ceylon tomorrow.' Though the development of the liberation struggle is in the early stages in our country . . . the basic tendencies are the same. . . ."

This, then, was the tenor of the Conference. There are a few more themes worth investigating to complete the revelation of the main lines of the strategy of Communism in Southeast Asia. The delegate from the Soviet Union, Solovyov, informed the Conference: "The Soviet Delegation supports the proposal that our conference should appeal to the working masses of France, Holland, Great Britain, and the United States, asking them to urge their governments to stop immediately the intervention in Indonesia, Vietnam, Burma, Malaya and South Korea and to withdraw their troops from these countries." This statement was echoed by Choi Ho Min, Chairman of the Central Committee of the North Korea Trade Unions. The demand for nonintervention by the "Imperialists" is clearly designed to enhance the efforts of the Communists to control all of Southeast Asia since the latter place no such limitation on their own behavior. Liu Shao-chi made this point clear at a rally for the Conference delegates on November 23.

The establishment of a World Federation of Trade Unions liaison bureau at Peking disposed of the third major point on the agenda of the Conference, which thereupon adjourned.

The importance of the decisions taken at this Conference cannot be overstated. Identical themes were stressed at a later regional conference of the Women's International Democratic Federation at Peking, December 10-16,1949; and the same material has been featured in the Chinese Communist and Soviet broadcasts to and concerning Southeast Asia. The decisions have a direct bearing on the behavior of the Communists within each of the countries represented here at the Conference. Indochina, however, deserves particular consideration because it is today the major area of Communist concentration in Southeast Asia. Moreover, the pattern of events in Indochina is a clear indication of the practical significance of the decisions taken.

Indochina generalized warfare between the Communist-led "Vietnam Democratic Republic" and a colonial French army has been going on for four years. Communist Ho Chi Minh, President of the "Republic," has been eminently successful in keeping together a broad Communist-nationalist front since August 1945. Although it is not within the scope of this paper to detail the events associated with the success of the Communists in Indochina, it is necessary to note that in November 1945 Ho Chi Minh dissolved the formal Indochinese Communist Party and organized in its stead an Association for the Study of Marxism, known as the Marxist Group. It is within the framework of the Viet Minh (Vietnam Independence League), the dominant political organization of the "Vietnam Democratic Republic," and through control of the governmental apparatus, that the Communists have either smashed, neutralized, or won the support of competitors for the leadership of the Vietnamese nationalist movement.

However, the new Communist line in Southeast Asia requires emphasis on the primary role of the working class, led overtly by Communists. The problem for the Communists in Vietnam is to adjust their tactics in such a way that they will comply with the new program and yet will not push their nationalist allies into the camp of ex-emperor Bao Dai, who is seeking to create a rival nationalist movement under French auspices. In their attempt to make this delicate adjustment, they have presented the Viet Nam Tong Cong Doan (Vietnam General Federation of Labor) as a leading force in the Vietnamese nationalist movement, cemented relations with the Chinese Communists, increased the number of tried and tested Communists in positions of leadership within the "Vietnam Democratic Republic," and exploited the Vietnam Radio for the dissemination of Communist propaganda. Today the "Vietnam Democratic Republic" is a full-fledged partner in the camp of the Soviet Union and Communist China. It has moved in this direction gradually, and the success of the Communist leadership in Vietnam was greatly aided by the Chinese Communist victories. The Indochinese Communist Party has not as yet been reconstituted officially. . . .

In late November 1949, Ho Chi Minh exchanged telegrams with Mao Tse-tung. As the Chinese Communist People's Liberation Army drove the defeated Nationalist troops south, forcing them to cross the border into Indochina, the Ho government sang a perfect duet with the Peking Radio. Although French officials in Indochina had announced a strict policy of interning Chinese Nationalist troops that crossed the border, they were charged with having made a secret agreement to do otherwise. The Ho government associated itself with Chinese Communist Foreign Minister Chou En-lai's warning statements to the French on December 7, 1949, and protested against "underhand machinations of the Chinese Kuomintang reactionaries and the French Imperialists aimed at violating Vietnamese national sovereignty."

Significantly, the Vietnamese radio spokesman threatened the French with the possibility of joint action by Vietnamese troops and Chinese Communist armed forces. He cautioned the French to "bear in mind the fact that democratic China never intended to send her army across the Vietnam border and that Vietnam never relied on the Chinese Liberation Army for winning the war against the French landgrabbers," but "should the French imperialists be boneheaded enough to harbor the enemies of New China and allow them to annoy the Vietnam people, then they would be held responsible for all the ensuing consequences." The Communists in Vietnam were somewhat less reticent about expressing their own views as to "ensuing consequences"; the late-December issue of their fortnightly review *Su That* (Truth) stated that "The Vietnam Army and the people would not only heartily welcome but also back up the Chinese Liberation Army should the latter deem it necessary to pursue the remnants of Kuomintang hordes into Vietnam." . . .

On January 14, 1950, Ho Chi Minh made public an official appeal to all of the governments in the world for recognition of the "Vietnam Democratic Republic," which "was ready to establish diplomatic relations with any government which would be willing to treat her on a basis of equality and mutual respect, of national sovereignty and territory." This appeal was followed on the next day by a formal telegram of recognition of Mao Tse-tung's Central People's Government of China from Hoang Minh Giam, Foreign Minister of the Vietnam "Republic," an action apparently designed to counter steps taken by the French, who were promoting a greater degree of international standing for the Bao Dai government in Indochina to aid it in its contest with Ho Chi Minh for nationalist support. Faced with the prospect of recognition of Bao Dai by non-Communist nations, the Communist world reacted to help its faithful supporters in Indochina.

On January 18, 1950, Chou En-lai acknowledged receipt of the telegram and notified the Vietnamese government of the Chinese Communists' willingness to establish diplomatic relations and exchange ambassadors. Diplomatic recognition represented a signal achievement for the Ho Chi Minh government. In contrast to the ill-fated Greek government of General Markos, the "Vietnam Democratic Republic" could now "legally" acquire arms and material from its strong northern Communist neighbor. It could hope that, with the recognition of Communist China by the Western powers and its admission into the United Nations, Vietnam might also benefit.

The Soviet Union officially recognized the "Vietnam Democratic Republic" on January 31, 1950. In short order, the various satellite regimes in Eastern Europe and the North Korean government followed suit. The decision of the Yugoslav regime to extend recognition must have caused mixed feelings in Vietnam in view of the treatment accorded the Tito heretics by the Communists internationally. The Ho government representative in Bangkok explained the event in terms of the "any government" statement in the official recognition formula. The Vietnam Radio, however, has been careful to broadcast several appropriately denunciatory repudiations of Tito made by the Vietnam General Federation of Labor.

Domestically, too, the Ho government has sought to reap the full benefits of its new relations with the Chinese Communists and the Soviet Union. A Sino-Vietnamese Friendship Association has been established; among its purposes is that of helping the Vietnamese people to understand the factors that led to Chinese Communist success. The leadership of the new Association is liberally adorned with prominent Vietnamese Communists, and its President is sep-tuagenarian Ho Tung Mau, a former member of the Chinese Communist Party and one of the original founders of the Indochinese Communist Party. Ho Tung Mau made the principal speech on February 18, 1950, designated as Sino-Vietnamese-Soviet Friendship Day by the Ho government. His appointment and new-found public prominence mirrors the trend within the "Vietnam Democratic Republic." Not only is the struggle and program of the "Republic" completely tied to the orthodox Communist international line, but also organizational control is entrusted to tested Stalinists. . . .

That the Communists in Vietnam understand this new situation can be seen in the statement in the January 25th issue of *Su That* to the effect that "The Democratic Republic of Vietnam has consistently been standing in the international democratic camp led by the Soviet Union. . . . This is an opportunity for us to contribute as much as we can to the worldwide struggle for peace and democracy under the leadership of the Soviet Union. This is also an opportunity for us to weld up our legitimate patriotism with righteous internationalism." In addressing themselves to the internal and external problems of the "Vietnam Democratic Republic," the various journals and numerous organizations of the resistance movement supporting Ho Chi Minh have subsequently used language that is indistinguishable from overt Communist propaganda. Vietnamese political life under the Ho government has indeed been "coordinated" and brought into line with the decisions of the Asian and Australasian Labor Conference.

The rise of Communist power in China has had a marked effect on the Chinese ethnic minorities throughout Southeast Asia. Tied by bonds of nationality and family to the mainland, many of the overseas Chinese are shifting their allegiance from the declining Kuomintang to the new Communist rulers in Peking. Living in highly organized and integrated communities within the various areas of Southeast Asia and often subject to discriminatory action by both native and colonial rulers, the Chinese have traditionally looked to and received support from the Chinese central government. In return, they have provided tremendous sums of money in the form of remittances to relatives in China, contributions, and investment capital—sums that have materially helped to meet the financial needs of the Chinese government. Although they number but an estimated 7.5 million of a total population of 156 million (less than 5 percent) in Southeast Asia, the Chinese play an extremely powerful role in the economy of the area. They also constitute a significant part of the industrial labor force in Southeast Asia and were among the first to be organized into both legal and illegal trade unions. Thus, for the Chinese Communists, control of the Chinese overseas is highly important. . . .

Because many of the overseas Chinese are urban dwellers and small businessmen who have not shown particular enthusiasm for the Chinese Communist Party, the principal political vehicles for Communist organization overseas have been the China Democratic League and the Kuomintang Revolutionary Committee. As Communist "fronts," they have apparently had more success than the Chinese Communist Party in winning adherents. Politically, they now stand on the same program as the Chinese Communist Party. The enlarged fourth plenary session of the China Democratic League declared that "the China Democratic League accepts wholeheartedly the leadership of the Chinese Communist Party and marches forward under the banner of Mao Tse-tung." The League set as its major objective the unity of "the broad masses of intelligentsia, enlightened industrialists and businessmen and democratic overseas Chinese to strive for the realization of the common program of the CPPC and the fulfillment of the new democratic revolution." "A resolution supporting the 1950 budgetary estimates of the Central People's Political Government and issuance of People's Victory bonds was also passed at this session."

Besides these avowed political leagues, there are numerous community groups, secret societies, and organizations that speak for the local Chinese throughout Southeast Asia. The Communists have managed to win support for their government from these Chinese who have suffered politically and economically from the great social upheavals in postwar Southeast Asia and want any protection that a strong Chinese central government can provide. By appealing to both patriotic feelings and the genuine concern of the Overseas Chinese for the welfare of their families within China, the Communists have already gained substantial support for specific objectives. It can be expected that they will find wider acceptance of their general propaganda line, thereby facilitating the overall Communist program of promoting "national liberation" struggles throughout Southeast Asia.

Communism in Southeast Asia, then, is today a coordinated movement whose objectives are the complete elimination of all Western influence and the immediate creation of Communist-controlled "people's democracies." To achieve these objectives, Communists in Burma, Malaya, Indochina, and the Philippines are actively engaged in armed conflict. These efforts have been successful enough to bring about the commitment of large sums of money, arms, matériel and men by the nationalist or colonial governments which the Communists are opposing. In these areas—unlike India and Indonesia, where Communist insurrectionary activities seem, at least for the moment, to have been suppressed—warfare against the Communists at present appears to be little more than a holding operation. As rim areas of a Communist-dominated China, they are and will remain vulnerable to Communist infiltration and attack to the extent that the Chinese Communists sponsor guerrilla operations. By its own efforts alone, nationalism in these areas cannot survive in the face of such combined internal and external pressures. Having recognized that Communist operations in Southeast Asia are integrated, the non-Communist world must still find the necessary combination of political and military means to reduce the active threat of Communism in the area.

John Foster Dulles

INTERNATIONAL COMMUNISM AND
THE KOREAN WAR

In the following address, delivered to the China Institute in New York City on May 18, 1951, John Foster Dulles developed the dual theme that the Soviet Union, after a quarter century of intensive effort, had gained control of China and then, through its influence in Peking, had driven China into the Korean war. Hu Shih, in reading five, had developed the first, and essential, idea. Dulles, then special consultant to the Secretary of State, took the lead in attributing Chinese aggression in Korea to the Soviet control of Chinese external policy. To Dulles Mao was the creature of the Soviet Politburo and thus under complete Soviet dominance. Thus in his view the Chinese involvement in Korea served Russian, not Chinese, interests. What disturbed Dulles especially was Mao's determination to turn the Chinese people into enemies of the United States. No American official developed the theme of Chinese subservience to international forces more dramatically than did Dulles in this speech. For him Chinese and American interests demanded the elimination of the Peking regime; he, no less than others, was totally incapable of defining the means to achieve that goal.

One of my most prized possessions is a letter I received when 8 years old from Li Hung Chang, then the great Chinese elder statesman. The opening sentence of the letter reads: "To the little grandchild of General Foster, my friend and counsellor in my hours of perplexity and trouble."

That letter is to me symbolic of what has been and always should be, the relations between our peoples.

It breathes the spirit of fraternal friendship between their old and our young society. It reflects the kindly good humor and respect for home and family ties which make it easy for Americans to understand and to love the Chinese character. It confesses the troubles and perplexities which inevitably confront an ancient civilization when it is pressed upon by the thrusts of a restless new outer world. It testifies to the value to be found in counsel which is understanding and loyal.

That, you may say, is sentiment. So it is. Sentiment, rather than

From "Sustaining Friendship with China," The Department of State *Bulletin,* May 28, 1951, pp. 843–845.

materialism, is, indeed, the essence of the relationship of the American people with the Chinese people. First, as colonists we came to know and admire Chinese art in terms of chinaware, wall paper, silks, and lacquer. Later, our clipper ships began directly to touch at China ports. But trade with China never grew to large proportions nor did Americans ever invest heavily in China. Always the contacts have been primarily cultural and spiritual, notably through missionaries.

The Tientsin treaty of 1858 freely gave Christianity a special invitation. During the nineteenth century, scarcely a community in the United States was without at least a share in a missionary to China. Our church people regularly gathered together to fill missionary boxes for China and to hear read aloud the story of their China missionary and his Chinese friends and of the growing spiritual kinship between them. Later, Americans founded in China many Christian colleges, medical schools, and hospitals, and many Chinese students came to this country.

Only when the Spanish war made us a western Pacific power did our relations with China become a matter of major governmental concern. We saw that the people of China should be allowed to develop in their own way which, we were confident, would be a peaceful way. We were fearful of the consequences if the Chinese became the tools of alien despots. So, Secretary Hay called for the "open door," Secretary Hughes made the Washington treaty to maintain China's integrity, Secretary Stimson proclaimed "nonrecognition of the fruits of aggression." Finally, we accepted the probability of war with Japan rather than accept Japanese domination of China through the puppet regimes which Japan had set up in Manchukuo and Nanking.

During the long, hard Pacific war, the United States helped China, both morally and materially, and we looked forward to victory as opening a new era of closer friendship between us.

It comes as a brutal shock that today much of China is under the control of a regime which fanatically hates the United States and which has sent Chinese armies to Korea to kill Americans who are there at the behest of the United Nations.

The Chinese Communist attitude is exemplified by a widely publicized pamphlet written last October. The first section is entitled *We Must Hate America, Because She is the Chinese People's Implacable*

Enemy. There follows a recital of alleged historic incidents which blames the United States for almost all of China's troubles, beginning with the opium war which was allegedly supported by the American Navy.

The second section is entitled *We Must Despise America, Because it is a Corrupt Imperialistic Nation, the World Center of Reaction and Decadency.* There follows a picture of the United States which is indeed startling: 18 million unemployed; 10 million with no housing whatsoever; 40 million who barely exist in slums; 14 thousand agents of the F.B.I. engaged in "the exclusive mission of persecuting the people"; 99 percent of the newspapers and magazines controlled by the National Association of Manufacturers and used for making the younger generation "spiritually decadent and halting their intellectual development, so that they may be driven to serve aggression and war."

The third section is entitled *We Must Look Down Upon America Because She is a Paper Tiger and Entirely Vulnerable to Defeat.* There follows a picture of America without friends or allies, internally divided and confronted by the closely knit 830 million peoples of China, Russia, and the Russian satellite states. Our great industrial capacity is admitted but, it is said, this will be offset when Western Europe is liberated and, further, our concentrated industry is said to be particularly vulnerable to the Soviet Union's atom bombs. It concludes America faces "defeat which will be more disastrous than that which befell Hitler and Japan."

That is the regular Party line. By print, by radio, by drama, by pictures, with all of the skills which communism has developed, "Hate America, Despise America" is the sentiment being pounded into the Chinese people.

How has this come to pass? In part, no doubt, because of some errors on our part. But, in a larger sense, the present situation is the Soviet's reward for 30 years of hard work.

In 1924, Stalin revealed it as basic strategy that "the road to victory over the West" would be sought in Asia, and particularly, China. The 450 million people of China must be made to serve the Soviet Communist program of world conquest. To this end, a Chinese Communist Party was formed under the guiding direction of the Russian, Borodin. That Party, Soviet Russia has nurtured until it has matured into today's regime of Mao Tse-tung which serves as the instrument of Soviet communism.

If any doubt that relationship, I remind them of these facts:

1. The Chinese Communist Party has consistently and publicly proclaimed its disciple-master relationship with Stalin and Soviet Russia. The following oft-repeated statement of Mao Tse-Tung, first made in 1939, is typical:

> *The fact that Stalin has come into the world is indeed fortunate. Today, when we have the Soviet Union, the Communist Party, and Stalin–all's right with the world.*

2. The Soviet Government paid a great price to bring the Chinese Communist regime into power and would only have done so to serve itself. Among other things, it openly dishonored its 1945 Treaty of Alliance and Friendship with National China whereby it undertook that for 20 years its "moral support and aid in military supplies and other material resources," would "be entirely given to the National Government as the Central Government of China."

3. Mao Tse-tung, after winning mainland victories with the Soviet help we have referred to, went to Moscow at the end of 1949 where he spent nearly 3 months in consultation with the Soviet leaders. On his return, he broadcast to the peoples of Southeast Asia, calling upon them to seek liberation through "armed struggle" as part of the "forces headed by the Soviet Union." There followed Communist-armed interventions in Korea, Indochina, Tibet, and the Philippines. These interventions conformed exactly with known Soviet wishes and, indeed, were forecast in advance by the Soviet official press.

4. These foreign policies of Mao Tse-tung are utterly irreconcilable with the interests of the Chinese people. After 14 years of exhausting war, they desperately need internal recuperation. No one in his senses could assert that it is in China's interest to shovel its youth and material resources into the fiery furnace of Korean war to gain South Korea, an area which means little to China, but which, since the czars, has been coveted by Russia because of its strategic value as against Japan.

By the test of conception, birth, nurture, and obedience, the Mao Tse-tung regime is a creature of the Moscow Politburo, and it is on behalf of Moscow, not of China, that it is destroying the friendship of the Chinese people toward the United States.

What has happened is precisely what Stalin planned. In his 1924 lectures on Leninism, Stalin discusses what he calls "The National Problem," that is, the problem of how aspirations for national independence can be fitted into the Soviet program of world conquest. Communist leaders in Asia must, he says, recognize that national independence is but a slogan wherewith to ride into power on anticolonial sentiment. But, once in power, the Communist leaders must fight against the tendency of the masses toward "national insularity" and must seek "the amalgamation of these masses into a single state union" which is the goal of "Soviet power."

That is what is going on in China now. Anti-American sentiment is being whipped up to eradicate the influence of the West, ostensibly in the interest of national independence. But this popular hysteria is sought as a front behind which the Chinese people are being deprived of their independence and being betrayed into amalgamation with the mass which serves Moscow.

It is inevitable that many Chinese should be fooled by what is going on. But the American peope and their Government should not be fooled. We should treat the Mao Tse-tung regime for what it is—a puppet regime. The relationship to Moscow is camouflaged more craftily than was the relationship between the Japanese and the Nanking regime of Wang Ching-wei. Recent developments in the technique of propaganda enable it to win greater popular support and to depend less openly upon foreign military power. But the doctrine and the iron discipline of the Communist Party, Bolshevik, bind Mao Tse-tung to the service of Moscow more completely than was Wang Ching-wei ever bound to the service of Japan.

That could change. The Chinese people are today being abused to a degree that is causing many Chinese Communist leaders to feel rebellious against the subserviency to Moscow. But, unless and until actual conduct gives clear proof of change, our national self-interest, our friendship for China, and the historic dedication of our Nation to the cause of human freedom combine to require that no act of ours shall contribute to a Mao Tse-tung success which could fasten the yoke of Moscow on the Chinese people.

My own official concern today is the Japanese peace treaty. I can assure you that, in negotiating the treaty, we shall not consider that the voice of Mao Tse-tung is the voice of China.

While we thus adopt a negative attitude toward Mao Tse-tung and all his ilk, we should adopt a positive attitude toward the many Chinese who remain loyal to the welfare of China and to the friendship between China and the United States which has in the past served China so well. Our own loyalty to those ideals should be demonstrated by deeds, public and private. It will not always be easy to find the way. But whatever the obstacles, however long and troubled be the way, we must be loyal to past and present friendships. We must work to preserve these friendships with persistence and resourcefulness at least equal to that which for 30 years Soviet communism has devoted to undermining Chinese-American friendship.

A great weakness is that we are not enough interested in long-range programs. Because elections come so frequently, there is a tendency on the part of government to seek shortcuts which can bear quick political fruit. There is a tendency to evade long, hard tasks.

That gives the Soviet Union a great advantage, for its planning is often in terms of what Stalin has referred to as "an entire historic era."

I am not advocating slow motion in the case of China. On the contrary, it is imperative that we move quickly, while we still have many friends not only on Formosa, but also on the mainland, and possibilities of access to them. But we must not only start fast, we must start with long vision and endurance because we cannot overnight undo what has been accomplished by the best brains and skills of the Soviet Communist Party working with substantial resources over a span of 30 years.

Generally, and particularly in the Orient, great results are not achieved quickly, and those who would succeed must dedicate themselves to sustained effort.

That is where our people come in. In the past, our churches, colleges, private organizations, and individuals have decisively molded and sustained our China policy. That must continue to be the case. Despite provocation and discouragements in China, the American people must persist in their faith in the Chinese people and the determination to find works which will express that faith. Thus hatred will succumb to friendship, servitude will give way to liberation, and warfare will subside into peace.

We have entered upon a period of long trial. But true friendship has the capacity to survive the strain of misunderstanding, provocation, and disappointment. It "beareth all things, hopeth all things, endureth all things."

Those who have been friends of China, who inherit and would preserve that great tradition, have often been mocked because their plans have gone awry, and their hopes have seemed vain. All of that is unimportant, so long as faith and determination persist. The friends of China may have been daily wrong—but they have been eternally right.

Wilbur W. Hitchcock

NORTH KOREA JUMPS THE GUN

Even before Dulles delivered his speech of May 1951, Wilbur W. Hitchcock, former member of the United States Military Government in Korea, challenged the official view that the invasion of South Korea was promoted by a Moscow-directed international conspiracy–that North Korea, like China and Ho's Vietnam Democratic Republic, was under the control of the Kremlin. What troubled Hitchcock was Washington's readiness to base all United States policies on the assumption that the real enemy in Korea was the U.S.S.R. In his effort to refute official United States suppositions regarding Communist aggression in the Far East, Hitchcock argued that the Soviet Union lost four distinct advantages because of the North Korean attack: (1) a favorable rearming-rate ratio; (2) the neutrality of certain countries; (3) the element of surprise; and (4) the U.N.'s possible recognition of the Peking regime (which the Kremlin seemed to favor). Hitchcock concluded that none of the assumed Russian gains from the North Korean invasion would compensate Russia for the four losses listed above. His conclusion followed logically: the Soviets did not order the North Korean action at all. The Korean War was an isolated incident, not a prelude to other assaults on the Western positions in Asia.

From "North Korea Jumps the Gun," *Current History* 20 (March 1951): 136–144. Reprinted by permission of the author and *Current History*, Inc.

"The attack upon Korea makes it plain beyond all doubt that Communism has passed beyond the use of subversion to conquer independent nations and will now use armed invasion and war." So the President of the United States stated at noon, June 27, 1950. He was announcing the commitment of American armed forces against those of North Korea 70 hours after the latter had stormed across the thirty-eighth parallel. Mr. Truman's remarks have been misinterpreted by no one. The President, while avoiding directness, fully intended to imply that the invasion was that of the Moscow-directed international conspiracy known as Communism, that the North Koreans were but dangerous stooges of the Kremlin and that the real aggressor was the Soviet Union. Moreover, his interpretation of the events unfolding in Korea was neither startling nor new. Mr. Truman merely made official the opinion that had gelled into its present form throughout the free world with the first electrifying reports of the attack: the Soviet Union, no longer feeling restrained from the use of armed force, had finally thrown the switch!

This interpretation of the conflict has had a profound influence upon the planners of the West. Should we give military assistance to the South Koreans? Having committed air and sea forces, should we introduce ground forces? Should the enemy be repulsed beyond his original border, the thirty-eighth parallel? Should he be pursued to the south bank of the Yalu River? Should the Communists from China be attacked in their own territory? Should Nationalist Chinese forces be utilized? Each of these questions, and many more, were answered in the light of what the Soviet Union's *next* move was most likely to be. At each step of decision-making, our planners carefully weighed the influence of the factor that, having thrown the switch in Korea, the Russians were very likely to throw other switches. . . .

Is it any wonder, then, that during the first few days of the conflict serious consideration was given the thought that the Soviet Union intended the North Korean invasion to be a prelude to all-out war with the West, either as a main thrust or as a feint for a main thrust elsewhere? This conclusion, that the Communist mission in Korea involved the initiation of a World War III, was further supported by the huge price paid by Communism for whatever was to be gained by the attack.

At least four major advantages held by Communism before the

conflict were sacrificed by North Korean aggression. This is not a matter of hindsight. Soviet planners had every reason to suspect in advance that a North Korean invasion would cost what it did in advantages lost. Forfeited by the Communist drive into South Korea were a favorable rearming-rate ratio, the neutrality of certain peoples, the element of surprise and the imminent recognition of Red Chinese delegates by the United Nations.

What Communism Lost

1. By the spring of 1950 it was appreciated by the foreign policy shapers of the Western Powers that vigorous Communist advocacy of peace was unreliable and that the Red Army would attack whenever it was felt that Communist strength would guarantee victory. Large segments of the population had yet to be convinced of this. And because the people were not wholeheartedly behind the necessity of sacrificing for the common defense, the rearming and reorganizing of Western defenses proceeded at a pitifully slow rate. Political leaders are not apt to call upon the people for extreme sacrifices, even for their defense, unless the people can be reasonably expected to support such measures. President Truman, for example, did not declare the existence of a national emergency until six months after the outbreak of the Korean war. Absence of data from behind the Iron Curtain precludes the use of accurate statistics but it is probably true that each day of peace was a day in Russia's favor. Every day saw Soviet strength that much greater than non-Soviet strength. And the masters in the Kremlin were not unaware of this phenomenon. Until that day in which Soviet power-on-hand would be so overwhelming that all-out war would be succesful, it was decidedly in their interest to keep friction with the West at a minimum so that the people would not be aroused into upsetting the rearming-rate ratio. Already Western public opinion was approaching that critical point at which the need for defense efforts great enough to reverse this ratio might be apparent. Greco-Turkish aid, the Marshall Plan, the North Atlantic Pact and the Schuman Plan were official expression of this shift in opinion; American ire over the loss of China to the Communists, an unofficial expression. One more false move by international Communism might so incense the masses of the West that their govern-

ments would be encouraged to take steps that would make each day of peace a day favoring the West. The Kremlin knew this well; the North Koreans attacked anyhow.

Even had the United Nations not approved intervention in South Korea's behalf, even had the United States not intervened in the first place, the Korean invasion would have so aroused the people of the West that governments thereafter would probably have had to take essentially the same steps for defense as those actually taken. Regardless of United Nations or United States intervention, then, the Korean war has directly caused the acceleration of Western defensive measures so that the rearming rate ratio now favors, or will soon favor, the West.

2. Not all non-Communist nations, of course, are augmenting their defenses. It is, however, reasonable to suppose that many other peoples who formerly proclaimed their neutrality in the East-West ideological conflict have been swung toward the West as a result of the brazen strike in Korea. The result of such shifts in allegiance can not be predicted exactly. Nevertheless, this factor is another obstacle to the successful execution of Soviet foreign policy, and one which the Soviet Union could have anticipated.

3. The loss of the element of surprise by the Soviets is directly attributable to the North Korean invasion. Other factors being equal, he who surprises his foe holds a distinct advantage while the surprise is being exploited. The Communist attack caught the West off guard but the advantage was not exploited fully. The Soviet potential for surprising their adversaries in the future has been markedly reduced. Part of this effort has been mentioned above: the West is preparing for Soviet aggression at a rate previously impossible. Over and above this, however, is the matter of alertness. The West has been alerted and, though some relaxation of the alert was to be expected after the shock of the initial blow had worn off, never again will the Soviet Union have at its disposal the element of complete surprise, so essential in an aggressive war. This could not have been unforeseen by Soviet strategists.

4. The Soviet Union has advocated and still desires the recognition of Communist Chinese delegates by the United Nations. In the spring of 1950, she had all but achieved that goal. The Communist government at Peiping was in almost complete control of the Chinese mainland and had indicated a desire to carry on business-

as-usual with other nations. Most deliberately the Peiping government had avoided antagonizing other nations by internal or external extremes of arbitrariness, once control of the mainland was acquired. The Peiping government had earned for itself several non-Communist advocates, including the United Kingdom and India. Her chief opponent, the Nationalist Chinese government, had lost favor even with the strongest of capitalist states, the United States. And the United States had gone on record that, though she would not vote for Red China's admission to the United Nations, she would not veto such admission either. In general, Communist China seemed to be behaving herself, and it would appear that the seating of the Red delegates was but a matter of time.

The Korean war, however, changed all this. Immediately strong storms of protest arose from every quarter over even considering replacement of the Nationalist delegates. So unlikely did it become that the Communists would be seated that on December 14, while Communist China held two additional bargaining points, her advancing armies in Korea and the visit of her representatives to the United Nations by invitation, the matter of seating her delegates was excluded from her terms for a peace settlement.

Thus in the spring of 1950 it would have seemed to Russia's advantage to provoke the West no further, to make no more false moves, until her strength was such that victory in an all-out war would be certain. But the Korean attack is not indicative that Soviet strength had reached that point, for the all-out war never came. . . .

What Was Russia's Aim?

We must look further, then, for Soviet purposes. Russia must have had in mind a goal more immediate and more local than the involvement of her resources in World War III. Our commentators have offered many suggestions. The invasion, for example, was merely a reconnaissance-in-force to determine the strength of South Korea and to learn the capabilities and intentions of the West. Or the invasion had the limited goal of merely bringing South Korea within the Soviet realm. Or the invasion was but a feint to conceal a more significant but limited (i.e., not involving all-out-war) attack elsewhere. Or the invasion was but a crowbar with which to pry concessions from the West. Or the invasion was but a scheme to exhibit the United States and her allies as imperialists and aggressors. Or the invasion was a clever device to wear down by attrition the military and economic potential of the West without so affecting that of the Soviet Union.

Each suggestion, however, either has been nullified by succeeding events or has been reached by its proponents without full consideration of the factors involved. Most fail only because they do not compensate for the loss of the four major advantages mentioned above. For whatever objective the Soviet Union had in instigating the North Korean thrust, it must have been a goal which she considered reasonably attainable and for which she was willing to trade these advantages, i.e., the favorable rearming-rate ratio, the neutrality of certain peoples, the element of surprise and the imminent United Nations recognition of Red Chinese delegates. Let us consider each suggested objective in detail.

The reconnaissance-in-force theory collapses because the cost of such an action would be excessive. It has other defects, however. Within a week after the invasion, although United Nations forces in quantity were not yet in Korea, the mission of such a reconnaissance would have been accomplished. Yet North Koreans continued the fight. In addition, the Soviet Union, having had disclosed to her the information sought by the reconnaissance, had sufficient time to prevent further United Nations action by her veto in the Security Council. In fact, to better her status as a "peace-loving nation," she might well have approved the United Nations resolutions for in no way would this have hindered a reconnaissance mission. The Russian delegate, however, did not appear in the Security Council until a month later. Further, a reconnaissance which by its own action drastically alters the enemy's dispositions can hardly be considered a reconnaissance, for the information it seeks would be out-dated by the enemy's reaction to the investigation. The reconnaissance in this case approaches a feint or a main thrust, to be treated below. In short, if one intends to capture a sleeping tiger, one does not awaken him first to determine how he will behave should he wake up!

The acquisition of South Korea, as a limited goal, has much to say for itself. Such a holding together with Sakhalin Island in the north would give Russia almost complete domination of the Sea of Japan, forcing the Western occupying powers in Japan to rearm that nation contrary to their plea that the Japanese were to remain disarmed. . . . South Korea per se, however, being completely agricultural and offering but three major seaports, was hardly worth the loss of the four great advantages mentioned above, and it might even be questioned that the increase in Japanese-Western friction just described would really be worth it. . . .

That the invasion could have been a feint for a more significant but limited attack elsewhere is disproved by the same reasoning that it could not have been a feint for a major war-provoking attack. Only one Communist invasion followed the Korean attack, the invasion of Tibet, and this is hardly more significant than the presumed feint. Even if the forces of the West were not tied down in Korea, under no circumstances could it have been supposed by Soviet planners that the West would, or could, defend Tibet.

More feasible is the possibility that the feint was intended to reduce the defenses of Formosa by sucking Nationalist Chinese troops into Korea and that the United States naval blockade of Formosa unexpectedly prevented the main attack. Once again we can question that the seizure of Formosa was worth the loss of the four major advantages held by the Communists prior to the Korean invasion. This theory, however, presumes that Red forces were massed for the attack prior to the Korean feint. An amphibious assault is the most difficult operation in the book. Even under optimum conditions a successful amphibious attack demands the maximum of fire-power and man-power. Yet, the Chinese Reds, hypothetically poised for assaults across the Taiwan Strait, preparing for another assault into Tibet, and located ominously near the French Indo-Chinese border, took five months to enter the Korean conflict in force once it was established that the United States Seventh Fleet would thwart all attempts Formosa-ward. (The very fact that so many Chinese troops were massed elsewhere, at the borders of Tibet and of French Indo-China, indicates that an invasion of Formosa was either not imminent or of low priority.)

We must conclude, then, that the Chinese Communists were not prepared to strike at Formosa and that this could not have been the operation for which the Korean attack was intended to be a feint. The feint-theory must be rejected, therefore, on the grounds that no significant attack was attempted elsewhere and that the feint must have more chronological proximity to the main thrust than is now possible if the main attack has not yet been initiated, as might be the case in French Indo-China.

If the Korean strike were to be a means of prying concessions from the West, such desired concessions should have been made public by now. Communists have made demands; but the methods of the Communists are hardly appropriate to these demands. The Soviet Union has insisted on the withdrawal of foreign troops from Korea and the United Nations recognition of Red China. Communist China, in her December demands for a peaceful settlement, has sought but a reversion to the prewar status quo: withdrawal of United Nations troops from Korea, withdrawal of American troops from Formosa and cessation by Western powers of all "armed expansion" and war preparation. The only terms for settlement offered by Communists, then, have either been made more difficult to attain because of, or would have been unnecessary to seek but for, the Korean assault. The crowbar theory must fail for lack of suitable concessions demanded. . . .

A War of Attrition?

Most popular of the explanations offered, however, is perhaps that which describes the Korean conflict as a clever means of wearing down our economic and military resources without so affecting Soviet potentialities. This attrition theory, however, is a contradiction in terms. It would have us believe that Stalin is able to expend his resources in a manner which will not expend his resources. For let us not lose sight of the fact that whatever military or economic potentialities are available for disposition by the Kremlin, be they Russian or satellite, they are military or economic potentialities available to the Kremlin! The use of such forces to wear away at the potential of the West cannot be justified on the grounds that Soviet potential is not affected. If, for example, the manpower of North Korea and of Communist China can be commanded by Moscow, and the attrition theory presumes this to be so, then any attrition is a direct loss to Moscow, for whatever manpower is expended in Korea cannot be utilized at some later date in another place. The same is true of economic and industrial potential, wherever located in the Communist realm. It is quite true that the military forces of the Soviet

Union are not yet directly involved in the shooting, and there is perhaps some slight diplomatic advantage to be gained by Moscow from that fact. Yet millions of Russians in slave-labor camps testify adequately that the Georgian Stalin has no special compunction about expending Russians per se. This attrition theory, however, fails to satisfy our requirements for even a more fundamental reason. Is there actually a wearing away of our resources? Seven United States Army divisions, at the moment of writing, are suffering a bad mauling in Korea. But seven divisions is hardly the total military potential of the United States. Eighty-nine divisions were mobilized in World War II. In return for our serious setbacks in Korea and the magnificent though bitter sacrifices of our troops there, the United States and her allies have been awakened to the realities of the international political order. The reconversion of industry to war production, the mobilization and training of fighting men, the planning and implementation of civilian defense and the accumulation of mutual defense arrangements have all been stepped up. These are gains in our favor. Compared with the relatively slight losses in Korea they stand out as net gains, no matter how tragically bitter our Korean losses are to the participants on the scene and their families at home. Perhaps in several years, when we have reached the saturation point in preparedness and need only maintain our defenses at that level by replacing expenditures, we can speak of a wearing away process. But not yet.

The attrition theory premises that Soviet schemers anticipated Western involvement in the war. If this assumption is false, the attrition theory has no foundation. If this assumption is true, we can not suppose that the planners in the Kremlin would overlook the tremendous stimulus to our rearmament programs that such involvement, with its accompanying expenditures of personnel and matériel and with the concomitant excitation of the man on the street, would inevitably bring. The attrition theory asks us to believe that the Soviet Union would deliberately cause the West to make more adequate preparations for war. It must therefore be rejected.

Thus each of the "explanations" for Soviet conduct in Korea are refuted. We cannot infer that the Kremlin, without considering carefully every factor, ordered the invasion erroneously. We cannot assume that Soviet planners are inept or uninformed. We must give the enemy the benefit of the doubt in regard to the soundness of his plans. It is a fundamental maxim of military intelligence that, irrefutable evidence to the contrary lacking, the enemy is mentally capable and plans his maneuvers in a logical fashion. Another maxim, that what appears logical to you is not necessarily logical to the enemy, might attenuate application of the first, but without a precise knowledge of the nature and extent of the intelligence upon which the enemy bases his strategies, our examination of his actions must of necessity be restricted by what appears to be reasonable and logical and by what information it would seem reasonable to suppose is in the enemy's possession. On these grounds each suggestion concerning Russia's immediate objective in the Korean war has failed to withstand analysis. On these grounds we can state that none of the suggestions would have been accepted by Soviet planners as goals to be reached feasibly or profitably by a North Korean attack.

Accordingly, we are led to either of two conclusions. The first is merely that we have not yet fathomed Russia's real purpose for the Korean war. This follows logically from the premise that the Soviets had such a purpose. The conclusion is negative, however, and not very useful since it clarifies little if anything. Furthermore, the conclusion is questionable inasmuch as it presumes a highly improbable, though not impossible, Soviet feat: that, her ultimate goal, world domination, well known, Russia was able to instigate and maintain a war for six months without revealing her immediate objectives. . . .

The alternate conclusion, startling as it may be, is simply that the Soviet Union had and may still have no war objective, that the Soviet Union in fact did not initiate the war, that the Soviet Union, far from throwing the switch, was just as surprised as was the Western world when the North Koreans threw the switch!

A Surprise for Stalin

We have become so accustomed to crediting Stalin for everything occurring within his domain that invariably we accept Moscow domination of all Communist activity as an unquestioned rule of thumb. That at least one Tito was able to break the rule should give us reason to hesitate before adhering to this premise so blindly.

This conclusion denies only that Moscow planned a North Korean invasion to commence June 25, 1950. It does not deny that the Soviets equipped, trained and indoctrinated the North Korean warrior. It does not deny that the Soviets may have contemplated a similar invasion at some later date either by itself or in conjunction with other operations. In fact, what evidence there is as to Soviet intentions indicates that the "liberation" of South Korea has long been the ultimate goal toward which all North Korean equipment, training and indoctrination have been directed. From 1945 to 1950 the Soviets had ample opportunity to impress the North Korean with this objective. There can be no doubt that the North Korean warrior fully understood his destiny and anxiously awaited the signal to spring into action to re-unite his homeland.

It is reasonable to suppose that even Kim Il Sung, North Korean Premier, grew tired of foreign (Soviet) domination and impatient about the long overdue signal from Moscow. In June came Premier Kim's opportunity. He had recently received much modern equipment from Russia. . . .

Stalin may have loaded the gun, but it was Kim Il Sung who seized upon it and pulled the trigger! With complete disregard for Stalin's chips in the bigger game, Kim took advantage of a favorable set of local circumstances. Koreans are but neophytes in the game of politics, either domestic or international. South Koreans have demonstrated that impulsiveness frequently outweighs their political expediency. Politicians in the North need not be unaffected by the same trait.

This conclusion clarifies the Soviet failure to return to the Security Council and veto in resolutions. The Soviet delegates had not strayed away; they were still in New York and could have re-entered the Security Council deliberations at any moment they desired. But the Soviet Government too had been caught off balance by the attack and was trying to piece the news together, to invent its account of the attack and to regain control of the situation. The Soviet delegates had not been pre-warned and had received no instructions from their government.

This conclusion explains why, contrary to its usual practice, the free world was able to act more swiftly than the Communist world in reporting the event. The first word from behind the Iron Curtain came hours after the Security Council had passed its first resolution based on reports of diplomatic agents and of the Sunday edition of *The New York Times.* The first Communist comment came from Pyongyang, the North Korean capital, via the (Communist) New China

News Agency and Berlin. It was only to the effect that the South Koreans had attacked first. Not until the next day did the Soviet Union comment, and then only that the first resolution of the Security Council was illegal since the Soviet and Red Chinese delegates were absent from the proceedings! On the day in which every other newspaper in the nation carried banner headlines, Sunday, June 25, the *Sunday Worker*, completely out-scooped, said nothing about the conflict! Not until the following day, along with the tardy comment from Moscow, did the *Daily Worker* proclaim indecisively, "Report fighting in Korea; North said to rebuff Rightist aggression."

For the masters of the coup d'etat and the propaganda lie, these attempts seem feeble indeed. To fabricate a more plausible account of the battle than the weak and patently ridiculous assertion that the other party shot first would have been child's play for the professionals. The clay from which to mold a less obvious fabrication was readily available: border incidents at the thirty-eighth parallel had been common for years. . . .

What of Kim Il Sung?

The conclusion indicates why full advantage was not taken of Soviet chairmanship of the Security Council in August. Had the invasion been held off by the instigators until the end of July, Chairman Malik, who very capably blocked all positive action by that body for a month, could have used his temporary role even more effectively.

Finally, the conclusion sheds light on the unusual silence of Kim Il Sung, about whose welfare we might well wonder. In October he was reported fleeing to Manchuria after conceding that the North Korean cause was lost. The picture, however, has been altered. Kim's Chinese allies have saved the day for him. But since his reported flight we have heard from Kim only once. On December 12, Moscow reported that Kim had exhorted his troops to continue the drive. It seems significant that at a time when all other reports from the Communist side of the battleground were being transmitted via Peiping, this report should come from Moscow. It seems significant that no account of Kim's location or of his activities was included in the report. It seems significant that there has been no glorious, well-photographed meeting, Hitler-Mussolini style, with Brother Kim greeting and thanking Brother Lin Piao, the Chinese commander.

Though braggadocio is to be expected of resuscitated has-beens, Kim, for all practical purposes, has disappeared! If presently it is revealed that Kim has succumbed to jungle rot, the meaning will be clear: his wild excursion to the South has brought more grief than joy to Moscow.

Thus, the conclusion that the North Korean regime began the war independently of the rulers in the Kremlin has great utility. Without introducing new uncertainties, it clarifies many issues inexplicable by its contradiction, that the Korean war is part and parcel of Soviet strategy. Our best intelligence efforts had produced the estimate that Russia would not be ready for all-out war until 1952. The North Korean attack, per se, does not revoke this estimate.

A new frame of reference, using this conclusion as a working hypothesis, must be erected for the planners of the West. That the Korean invasion was not a part of Moscow's grand strategy does not mean, of course, that Soviet strategy has not been adjusted meanwhile to accord with events. It does mean that since June 25, 1950, Soviet strategy in Asia has been at best a salvage operation for the purpose of extricating international Communism from what was at the time, and may still be, a bad situation not of its choosing. . . .

IV NATIONALISM AND COMMUNISM IN A CHANGING WORLD

Richard Harris

THE LIMITS OF COMMUNIST EXPANSION

In this essay Richard Harris, Far East specialist of The Times *(London), focused on the Western (especially American) tendency to detect Communist expansion, or at least the Communist aim of world conquest, in every Asian crisis. Writing in the early sixties, Harris noted the vast discrepancy between the limited Communist successes (no new Communist governments after 1949) and the ubiquitous assumption of Communist expansionism. Where communism had succeeded, it had done so on the crest of nationalism. The Sino-Soviet split, believed Harris, was enough to put an end to the concept of a monolithic world communism. Besides, the triumph of communism in any country required the existence of a strong Communist party. In most countries such a party did not even exist, for an effective Communist organization demanded people willing to suffer privation for political causes. Poverty itself had stimulated no revolution. As a highly sophisticated philosophy, communism required an educated leadership. With much of Asia thus insulated from communism, Harris believed it time that Western leaders reexamine the term "Communist threat." For him the very concept of a monolith resulted from slipshod thinking.*

"Communist expansion," the Communist aim of "world domination" or other phrases of the same intent, have fed the roots of Western political thinking ever since 1948. The absorption of Czechoslovakia in that year, and the addition of China to the Communist world in 1949, were thought to be sufficient proof of a world conspiracy. The recent serious fighting over the border between India and China has given yet another fillip to such generalizations. Yet by now it is acknowledged that the Communist success in China was brought about in spite of Stalin and not at all from any aid he gave the Chinese Communist Party. There are other assumptions about the nature of Asian revolution current at that time which are also being revised. But the fear of Communism spreading, especially in the developing world, still permeates Western thinking, above all American thinking. Laos and the Congo are two among many examples of crisis in which this fear has prompted Western action of some kind. British and American troops were committed in Lebanon and

Reprinted by permission from "Communism and Asia: Illusions and Misconceptions," *International Affairs* 39 (January 1963): 13–23.

Jordan in 1958 when the supposed Communist influence of revolution in Iraq had to be contained.

Surely it is time we looked a little more closely at this threat, if only to inquire whether Western policies may do more harm than good in forcefully shaping up against a threat that may be far less than they imagine. Africa and Latin America are still raw areas in the age of nationalism and revolution; but if such areas are still too agitated for cool analysis perhaps we can now look at Asia where the dust of battle has settled a little.

The first obvious but rarely noted fact is that no Communist government has come to power in Asia since 1949. (North Vietnam emerging from the Geneva agreement of 1954 ratified conditions that had existed for years before.) Thus 14 years have passed since Chinese Communist armies entered Peking. Surely time enough to examine the facts on which these fears are supposed to be based. In this article an attempt is made, first, to set out the methods by which Communist governments have gained power hitherto; second, to examine the conditions under which Communist parties thrive and, by contrast, to suggest those in which they cannot thrive and are never likely to. These arguments are then illustrated in a particular area of suspicion, Southeast Asia. It should be obvious from the approach that though expounded in Asian terms the method is equally applicable to conditions in the Middle East, Africa and Latin America.

The fears of Communist expansion in Asia have rested in the past on propositions as little defined as Communist expansion itself is. The first was that Communism was by its creed determined to expand, and that therefore all Communist governments shared this determination. When they were not plainly "expanding" their retreat or inaction was tactical; there could be no doubt of their eventual aim of world domination. The second proposition matched intention to probability by pointing to Asia's acute poverty. Since poverty and Communism marched together it was only natural that the Asian masses would "turn" to Communism for the satisfaction of their desires. From the Communist world—China especially—would come the impulse, the subversion (another remarkably ill-defined word) or the arms, and from the Asian masses would come the response. . . .

We must get some clichés out of the way first. There is no need to appeal to a linguistic philosopher to dismiss the phrase Communist expansion as meaningless in itself. Communism as an idea may spread like other ideas or tastes; like Protestantism or jazz, like abstract expressionism or the Gregorian calendar. And if Communism were to spread in this way it could certainly be a threat. But these threats only become a reality when a country has a Communist government. If Communist expansion is to mean anything it must then mean the action of Communist governments or Communist parties. This may seem obvious, yet it is astonishing how many statements are made in circumstances where no such entity exists; Communism becomes personified as a marauding monster.

In what ways therefore has Communism come to power hitherto? Since 1917 (*pace* Cuba) there have been three roads to power. First is the revolutionary *coup d'état* of some kind as in Russia itself, and, in a different way, in Czechoslovakia. Second is the guerilla or civil war, usually long drawn out, in which Communist-led armies win the day, as in China and Yugoslavia. The third is the promotion of Communist governments by the occupying army of a Communist state, as in Eastern Europe and in Korea. This last method could only result from the military invasion of Communist arms and, whatever its likelihood, lies outside the scope of this article.

Now both the first and second methods require one thing: there must be a strong, well-organized Communist party in existence in any country if a Communist government is to be predicted. It need not necessarily be large in numbers especially if the *coup d'état* is the means to power, but it must all the same be strong. The belief that Communism is successfully fomented from outside by subversion or that arms cross a frontier and in themselves create a threat has no evidence to support it. Both the first and the second methods depend on the existence of a Communist party in and of the country in question. If such a party does not now exist in any country, and if the growth of such a party seems highly improbable, then the possibility of Communism coming to power in that country may be dismissed. And since precision is necessary let it be said that Communism coming to power means a government formed and led by the Communist party of the country.

The argument, in short, is that Communism is a particular kind of plant, a political species that came into being long enough ago both for its characteristics to be subject to analysis, and for the variants of the species to be studied. Already variants other than *c. sovietica* and *c. sinica* are beginning to appear, and certainly by now the soil in which the plant will or will not thrive can be analyzed.

Communism is a highly sophisticated philosophy. However simply it may be presented by a Communist party to the masses, its leading adherents must be highly sophisticated men. To the masses the Communist party will no doubt represent itself as serving the cause of justice, equality, social revolution, economic advance or national regeneration; its leaders will not have become *Communists*, however, unless its philosophy had attracted them. Otherwise they would have been Socialists or revolutionaries of some other kind as all leaders of Asian and African countries tend to be; but Communism is precise, is sophisticated and appeals to the educated man. However large a Communist party may be, at its core will be such educated, doctrinally convinced men, otherwise there may be a revolutionary movement but it will not be a Communist party. And if this hard core of believers must exist, so too must their hardness. As the phrase implies they will not be "soft" men. They will be dedicated, tireless, devoted, convinced believers; prepared to suffer defeat and temporary setbacks.

This distinction between a hard and a soft culture is convenient and relevant to this inquiry. Why are some societies hard-working, intelligent and well-educated and others lazy, casual and without serious aspirations? It is not of course a racial question as some think; history, climate, religion, diet, natural resources—all these can play a part. The charm so many people find in Southeast Asian countries is the charm of a "soft" culture, especially appealing as such to the *angst*-ridden European. Calcutta on the other hand is not charming; but Calcutta is "hard" and it has Communists. What can be said, and with conviction, is that there are certain countries where the degree of dedication, hard work and readiness to suffer for political ends simply does not exist in sufficient quantity, either now or in the foreseeable future, for that country ever to produce a Communist party. In such countries the threat of Communism may be discounted.

Having made this general distinction between the hard and soft cultures we may turn to the separate ingredients that go to the making of the political soil. The first is religion, and the warning must immediately follow that religion as a barrier to Communism is an altogether too simple view. What does matter, since it diffuses the appeal of Communism, is the degree to which religion touches life at every point and governs the whole social structure, at least at the village level. In such cases Communism is unlikely to be anti-religious; if it were it would seem to be undermining too much for any peasant. In such cases Communist parties will work within the confines of tradition, even if they attack some aspects of the social structure. This is true of Buddhism in Laos, Cambodia, Thailand, Burma and Ceylon; of Islam in Indonesia, Malaya and Pakistan. It is even more true of Hinduism in India. But this need not mean that Communist parties cannot get votes; Muslims in Java will vote Communist as Catholics in Italy do.

Education is almost as important. Communist parties cannot do without a core of educated men, and the larger the number of educated in a country the more potential recruits to Communism, though it is important to remember that aspiration to education matters almost as much. There are marked differences between countries where everyone gets as much education as they can and those where it is little regarded; it might almost be the criterion between the hard and the soft cultures. Naturally, university education tends to be the key level for the Communist appeal.

But at this point a warning needs to be inserted for those trying to calculate the present appeal of Communism in Asia. Communism as a political dogma co-exists in time almost exactly with Asian nationalism. Thus Communist parties that rode on the advancing wave of anti-imperialist nationalism might gain control as the Vietnamese did. If they did not, or ran against it for a time as the Indian party did, they lost heavily. Now that era is past, and Communism has to appeal as a dogma against other forms of socialism loosely expressed. Asian nationalism throughout the whole of this formative period looked to the West as a source of political ideas as much as it looked for technology. Western institutions were imported. And in the days when Communism as an idea had a large following among Western intellectuals it made inroads in Asia too. That is no longer true in Western Europe (or in the United States today), hence the influences in Asian universities and among those attending Western universities from Asia are more often pacifist and anarchist than

Communist. As a total revolutionary solution Communism has less appeal to the young in Asia, not least because they no longer want total revolution.

The other factors that influence the growth and vigor of Communist parties are those that affect growth of any kind. Climate, pressure of people on land, concentrations of urban population, adequate communications; not least, since it is often overlooked in thinking about Asia, is the cultural unity which such a universalist movement needs, if it is to spread. A common language and a sense of common culture matter to a party so much dependent on speech and the written word. The Chinese had a tremendous advantage here; the Indian party suffers a great disadvantage. Try as they will the Chinese Communists in Malaya cannot make a national Malayan party of something that is bound to remain obstinately Chinese and that can only communicate its flavor through that language. To conclude: the lesson should be that the growth of Communism is almost wholly determined by conditions within any one country, and each country needs to be studied in its own right. Generalizations about Asia are often misleading.

The most misleading generalization of all is the one based perhaps on the only common thing "Asia" has at all (though we must except Japan), and that is its poverty. The materialist obsessions of the West see this and little else and from it the unverified conclusion is drawn of Communism and poverty going hand in hand. Marx's proletariat with nothing to loose but its chains looks an even more alarming horde when translated into the poverty of the Asian peasant masses. Yet who can point to a single revolutionary movement in Asia of which poverty has been the prime stimulus? It was not poverty but the landlords' injustice that brought Chinese peasants in their millions to follow Mao Tse-tung; and elsewhere in Asia it might be said that injustice rather than poverty is the cause of revolt. The moneylender, the landlord and the buyer of his produce, the exactions of a petty official or a village boss—these seem a greater burden on the life of the peasant than poverty alone. The village, after all, is a complex and largely self-contained organism. Prolonged disorder and maladministration may make for a rebellious temper, but on the whole political doctrine does not penetrate easily into this tenaciously resilient spider's web of obligation and tradition, least of all a doctrine that proposes so great a change in attitudes. When Communists have made progress among peasants it has been on the narrow front of a campaign against a particular evil.

This cliché about poverty and Communism used to be the main argument for economic aid, and in some minds still is. I doubt if it could be shown that economic aid has made the slightest difference in any Asian country to the growth or otherwise of a Communist party any more than has a military alliance such as SEATO; these supposed Western weapons against Communism beat the air. The arguments for economic aid at least can rest on better ground than stopping Communism.

Before applying these arguments to particular Asian countries the major distinction between East Asia and the rest of Asia must be made because it is even more relevant to a discussion of Communism than to other differences between the two areas. East Asia is preeminently the civilization in which rule through a state doctrine is a firm tradition. The political outlook which took shape as Confucianism spread through East Asia to Korea, Vietnam and Japan, and remained the establishment doctrine in China for the last 1000 years. Often an other-worldly religion such as Buddhism might threaten its supremacy, in which case some religious elements were absorbed into a new recension of the doctrine. When this doctrine finally came to be questioned at the turn of the century it was not long before the need for an alternative was felt, and an alternative equally fundamental in its ordering of man and society.

Thus Communism has an advantage in East Asia which it has in no other world civilization, and when we look at the other factors—education, a sophisticated philosophical tradition, earnestness, pressure of population on land, the lack of any serious religious impediment—it is no wonder that East Asian civilization is the most responsive to Communism. And it is in East Asia alone that Communist governments are in power: China, North Korea and North Vietnam. . . .

Let us then apply the arguments to South Asia. Where do powerful Communist parties exist and why? Where do they not exist and why not? Part of the answer must obviously depend on the rigor with which some governments repress Communist parties. Thailand, the

Philippines, Malaya are such cases, though in Malaya Communism is so much a Chinese force that it can hardly be considered outside the Chinese context. Leaving it aside for the moment, we are left with two Communist parties of any size, the Indian and the Indonesian. In neither case can they be regarded as strong national parties; their strength is much more regional.

The Indian party was a bad growth from the start, semicolonial in its tutelage from British and Russian leaders. It was not until the 1950s that it even began to reshape itself as an Indian political party, crawling slowly out of its dogmatic shell and its strictly inter-nationalist tradition. In the last 10 years it has begun to gain strength, but it is significant that the largest concentrations are in Kerala and West Bengal, the two states with the heaviest population per square mile and, most certainly in Kerala's case, the highest standards of education. A map showing other areas of Communist strength in India can also be related to one or other of the factors mentioned. The Communists in fact are not the only political party in India that finds itself thriving on regional differences.

The same applies to Indonesia where the party began to recover from the old-style Madiun uprising of 1948 when a new and younger leadership took charge in 1952. Thenceforward it has grown but the strength is almost entirely in Java, not at all in Sumatra or the outer islands. Java is thickly populated with almost three-quarters of In-donesia's population of 95 million. Assuming Indonesia returned to a system of free elections, could the Communists win the day? In parts of Java the answer is that they could. Just as in Kerala the Com-munists have been elected to state power, and may be elected again, so in Java, there could be pockets of Communist rule. It is doubtful if rule in such pockets could ever be translated into rule over the whole country. The very essence of this regional strength is that either it must accept the rules of the national game—in a democratic sense—or, if it tries to assert power nakedly in the old Communist fashion, it can only mean the break-up of national unity. In other words, that Communism coming to power by parliamentary means is a possibility but one which will itself condition such parties towards a democratic system.

One should not overlook the imperial legacy on the political sys-tems in these countries of South Asia. The Dutch may have left little behind in Indonesia, but the British deposit on Indian political life will certainly be absorbed. While parliamentary democracy survives the Indian Communists will be part of it, and the longer it lasts the longer they will be molded by the system.

A glance at some other countries in South Asia shows examples of Communist parties that began in the old days of international Communism based on revolution of the urban proletariat and have never since succeeded in transforming themselves in accordance with national conditions. This is true in Ceylon, and it is true in Burma where an insurrection begun in 1948 drags weakly on for lack of an alternative way forward. In neither of these Buddhist countries does a Communist party ever look like building a mass following.

But the area that most needs clarification by this form of analysis is Southeast Asia. Ever since Communism first came to power in China in 1949 a threat to Southeast Asia has been unquestioningly assumed; it has dictated American policy entirely, and still does. Even if Chinese policy were directed towards setting up Communist régimes in these countries (and there is no evidence to support this and much to disprove it) it would follow from the foregoing arguments that without strong local Communist parties they would have nothing to work with.

Malaya—and Singapore in particular—offers one case of a strong Communist undercurrent, and to explain it one need do nothing more than point to the outlook of the Chinese concentrated there, and concentrated, it may be noted, in circumstances differing from those in Indonesia or Thailand or Burma. In all other Southeast Asian countries the Chinese are in an obvious minority and there is a society in which to varying degrees they can assimilate. This is not true of Malaya where the ethnic and religious division is enforced by a virtual prohibition on intermarriage, though it may slowly become true as an English-educated Chinese element begins to merge into some kind of Malayan personality. The point to emphasize is that it is a Chinese education that makes the Chinese outlook, and given the outlook the Communism will flourish without any "direction" or stimulus from the Chinese mainland. In Malaya, too, a failed Communist insurrection has left the Malayan Communist Party weakened, and it is more in the concentrated, and on the whole more highly educated, Chinese of Singapore that the Communist pull operates.

In the rest of Southeast Asia we have Thailand and the three states

once under French rule and known as French Indochina. It is imperative to separate these constituent countries to see where Communist
strength lies. No Communist party is allowed in Thailand, and no one
acquainted with the country would rate its political consciousness
very highly. It may not be just to put it in the "soft" class as a
culture, yet not unjust, either, to find its attitude and tastes closer to
the Light than to the Third program. A succession of repressive
military dictatorships has prevented any clear picture of political
activity. From time to time "Communists" are arrested, but the
epithet is too commonly used to provide any evidence. Suffice it to
say that, by any of the criteria adumbrated, a strong Communist party
in Thailand is improbable. The same applies with considerably more
certainty to Cambodia, a country only slowly moving towards even
the elements of sophistication. And Laos. Why should the question
not be asked of Laos? Can it really be believed that a country as
primitive and backward, as apathetic and given to as much ease as
can be had from life—can it be imagined that this country can
produce a strong and effective Communist party?

Unfortunately, years of guerilla warfare have clouded the purely
political issues. Anyone who believes that China is pulling all the
strings thinks it unnecessary to ask questions about the puppets who
are being pulled. But what precisely is the *Communist* strength of the
Pathet Lao (or the Neo Lao Haxsat Party)? Its pronouncements and
policies are Communist, but are its leading cadres all of the dedicated type one would expect?

For the answer to these questions one has to look across the
border where the wholly different East Asian-type Communism of
Vietnam is at work. In its origins the Pathet Lao guerilla movement
was no more Communist than any other of the nationalist movements
of the area. It was in 1951 that the Vietminh drew under their wing
the guerillas of Laos and Cambodia. Since then, though their connections in Cambodia seem to have been severed, the guardianship
of the Pathet Lao has been maintained. There are historical as well as
Communist reasons for this. The French were unaware of the possible consequences of bringing Cambodia and Laos, which are part of
the Buddhist cultures of Southeast Asia, under the same rule as
Vietnam which is part of the radically different civilization of East
Asia. Under French rule the Vietnamese were the entrepreneurs who
spread into these notably "soft" cultures; but the Vietnamese, unlike

the Chinese who emigrated from their homeland all over Southeast Asia, never saw themselves as "overseas Vietnamese" in Cambodia or Laos. For a century and more before the French arrived on the scene the Vietnamese had themselves been in conflict with the Thais over the influence they exerted in Laos and Cambodia. In Laos rather more than Cambodia a Vietnamese expatriate stiffening existed, and it is this influence rather than anything purely Laotian that makes the Laotian crisis of more than a decade even credible.

The point to be made here is simple. It was an unforeseen error of France to spread its rule across this vital boundary between two civilizations rather than to make the boundary even more distinct than it was. American policy, posing a "Communist threat" which has its vague origins in Moscow, or if not Moscow then Peking, has done exactly the same and thereby spread the very virus it should seek to isolate. Detach Vietnam from Laos and Cambodia and any Communist threat is detached with it. Laos for the Laotians, far from leaving the country wide open to "aggression," would ensure the existence of a unit in which revolution of some kind might be probable. But an effective Laotian Communist Party—no.

For Vietnam itself the conclusion follows. Here we have a typical example of East Asian Communism at work. No failure of crops, no dissatisfaction over collectivism, no outcry over freedom of speech, none of the other evidence of failure in the northern Communist regime has stopped Vietnamese in the south from gravitating to an ideological platform. To believe that but for subversion from the north Communism would not exist in South Vietnam is another of the typical illusions on which so much Western thinking is founded.

There is another damaging illusion that springs from the belief that Communism is always being injected from without. It is the view of Southeast Asia as a series of small states liable to fall one by one into the lap of "the Communists"—what government or party is meant is never defined. Ever since 1949, therefore, policy has been based on the fear that a Communist China leads to a Communist Vietnam which leads to a Communist Laos which leads to a Communist Thailand and Cambodia, and so right down south until all Australia is aghast at the prospect that faces it. This is no more than an argument by contiguity plus vague assumptions about "Communist" policy, again without any definition of what government or party is meant.

So long as the monolithic character of world Communism passed unquestioned this kind of slipshod thinking went on. Now that the Sino-Soviet split has at last destroyed such assumptions a little more precision can be introduced into the question of whether or not, and if so where, there is a "Communist threat." If the argument is accepted that without a strong (and it need not be numerically strong) Communist party no outside Communist government can foment successful *Communist* revolution, then the actual strength of Communist parties can be examined and some more accurate and less ∨ague deductions made. And this means looking at each individual country and setting aside woolly generalizations about "Asia." Of all Western misconceptions "Asia" is perhaps the one with least substance.

Benjamin Schwartz

IDEOLOGY AND THE SINO-SOVIET ALLIANCE

Many scholars as well as journalists and officials assumed a powerful Soviet voice in Communist affairs outside Russia during Stalin's rule. Some even referred to this condition as a monolithic communism. But Benjamin Schwartz, the noted Soviet expert, reveals in the following essay that Soviet and Chinese ideology diverged from the beginning despite Stalin's effort to bridge the chasm or deny its existence. Schwartz insisted, moreover, that the Communist Party of China was no less in control of China than was the Communist Party in control of Russia. In the Twentieth Congress of 1956 Nikita Khrushchev acknowledged the ideological split between Moscow and Peking. The absence of a core of ideological agreement, predicted Schwartz, would cause the Sino-Soviet alliance to weaken even further under the impact of conflicting interests. What matters in any ideological affinity is the extent to which individual states are autonomous. To Schwartz, Stalin recognized the political independence of both Yugoslavia and China, but still attempted to assert the Kremlin's ideological supremacy. What that assertion meant in the control of national policy within other states remained unclear.

Abridged from pp. 125–141 in "Ideology and the Sino-Soviet Alliance," by Benjamin Schwartz, from *Moscow-Peking Axis: Strengths and Strains,* by Howard L. Boorman et al. Copyright © 1957 by Council on Foreign Relations, Inc. By permission of Harper & Row, Publishers, Inc.

The rise of the Chinese Communists to power followed hard on the heels of the crisis which had been touched off by the break with Tito. Mao's assumption of power in China may well have coincided with a certain disturbance in Stalin's image of a "socialist camp." As Professor [Adam] Ulam has pointed out in *Tito and the Cominform*, previous experience had probably led Stalin to believe that a mere assertion of his displeasure, a mere verbal chastisement by the Kremlin, would be sufficient to undermine Tito's power. Subsequent events demonstrated that a Communist party which had created its own dynamic leader fully familiar with Communist techniques of control, could not easily be captured from within once it had achieved state power. . . .

If Stalin's ultimate image of the "Socialist camp" continued to be that of a world tightly controlled from the Kremlin, one may surmise that after 1949 he postponed, rather than renounced, his hope of ultimately gaining control of the Chinese Communist Party. Up to his death, he seems to have accepted, however reluctantly, the necessity in practice of treating the Chinese Communist regime as an autonomous center of power.

While not much could be done toward instituting organizational control over China, every effort was made to reassert the Kremlin's ideological supremacy. Every Soviet account written before Stalin's death of Chinese Communist history stressed again and again that all the theoretical foundations of the Chinese Communist victory had been laid by Stalin. Moscow made no concessions to Chinese that Mao had made original theoretical contributions to the storehouse of Marxism-Leninism. In all Soviet accounts, Mao figured, at most, as the talented executor of Stalin's theoretical teachings.

At the same time, every effort was made by Moscow to fit Communist China into the category of the "people's democracies" as that concept was interpreted after 1948. This very effort disclosed an ideological gap between the two leaderships. . . .

After the break with Tito, Moscow announced clearly and abruptly that there was only one road to socialism, the Soviet road, and that all the "people's democracies" would have to tread that path. The Soviet Union had been able to make the transition from the quasi-capitalist stage of the New Economic Policy to the Sovialist stage only because its state was based on the "dictatorship of the proletariat." According to Lenin's dictum, while different countries might display certain variations in their forms of government during the period of transition to socialism, in essence all governments of this type would have to be dictatorships of the proletariat. After 1948 Moscow constantly reiterated that the regimes of Eastern Europe were, in their essence, dictatorships of the proletariat on the road to socialism and that they should behave accordingly. Again, to Stalin's mind, effective organizational control involved firm ideological control, and firm ideological control involved a total acceptance of the Soviet model of development. The whole Soviet development had, after all, been merely the "historic actualization" of the truths of Marxism-Leninism-Stalinism. . . .

Having decreed that the "people's democracies" were, in essence, "dictatorships of the proletariat," the Kremlin was not slow to extend this concept to the new developments in Asia. There were, to be sure, differences between North Korea, China and Eastern Europe. Because of their backwardness, the Asian states of the "Socialist camp" still had many "bourgeois-democratic" tasks to complete. However, once these states approached the period of the transition to socialism, they would necessarily become dictatorships of the proletariat.

It was precisely on this issue that a marked gap continued to exist between Chinese Communist and Soviet theory throughout the period from 1949 to the Twentieth Congress of the Communist Party of the Soviet Union in February 1956. While the Chinese were willing to accept the term of "people's democracy" as equivalent to their own "new democracy," they did not accept the post-1948 interpretation of this concept. In the interests of ideological harmony, the gap was not advertised. Nevertheless, it persisted and was even enshrined in the preamble to the Chinese Constitution of 1954.

As early as 1952, the Chinese Communists proclaimed the beginning of the period of transition to socialism, but they failed to acknowledge the necessity for a dictatorship of the proletariat in China. On the contrary, in China the party of the proletariat would proceed all the way to socialism in alliance with the peasantry, the petty bourgeoisie, and the national bourgeoisie under the "hegemony of the proletariat." The "bourgeois" sectors of the economy and even the minds of the bourgeoisie would be peacefully transformed, step by step, until they merged into socialism. During the last months of 1956, the Chinese Communists speeded up this "peaceful transformation." Private industry was converted into "state capitalist enter-prises" at a greatly accelerated rate and the bulk of the "national bourgeoisie" were pictured as joyfully welcoming the new order, thanks to the intense "education" which they had undergone. The novel notion here is that an "exploiting class" may be "educated" into accepting socialism. It is interesting to note that not only has the façade of coalition government been maintained, but in recent months there has been a new propaganda emphasis on the partici-pation of non-Communist "democratic groups" in this government, thus emphasizing the compatibility of such groups with "social-ism." . . .

The *New China Monthly Gazette* developed the notion that the Soviet Union had required a dictatorship of the proletariat because the Russian bourgeoisie had proved formidable and hostile in the revolution of 1917. The same was true of Eastern Europe. In China, however, the national bourgeoisie had been weak and tended to cooperate with the proletariat; hence, the possibility of a "peaceful transformation" of the bourgeois class. The concept of the "dictator-ship of the proletariat" is here reduced from the status of a universal truth to that of a local Russian response to a parochial Russian situation. It implies that in China the whole "people," and not the industrial proletariat alone, is "building socialism." There is a kind of straining toward the notion that the Communist party is not merely the class party of the proletariat (although this is always mentioned), but somehow an embodiment of the "general will" of the Chinese nation as a whole, with the exception of those labeled as "counter-revolutionaries."

What, if any, have been the practical consequences of this ideological divergence? It may be reflected in certain features of the Chinese scene. The extraordinary emphasis on "ideological remold-ing" and on "persuasion" (in the Chinese sense), the genuine desire to make maximum use of the talents of the so-called "national bourgeoisie," the sedulous maintenance of the outward trappings of coalition government, the recent courting of the so-called democratic groups and parties, are all reflections of it.

On the other hand, whether the Chinese Communist Party calls its rule "hegemony of the proletariat" or "dictatorship of the pro-letariat," its effective control of China is not one whit less absolute than that of the Communist Party in the Soviet Union. While a façade of coalition government is maintained, the so-called democratic parties echo the Communist party line with parrot-like monotony. Furthermore, the Chinese seem to be implementing the Soviet model of economic development far more vigorously than any of the avowedly "proletarian dictatorships" of Eastern Europe.

The persistence with which the Chinese have clung to their "difference" may well have a significance above and beyond its implications for domestic policy. It has maintained and magnified the image of Mao Tse-tung as a great theoretical innovator in his own right. By the same token, it has reaffirmed the ideological autonomy of the Chinese Communists within the "Socialist camp." Further, by stressing the "peculiarity" of China's path to socialism—the ability of the Chinese Communists to march to socialism at the head of the "whole people"—Peking tacitly indicates to non-Communist Asia that China offers its peoples a uniquely relevant message, distinct from that of Russian Communism. . . .

Immediately after [Stalin's] death, there began, within Russia, a relatively cautious diminution of the Stalin image. With this, it became possible to drop the previous insistence on Stalin's decisive role as the theoretical engineer of the Chinese Communist victory. It immediately became possible to make some concessions to the claims made in China for Mao as a theoretical leader in his own right. Both before and after Stalin's death, Mao's writings were being translated into Russian and were reviewed extensively. While the reviewers conceded that Mao had "creatively" applied Marxism-Leninism to Chinese conditions, they did not go so far as to specify his concrete contribution to the "storehouse of Marxism-Leninism."

Considerable credit was now being given to Mao as the architect of the Chinese Communist victory, but the gap still remained between the Soviet concept of "people's democracy" and the Chinese interpretation. Although the years 1952–55 were marked by a sharp diminution in Soviet discussions of ideology, whenever the issue was discussed, as in the 1954 party textbook on *Political Economy*, Moscow reaffirmed emphatically the standard dogma of the universal necessity for the dictatorship of the proletariat during the period of transition to socialism.

Strangely enough, during the last few months of 1955, on the very eve of the epoch-making Twentieth Party Congress, there was actually a revival of emphasis on this dogma. An article by Dubina, published in *Kommunist* (October, 1955), on "The Leninist Theory of Socialist Revolution," restated the Soviet position with renewed vehemence. "The experience of building socialism in the countries of the people's democracy," he wrote, "has clearly demonstrated the utter groundlessness of the chatter on the part of nationalist, opportunist elements who assert that their countries are proceeding to socialism by some special path, new in principle as it were and excluding class war, by the path of a peaceful growing over of capitalism into socialism." The universal necessity of the "dictatorship of the proletariat" was again stressed as the be-all-and-end-all of Communist orthodoxy. . . .

The fact that these reassertions of orthodoxy were being pressed on the very eve of the Twentieth Party Congress, which was so soon to move in precisely the opposite direction, lends much weight to the hypothesis that deep differences of opinion on these ideological issues were being fought out in the highest policy-making circles. If Khrushchev and those close to him were then pressing for the adoption of the more elastic formulas which finally prevailed at the Twentieth Congress, it is conceivable that the more orthodox views expressed just prior to it reflected the vehement feelings of the opposition group. . . .

The real turning point was the Twentieth Congress of the C.P.S.U. Not only were the Chinese and Yugoslav paths to socialism declared fully legitimate, but Khrushchev himself went far beyond the Chinese in asserting "the possibility of employing the parliamentary form for the transition to socialism." This formulation, it is true, was by no means unambiguous. The notion that parliaments and united fronts might properly be utilized by Communist parties in their march to power is by no means an original one. What Khrushchev seemed to be suggesting, however, was that Communist parties operating in countries of "bourgeois democracy" could now legitimately claim that the achievement of socialism did not necessarily require "the smashing of the old state apparatus." The Soviet path to socialism, Khrushchev now states, was simply a Russian response to Russian conditions, to the intransigence of the Russian bourgeoisie at the time of the revolution. . . . So far as both China and Yugoslavia are concerned, the new line . . . constitutes a striking admission of their claim to enjoy ideological autonomy, if not outright ideological independence. . . .

Whatever Khrushchev's calculations as to the effects elsewhere of his revisions of dogma, the Kremlin's desire to close the ideological gap with Communist China was certainly of primary importance. Peking's assertion of China's unique path to socialism, in one sense, presented Moscow with a more pressing problem than did the case of Yugoslavia, precisely because China was in the "Socialist camp," whereas Yugoslavia, by its own declaration, was not. At the Twentieth Congress, the Chinese case was mentioned repeatedly as an illustration of the "creative application of Marxism-Leninism." Shepilov, who became Foreign Minister three months later, dwelt in some detail on the peculiar features of the Chinese path and added, significantly, that "from the viewpoint of scholastics of Marxism, such an approach to the problem of transforming exploiting ownership into Socialist ownership is tantamount to trampling underfoot the principles of Marxism-Leninism; in actual fact this is creative Marxism-Leninism in action." In discussing the question of "paths to socialism," the Resolutions of the Twentieth Congress singled out China as the test case par excellence:

> The Chinese People's Republic has introduced many special features into its form of Socialist construction. Before the victory of the revolution, the economy was extremely backward and was semi-feudal and semi-colonial in character. On the basis of its ability to capture the decisive commanding heights, the People's Democratic Government is now bringing about a peaceful transformation of private industry and commerce and their step-by-step conversion into component parts of socialism.

The Soviet leadership has conceded China's right to follow its own path to socialism, and it has thus closed the ideological gap, even though the verbal formula, "dictatorship of the proletariat," has not been dropped. An indication that the Chinese Communists interpret the Congress's action in this light is furnished by the Chinese Politbureau statement of April 4, 1956, entitled "On the Historical Experience Concerning the Dictatorship of the Proletariat." It specifically equates China's "people's democratic dictatorship" with the dictatorship of the proletariat. Since the Soviets have now redefined this term in such a way as to remove all its meaning content, the Chinese are able to reciprocate by accepting the term, for in accepting it, they have conceded nothing of their own views concerning China's "peculiar path." The gap has been closed, not by bringing the

Chinese ideological formula into line with Moscow's orthodoxy, but by adjusting Soviet ideology to accommodate the Chinese innovations. Ideological solidarity has, thereby, been reaffirmed.

The price, however, has been the reaffirmation of China's ideological autonomy and a further tampering with what remains of Marxist-Leninist ideology. In the short run, ideological solidarity can, presumably, be maintained only through ideological concessions; in the long run, the weakening of the ideology as a coherent whole cannot but exercise a weakening effect. If the ideological link has been a crucial one in Sino-Soviet relations, the constant wearing away of the core of shared ideological beliefs must inevitably weaken that core, and the alliance must come to rest more and more on the shifting sands of power interest. . . .

Robert A. Scalapino

MOSCOW, PEKING, AND ASIAN COMMUNISM

Unlike Milton Sacks, who wrote the selection included above in 1950, Robert A. Scalapino did not attempt in the following essay written in 1963, to attribute local Communist policies and purposes to the influence of Moscow or Peking. Nor did Scalapino deal with the issue raised by Richard Harris in the tenth reading regarding the strength and nature of the Asian Communist parties. This essay recognizes only that the Sino-Soviet ideological disagreements of necessity troubled the Communist parties of Asia, whether in power or not, and compelled them to choose sides or declare their neutrality. Most parties expressed their intellectual preferences for either the Soviet or the Chinese positions on such issues as Albania, Yugoslavia, and Soviet revisionism. The Asian parties, with the exception of Outer Mongolia and Ceylon, generally favored the Peking line. But this in no way countered Harris's contention that the Asian parties were independent of both Moscow and Peking. Scalapino assumed that Communist leaders could identify with their own countries and still remain committed to an international movement. But how they could serve interests which would ultimately conflict was not clear.

Excerpted by permission from "Moscow, Peking and the Communist Parties of Asia," *Foreign Affairs* 41 (January 1963): 323–343. Copyright © 1962 by Council on Foreign Relations, Inc.

Never before have we seen such an extraordinary display of disunity in the Communist world. Moscow's policy of rapprochement with Tito is regarded by Peking and its supporters as further proof of the fundamentally revisionist, anti-Marxian character of "the Khrushchev group." Peking views the indecisive Soviet policy regarding the Sino-Indian conflict—Moscow's precarious attempt to carry water on both shoulders—as a typical failure of Khrushchev to give full support to a "fraternal socialist ally." It brands the Soviet decision to withdraw missiles from Cuba as appeasement of American imperialism, a clear manifestation of the pacifism and fear that it now regularly describes as the trademarks of Russian diplomacy.

The Soviet Premier and his friends have answers to these charges. To them, the foremost enemies of Marx-Leninism at present are dogmatists who pursue a narrow nationalism, emulate Stalinism in its worst aspects and follow adventurist policies that risk global war. In Khrushchevian circles, the tendency is growing to divide the Communist world into its "advanced" and "backward" components, into categories of "friendly" and "unfriendly" socialist states or factions.

Clearly, the strenuous efforts of Communist intermediaries during recent months to bring about some understanding—or at least a *modus vivendi*—between Russia and China have borne little fruit. Thus the events that followed immediately after the 22nd Congress of the Communist Party of the Soviet Union (C.P.S.U.) acquire additional significance. For five months after October 1961 the Communist bloc quarreled publicly among themselves before the world. The era of open struggle was inaugurated when Chou En-lai departed from Moscow in a huff at the height of the Congress, having earlier left a wreath on the tomb of that "great Marxist-Leninist," J. V. Stalin, and having upbraided Khrushchev in stinging fashion for his public criticism of Albania. There followed the steady development of the Sino-Albanian alliance in the face of withering Soviet blasts against Albanian leaders and the severance of Russian-Albanian diplomatic relations. And throughout this period, although the Soviet Union and its allies repeatedly proclaimed that their position had the support of "the overwhelming majority" of the Communist parties of the world, most Asian Communist parties firmly refused to give Moscow their support on the crucial issues. . . .

History may well record that the truly significant aspect of this great crisis in the Communist world has been the attitudes and policies of Asian Communist leaders—not just those of Peking, but those of Djakarta, Pyongyang, Hanoi and Tokyo as well. If Khrushchev had hoped to isolate China on the issue of Albania, he failed. And nowhere did he fail more resoundingly than in Eastern Asia where only the parties of Outer Mongolia and Ceylon came quickly to his side. Elsewhere he called for full support in vain. A new phenomenon emerged—neutralism within the Communist bloc. The great bulk of the Asian Communist movement chose to remain nonaligned between Moscow and Peking, and this was in itself a defeat for Khrushchev, especially when, as in many cases, it was nonalignment that leaned toward Peking.

II

Khrushchev garnered two allies in the Far East at an early point, the parties of Outer Mongolia and Ceylon. On October 21, 1961, two days after Khrushchev's famous October 19 speech to the 22nd Congress, Premier Tsedenbal, head of the Mongolian People's Revolutionary Party delegation, spoke in firm support of the Soviet position. He congratulated the Congress for its "decisive struggle" against the harmful cult of personality and openly condemned the Albanian party leaders for their divisive "anti-Marxist" activities. These views were subsequently extended and sharpened in Ulan Bator. In late November, Chairman Tsend of the Great People's Hural (Mongolian People's Assembly) bitterly attacked Premier Hoxha of Albania and his stooges for sliding into the bog of nationalism. Nor did he ignore China, but bluntly commented that Chinese insistence upon handling the problems privately was a futile approach "deviating from the truth," since the cleavage was public knowledge. The party position was made official in January 1962 when Tsedenbal reported on the 22nd Congress to the Central Committee. He again rigorously censured Albania and, following the Khrushchev lead, called for a liquidation of the cult of personality that had formed around former Premier Choibalsan, dead since 1952. Clearly, the Outer Mongolian leaders had gone all the way.

The actions of the Ceylonese Communist Party must also have been gratifying to Khrushchev. On October 25, 1961, Mr. Pieter Keuneman, Secretary-General, addressed the Congress as a leader of the Ceylonese delegation. His remarks were brief, but included adverse comments on the personality cult and on Albanian party leaders who were accused of taking a position "incompatible with proletarian internationalism." A lengthy party statement, issued April 8, 1962, sustained and expanded these remarks. The Ceylonese Party regarded it as "inconceivable" that Hoxha could "basely accuse the C.P.S.U. and its leaders of revisionism and fawning upon imperialism; justify and extol some of the worst features of the personality cult; openly challenge the agreed conclusions of the international Communist movement on such basic questions as peaceful coexistence and the importance of the decisions and course of the 20th Congress. . . .

III

Nowhere else in Eastern Asia, however, did Khrushchev get this kind of support, setting aside the special case of India with which we shall deal later. The position of other Far Eastern Communist parties on these and related issues ranged from silence to open disapproval. Let us look briefly at the facts, starting with Indonesia.

The attitude of the Communist Party of Indonesia (P.K.I.) on such issues as Albania and de-Stalinization is of real significance in the Communist world. This party, with some two million members and additional millions in its front organizations, is the most important Communist Party currently existing in a non-Communist nation. When its position was clarified, Khrushchev had little reason to be happy. On the key issues it stood remarkably close to Peking, although the official stance can be described as one of nonalignment. . . .

The main danger to the Communist world is revisionism, they conclude, and they cite Yugoslavia as a prime example. Yugoslav support for the 22nd Congress is a trick to sow "the poison of division" within the Communist camp. Yugoslavia is completely outside the pale, "a tool of American imperialism." Albania, on the other hand, is a genuinely socialist society, not to be ousted from the fraternity by Soviet fiat.

Some of these positions are taken from the Moscow Statement of 1960, but the particular themes chosen for emphasis are most revealing, as are the various parallels in tactics and strategy between the Indonesian and the Chinese parties. In recent months, moreover, the P.K.I. has reinforced its pro-Peking orientation by strongly supporting the Chinese position on Yugoslavia, the Indian border issue and Cuba. Aidit called the dismantling of missiles "a regrettable sacrifice" forced upon the Cubans against their will. His statement left no doubt concerning his party's support for a "tough line," and it was widely circulated by the Chinese. For Moscow, nonalignment in any form is difficult to accept, but the Indonesian variety must seem especially grim.

Can Soviet leaders take greater solace from the forms of neutralism exhibited by North Korea and North Viet Nam?

North Korea today is under the iron rule of one man, Kim Il-song. After more than a decade of fierce intra-party struggle, Kim appears to have leveled all opposition. At the top, there is only one significant faction in North Korean politics, the Kim faction, composed mainly of the old partisan fighters who served with Kim in Manchuria; they have one characteristic in common: complete loyalty to the leader. Kim, now 50 years of age, holds the posts of Premier, Marshal of the Korean People's Army and Chairman of the Central Committee of the Korean Workers' Party (K.W.P.), which claims over 1.3 million members. North Korea is in the midst of a Stalinist phase of development.

The initial North Korean stand on Albania was that relations between the Soviet Communist Party and Albania were "abnormal," and that if this situation continued it would cause "grave damage" to the Communist movement. The solution, according to Kim, lay in discussions and mutual understanding, using the formula provided by the Moscow conferences of 1957 and 1960. . . .

The North Koreans gave full support to China against India and to Cuba against the United States. Significantly, Kim proclaimed that peace could not be begged for, but had to be won through struggle—by dealing the imperialists blows everywhere. Thus North Korean "neutralism" must also have an ominous ring in Soviet ears.

The tactics of the North Korean Communists following the 22nd Congress are also revealing. Selecting two ceremonial occasions, spaced only one day apart, they sought to portray their nonalignment unmistakably. On November 7, 1961, an effusive message of congratulations and praise was sent to Soviet leaders on the occasion of the 44th anniversary of the October Revolution. On November 8, a message of congratulations was sent to the Albanian Workers' Party on the 20th anniversary of the founding of the party. This praised the Albanian Party for having struggled successfully to construct a progressive socialist state and having opposed courageously the imperialists "and their lackeys, the Yugoslav revisionists." Eternal friendship between the Korean and Albanian people was pledged "within the great family of the socialist camp headed by the U.S.S.R."

Before seeking to generalize upon the tactics of Communist neutralism, let us look briefly at the policies of the Workers' Party of North Vietnam (V.W.P.), which has perhaps achieved the most perfect neutral position in public that was possible. Once again, this is an important Communist party. It is in firm control in North Vietnam, has extended its cadres deeply into the south, renders "fraternal assistance" to the Pathet Lao and probably has substantial contacts in Cambodia. With about 500,000 members, it is the most significant Communist party in continental Southeast Asia. In Ho Chi Minh, moreover, it has a national treasure. This Communist veteran, now more than 70, can claim to have known Lenin. He antedates both Khrushchev and Mao. And perhaps as much as any Communist leader, Ho has held a dual image as nationalist and internationalist, as Father of the Country and experienced Comintern agent. The Communist world does not possess a better mediator, and Ho's talents have been extensively used in recent months—seemingly in vain. . . .

Recent events suggest that the "perfect neutrality" of North Vietnam may be in jeopardy. In October 1962, amidst the many crises involving the Communist world, a delegation from the Chinese National People's Congress, headed by Peng Chen, visited North Vietnam. The speeches that ensued were models of cordiality. Peng asserted pointedly that Chinese-Vietnamese friendship had withstood all tests, survived despite great storms. Vietnamese spokesmen reciprocated by giving unstinting praise to "the correct foreign policy of the Chinese government and people," which, they asserted, had contributed to the strengthening of the socialist camp, the promotion of national liberation movements and the defense of world peace. Subsequently, Hanoi fully supported "the correct stand" of China on the Sino-Indian border conflict and also indicated its complete agreement with a policy of all-out support for Cuba. . . .

IV

Which other Communist parties of Eastern Asia can be placed in the same general category with those of Indonesia, North Korea and North Vietnam?

Let us first consider the Communist Party of Japan (J.C.P.). None of the parties of Asia has had more trouble than it, and in a relative sense few are weaker, suggesting once again that the Communist movement has its greatest opportunities in the early stages of the modernization process. Normally, the Japanese Party polls less than 3 percent of the total Japanese vote. Moreover, it has been badly factionalized in recent years. But if currently it is weak and divided, it still exists in a nation that is strategically important to the world balance of power.

The evidence suggests that the J.C.P. belongs to the neutralist group, with clear indications that a leaning toward Peking has now developed among a majority of the leaders. In the past, the J.C.P. has been reluctant to take a forthright public stand or has been unable to do so because of internal differences. Official statements have generally been marked by silence on the burning issues or by cloudiness. Sanzo Nosaka, veteran Secretary-General and leader of the delegation to Moscow, did not touch upon Albania or de-Stalinization in his speech before the Congress, and barely mentioned the subject upon his return when he insisted that Communist parties, "linked by the blood of Marx-Leninism," had an indestructible unity which "no imperialist machinations could destroy." . . .

In mid-1961, a small group of Communists left the J.C.P. and formed a separatist movement that took an anti-Stalinist, anti-Peking line. This group has repeatedly charged that a majority of party leaders back Peking on the critical issues. Recent actions and statements of the party, while generally guarded, emphatically support that contention. On issues ranging from the general problems of disarmament and peaceful coexistence to the specific problems of India and Cuba, its pronouncements currently have a pro-Peking flavor. Clearly, Khrushchev is in serious trouble with many Japanese comrades.

The picture within the Burmese Communist movement is even more chaotic. This movement has been openly split for more than a decade. There are the Red Flag Communists, a small group led by

Thakin Soe which has been fighting the government since 1946. Mistakenly called Trotskyites, this group in fact represents indigenous Burmese Communists molded ideologically by the purist, creative, egocentric mind of Soe. Soe's theoretical inclinations, however, have long been away from men like Khrushchev. Meanwhile a rival group has existed, the White Flag Communists, led by Than Tun. It is this group that is recognized internationally as the Burmese Communist Party (B.C.P.). Finally, there are certain separate Marxist, proto-Communist associations, notably the National Unity Front (N.U.F.).

In the aftermath of the 22nd Congress, Soe's Red Flag Communists have conducted an all-out campaign against Khrushchev and the current Soviet leaders. At the end of 1961, the Youth Front, a group affiliated with Soe, announced that it intended to burn Khrushchev's effigy on January 1, 1962, because he was an "arch-revisionist." Immediately, Thein Pe Myint, veteran Marxist and currently affiliated with the N.U.F., attacked the Youth Front for its plans. Charges and countercharges flew fast. The Youth Front accused Thein Pe Myint of "Browderism," of being a traitor to the Marx-Leninist cause and of becoming a mercenary in the pay of the Rangoon Soviet Embassy. It asserted that as editor of the *Vanguard*, Thein Pe Myint had been given 1,000 Kyat by the Russian Embassy to publish "a highly scandalous article on Stalin" previously rejected. . . .

Information about the attitudes and actions of the Communist movement elsewhere in Southeast Asia is sparse and often unreliable. However, the evidence generally points to gains for Peking. In Thailand, where the Communist movement appears to be growing, primary support comes from two sources: the Pathet Lao-Vietnamese Communist forces in the immediate vicinity—and Peking. Captured Communist leaders have indicated that their tactics and strategy are modeled extensively after the historic Chinese Communist experience: an appeal to the peasantry; the attempt to build a homogenized national-Communist movement, United Front in type; and the eventual establishment of an "independent base" from which to conduct military operations. Similar tactics prevail in the Communist movement of Malaysia. Communist leaders of this area, overwhelmingly Chinese in racial origin, also draw primary support from two sources: the Indonesian Communist Party and Communist China.

Both the Thai and Malayan Communist parties, as noted earlier, sent congratulatory telegrams to Albania in November 1961.

V

Soviet losses in Southeast Asia have perhaps been offset to some extent by a recent victory scored within the Communist Party of India (C.P.I.). This victory did not come quickly or easily, nor was it complete. After many months of delay, however, the party finally set forth its official position in such a fashion as to align itself primarily with Moscow. And this was important. Despite its many difficulties, it is a major political force in India. In the February 1962 elections, the party maintained its position as the leading opposition to the massive Congress Party.

Until mid-1962, the Indian Communists had not been able to take an official party position on the issues of Albania and de-Stalinization due to serious internal differences of opinion. It has been obvious for many months that a loose "Center-Right" coalition controlled the party at national levels and that this coalition leaned toward Moscow. Like other Indian parties, however, the C.P.I. has been undergoing a significant change: leadership at the all-India level is giving way to state-based leadership, and this transition represents a strong centrifugal pull upon the party. In some states, such as West Bengal for example, local Communist leadership has been openly and vigorously "pro-China."

Until his death in January 1962, Ajoy Ghosh served as general secretary and moderator between factions. His public speech at the 22nd Congress ignored the burning issues, and there were indications that heated debates were going on within the Indian delegation. In the following months the national party organs published many speeches by Soviet leaders attacking the cult of personality and the Albanian leaders. No coverage was given to the opposition. On December 10, 1961, Ghosh published a lengthy statement on the 22nd Congress which was generally favorable to Moscow. It was cautiously worded and did not purport to be an official party position, but it clearly indicated Ghosh's personal leanings.

Meanwhile, Ghosh had become involved in an open dispute with Peking over the border issue. When the Indian Government charged the Chinese Communists with new border incursions in late

November 1961, Ghosh issued a sharp demand on behalf of the C.P.I. that the Chinese Government stop such acts and in subsequent statements asserted that the Indian Government should defend its territory against aggression from any quarter. From this point until his death on January 13, 1962, Ghosh was involved in a running battle with Peking in which both sides used sharp words. The Peking radio strongly criticized Ghosh in the course of a 45-minute broadcast on the Indian problem; and in his last party appearance, on January 3, Ghosh firmly held his ground. He asserted that India's seizure of Goa had proven that the Indian Party's assessment of Indian foreign policy was correct and that of the Chinese Party was incorrect. He also bluntly stated that the Chinese charges against the Indian Party constituted an unwarranted interference in the internal affairs of a fraternal party. Ten days later, Ghosh was dead. It is not surprising that the Chinese note of sympathy was extremely brief.

Though Ghosh undoubtedly spoke for a majority of the party leaders there was strong opposition from the "left," as was illustrated by a number of events. The organ of the Kerala State Communist Party protested angrily against the removal of Stalin's body from the mausoleum. . . .

The official position of the Indian Communist Party on Albania and de-Stalinization can be summarized as follows:

Differences within the international Communist movement as a result of the striking new trends inaugurated by the 20th Congress were inevitable, but the Albanian attack upon Soviet leaders was regrettable and "highly unjustified." Only the imperialists and reactionaries of the world can profit from the present state of affairs in the international Communist movement. Differences should be resolved in accordance with the methods outlined by the Moscow Statement of 1960.

On the second of the two main issues, the cult of personality, the Soviet leaders are said to have acted with exceptional courage. It is necessary, of course, to keep both aspects of Stalin's character and role in mind. He was a great Marx-Leninist who made valuable contributions toward the building of socialism in the Soviet Union and the growth of the world Communist movement. These facts cannot be erased from history. At the same time, toward the later part of his life, the negative side of his character developed and the cult of personality went from bad to worse. Various excesses and crimes took place which had to be exposed. Indeed, more objective and self-critical examinations of this problem than have yet been undertaken need to be made. It was not denied that the struggle against Stalin created "a measure of confusion within the ranks of our party." While not necessarily endorsing every statement or action of the Soviet leaders in this connection, such as the removal of Stalin's body from the mausoleum or the change in names of cities, the party could, however, welcome and seek to emulate the basic Soviet trend toward greater party democracy in leadership and organization.

Read carefully, the statement of the Indian Communist Party indicated a tendency to conciliate the "left" and gave evidence of the extraordinary caution used in choosing each word and phrase. For this reason, much of the Indian press referred to the statement as a "compromise." However, it represented a "compromise" clearly leaning toward Moscow, reflecting the general balance of power prevailing within the top party echelons.

Then came the enlarged border conflict. On November 1, 1962, after two days of bitter debate, the C.P.I. National Council passed a resolution appealing to *all* Indians to unite in defense of the motherland against Chinese aggression. The pro-China element in the party had urged a resolution demanding immediate negotiations. But the anti-China faction won, apparently by a two-to-one margin, after a most acrimonious struggle. The Communist Party of India has never been so deeply divided.

VI

Perhaps we are now in a position to formulate some general propositions about the struggle between the Soviet and Chinese Communists for ideological and political leadership of the Communist movement in Asia. In this struggle, Nikita Khrushchev is not at this point doing well. At present, he has the upper hand in Outer Mongolia and Ceylon (though the Ceylonese Communists have been rocked by recent events and appear uncertain as to course). Perhaps he can gain a lasting advantage in India, although the situation there is explosive for all Communist factions, domestic and foreign. But everywhere else—in Indonesia, North Korea, North Vietnam, Japan, Burma, Thailand and Malaya—he has not been able to get acceptance of his position on Albania, de-Stalinization or various other issues, large and small. In general, the stance of these parties is one of nonalignment, but often a nonalignment that favors Peking.

Many Asian Communist leaders were antagonized by Khrushchev's decision to attack the Albanian leaders publicly and to seek to purge them. This action was privately interpreted as unilateral action on his part, Soviet "big power chauvinism" and direct interference in the internal affairs of another party. Some Asian Communists view Albania as a case of "There, but for the grace of China, go I." . . .

VII

Four facts in particular help to account for the problem the Soviet Union faces in Asia.

The first is the physical presence of Communist China—a huge, new state, struggling with gigantic problems but doing it with defiant pride and determination. Under any ideological banner, China would cast a shadow over the rest of Asia to the full extent of its physical power. It is natural, things being as they are, that this shadow should fall heavily upon the Communist parties of North Korea and North Vietnam, countries that share a common border with China. No doubt the Chinese have heightened their influence by an extensive program of economic and technical assistance to nearby states and "fraternal parties." Despite the serious domestic crises of recent years, Communist China has rendered major service to many states. Its aid to North Korea and North Vietnam may exceed that of the Soviet Union at present, and probably aid of a different sort flows to the Communist parties of Indonesia, Japan, Thailand and Malaya. It is significant that Communist "neutralism" generally follows the contours of the historic sphere of Chinese influence in days when China was powerful.

The degree to which Communist China can be a model for aspiring Asian Communists provides another gravitational pull toward Peking. In their march toward victory, the Maoists developed a serviceable tactic and strategy of revolution for much of the non-Western world: cultivation of the peasantry in order to acquire a mass base; the attempt to combine with the nationalist movement, if possible to capture its charismatic leader, in any case to seek to control it, combining 90 percent—"the people"—against 10 percent—"their enemies"; and, finally, the perfection of guerilla-war techniques, combining force with politics.

These concepts are not original with Mao, but it was his disciples who made them work, and now they are being followed by most of the Asian Communist parties. This combines with the extraordinary ignorance of the Soviet Union concerning things Asian to eat heavily into Soviet influence among the contemporary generation of Asian revolutionaries.

Connected with this second factor is a third—the Chinese world view, which is more closely attuned to the interests and attitudes of most Asian Communists than that of the Soviet Union. Three main issues between China and Russia stand out: decision-making within the bloc; tactics and policies toward the West and toward the emergent, nonaligned nations; and assistance to be given "fraternal socialist allies." Despite the verbal agreements reached in Moscow in 1957 and 1960, none of these basic issues has been resolved.

For the moment, at least, China is cast in the role of foremost challenger of Soviet monolithism. The themes of equality, independence and separate routes to revolutionary success for each Communist party were pioneered both in theory and in action by the Chinese Communists; now they are the common property of other Asian parties. . . .

It is also understandable why Asian Communists who are deeply dissatisfied with the status quo and feel thwarted, directly or indirectly, by American power, would want the Soviet Union to adopt the strongest possible anti-Western policy and give special priority for the "national liberation movement." The Soviet Union can compete with the United States directly, as a nation-state, in economic, political and military terms. Indeed, it must. But the Communists of North Vietnam, for instance, like those of China herself, can compete only indirectly—as the world revolution is forwarded or as the Soviets successfully challenge American strength in one form or another. In their eyes any Soviet accommodation with the United States—or lethargy toward the emerging world—represents a threat to their own interests. . . .

In short, the Communists of China, because of the timing of their revolution and the circumstances under which it has developed, have vastly more in common in terms of world outlook with the Communists of the emerging world than those of the second-generation revolutionary leadership of Moscow—a Moscow, it might be added, that must now assume all of the solemnity and caution that accrue to any global leader.

There is a final consideration, one involving personality or perhaps "national character": Khrushchevian diplomacy is considered crude and overbearing and Soviet knowledge regarding Asia is felt to be inadequate, with the result that the Communist cause is damaged. . . .

In this context, China has one advantage over the Soviet Union in Asia. Despite their ethnocentrism and xenophobia, the Chinese leaders do know much about their neighbors. The Soviet Union, on the other hand, is basically ignorant about the non-Western world, and Khrushchev often seems to ignore Asian Communist needs and sensitivities. This problem is magnified by the differences between first-generation and second-generation Communist leadership. The Asian Communist leaders, who are first-generation and intellectuals, find Khrushchev, a second-generation bureaucrat of peasant stock, impetuous and vulgar. The suavity of a Chou En-lai or the classical intellectualism of a Mao Tse-tung is more in tune with the contemporary Communist élite of Asia. One must not rule out personal and "esthetic" considerations like these in appraising the roles of Moscow versus Peking in the Communist world. The East-West division within the Communist ranks is in part a division in timing and in culture.

It would be wrong, however, to assume that the Communist leaders of Asia want to establish their independence from Moscow only to fall under the control of Peking. Many of them no doubt hope to make a virtue out of a necessity; they hope to establish a nonaligned position which will give them greater maneuverability than any small Communist state or party has ever been able to attain. In this, of course, they share hopes with a number of their European comrades. It seems very likely, for example, that Ho Chi Minh and Kim Il-song desire to keep Chinese control at a minimum and if possible to play the classical role of the small buffer state between two major powers.

There is the great danger for the Communist parties in Asia that if Moscow and Peking exert increased pressure—and perhaps even if they do not—the Sino-Soviet cleavage will result in new or widened splits in every Communist movement. The evidence suggests strongly that what has already happened in India and Burma, and is indicated in North Vietnam and Japan, is occurring almost everywhere. This is the major reason, of course, why the Asian Communists have exerted the greatest pressure to ensure that the tactics of dispute will not create harmful explosions even if the issues themselves cannot be resolved.

Thus Sino-Soviet differences offer one major opportunity for the "small" Communists, and hold out one major threat. The opportunity is to secure greater independence through nonalignment; the threat is internal schism. Both are now apparent on the Asian Communist horizon.

What are the implications of these facts for American foreign policy? In some respects we face significant new dangers. Generally speaking, Communism has succeeded in Asia only where it has been able to capture and use the nationalist movement. It may find greater opportunities to do this under present circumstances. In earlier times when international Communism was monolithic and centered in Moscow it was difficult for a foreign Communist party to take on the image of nationalism and independence or to follow pragmatic and realistic policies suited to local conditions. Asia is strewn with the remains of Communist men and movements that fell in the service of the Soviet Union—only to be repudiated by Soviet leaders in the end because they had failed. Now we are in a new era. In many parts of the world Communism is developing a greater rapport with its own society and increased flexibility in tactics and strategy, while at the same time retaining its thorough commitment to internationalism. . . .

V PERCEPTIONS OF THE CHINESE THREAT

Lin Piao

CHINA AND THE PEOPLE'S WAR

Marshal Lin Piao, then Vice Premier of China, published this doctrinal essay amid the ideological frenzy of the Great Chinese Cultural Revolution of the mid-sixties. Its bitter denunciation of the United States and its "lackeys" troubled those Americans who were inclined to view China as a profound revolutionary threat to the peace and stability of Asia. That Lin condemned the Kremlin revisionists as betrayers of the Marxist-Leninist revolution demonstrated the magnitude of the Sino-Soviet split, but it in no way eliminated the fear of those who chose to take this essay seriously. Commemorating the twentieth anniversary of the Chinese victory over Japan, Lin attributed that victory to Mao Tse-tung's concept of people's war. This triumph of the weak over the strong demonstrated, for Lin, the power which a self-reliant, determined Asia, Africa, and Latin America—the world's backward, rural areas—could generate through the strategy of a people's war. The superior military preparations of the "imperialist" countries, led by the United States, would in the long run prove ineffective against peasants organized under Mao's precepts. Even as Lin predicted victory for the revolution, he promised the revolutionaries theory and encouragement, but nothing more.

Full twenty years have elapsed since our victory in the great War of Resistance Against Japan.

After a long period of heroic struggle, the Chinese people, under the leadership of the Communist Party of China and Comrade Mao Tse-tung, won final victory two decades ago in their war against the Japanese imperialists who had attempted to subjugate China and swallow up the whole of Asia.

The Chinese people's War of Resistance was an important part of the world war against German, Japanese and Italian fascism. The Chinese people received support from the people and the anti-fascist forces all over the world. And in their turn, the Chinese people made an important contribution to victory in the Anti-Fascist War as a whole.

Of the innumerable anti-imperialist wars waged by the Chinese people in the past hundred years, the War of Resistance Against Japan was the first to end in complete victory. It occupies an ex-

From "Long Live the Victory of People's War!" *Peking Review*, September 3, 1965, pp. 9–30.

tremely important place in the annals of war, in the annals of both the revolutionary wars of the Chinese people and the wars of the oppressed nations of the world against imperialist aggression. . . .

How was it possible for a weak country finally to defeat a strong country? How was it possible for a seemingly weak army to become the main force in the war?

The basic reasons were that the War of Resistance Against Japan was a genuine people's war led by the Communist Party of China and Comrade Mao Tse-tung, a war in which the correct Marxist-Leninist political and military lines were put into effect, and that the Eighth Route and New Fourth Armies were genuine people's armies which applied the whole range of strategy and tactics of people's war as formulated by Comrade Mao Tse-tung. . . .

The victory of the Chinese people's revolutionary war breached the imperialist front in the East, wrought a great change in the world balance of forces, and accelerated the revolutionary movement among the people of all countries. From then on, the national-liberation movement in Asia, Africa, and Latin America entered a new historical period.

Today, the U.S. imperialists are repeating on a worldwide scale the past actions of the Japanese imperialists in China and other parts of Asia. It has become an urgent necessity for the people in many countries to master and use people's war as a weapon against U.S. imperialism and its lackeys. In every conceivable way U.S. imperialism and its lackeys are trying to extinguish the revolutionary flames of people's war. The Khrushchev revisionists, fearing people's war like the plague, are heaping abuse on it. The two are colluding to prevent and sabotage people's war. In these circumstances, it is of vital practical importance to review the historical experience of the great victory of the people's war in China and to recapitulate Comrade Mao Tse-tung's theory of people's war. . . .

In his celebrated work *On Protracted War*, Comrade Mao Tse-tung pointed out the contrasting features of China and Japan, the two sides in the war. Japan was a powerful imperialist country. But Japanese imperialism was in its era of decline and doom. The war it had unleashed was a war of aggression, a war that was retrogressive and barbarous; it was deficient in manpower and material resources and could not stand a protracted war; it was engaged in an unjust cause and therefore had meager support internationally. China, on the other hand, was a weak semi-colonial and semi-feudal country. But she was in her era of progress. She was fighting a war against aggression, a war that was progressive and just; she had sufficient manpower and material resources to sustain a protracted war; internationally, China enjoyed extensive sympathy and support. These comprised all the basic factors in the Sino-Japanese war.

He went on to show how these factors would influence the course of the war. Japan's advantage was temporary and would gradually diminish as a result of our efforts. Her disadvantages were fundamental; they could not be overcome and would gradually grow in the course of the war. China's disadvantage was temporary and could be gradually overcome. China's advantages were fundamental and would play an increasingly positive role in the course of the war. Japan's advantage and China's disadvantage determined the impossibility of quick victory for China. China's advantages and Japan's disadvantages determined the inevitability of Japan's defeat and China's ultimate victory.

On the basis of this analysis Comrade Mao Tse-tung formulated the strategy for a protracted war. China's War of Resistance would be protracted, and prolonged efforts would be needed gradually to weaken the enemy's forces and expand our own, so that the enemy would change from being strong to being weak and we would change from being weak to being strong and accumulate sufficient strength finally to defeat him. Comrade Mao Tse-tung pointed out that with the change in the balance of forces between the enemy and ourselves the War of Resistance would pass through three stages, namely, the strategic defensive, the strategic stalemate and the strategic offensive. The protracted war was also a process of mobilizing, organizing and arming the people. It was only by mobilizing the entire people to fight a people's war that the War of Resistance could be persevered in and the Japanese aggressors defeated.

In order to turn the anti-Japanese war into a genuine people's war, our Party firmly relied on the broadest masses of the people, united with all the anti-Japanese forces that could be united, and consolidated and expanded the Anti-Japanese National United Front. The basic line of our Party was: boldly to arouse the masses of the people and expand the people's forces so that, under the leadership of the Party, they could defeat the aggressors and build a new China. . . .

The peasantry constituted more than 80 percent of the entire population of semi-colonial and semi-feudal China. They were subjected to threefold oppression and exploitation by imperialism, feudalism and bureaucrat-capitalism, and they were eager for resistance against Japan and for revolution. It was essential to rely mainly on the peasants if the people's war was to be won. . . .

As far back as the period of the First Revolutionary Civil War, Comrade Mao Tse-tung had pointed out that the peasant question occupied an extremely important position in the Chinese revolution, that the bourgeois-democratic revolution against imperialism and feudalism was in essence a peasant revolution and that the basic task of the Chinese proletariat in the bourgeois-democratic revolution was to give leadership to the peasants' struggle.

In the period of the War of Resistance Against Japan, Comrade Mao Tse-tung again stressed that the peasants were the most reliable and the most numerous ally of the proletariat and constituted the main force in the War of Resistance. The peasants were the main source of manpower for China's armies. The funds and the supplies needed for a protracted war came chiefly from the peasants. In the anti-Japanese war it was imperative to rely mainly on the peasants and to arouse them to participate in the war on the broadest scale.

The War of Resistance Against Japan was in essence a peasant revolutionary war led by our Party. By arousing and organizing the peasant masses and integrating them with the proletariat, our Party created a powerful force capable of defeating the strongest enemy. . . .

The essence of Comrade Mao Tse-tung's theory of army-building is that in building a people's army prominence must be given to politics, i.e., the army must first and foremost be built on a political basis. Politics is the commander, politics is the soul of everything. Political work is the lifeline of our army. True, a people's army must pay attention to the constant improvement of its weapons and equipment and its military technique, but in its fighting it does not rely purely on weapons and technique, it relies mainly on politics, on the proletarian revolutionary consciousness and courage of the commanders and fighters, on the support and backing of the masses.

Owing to the application of Comrade Mao Tse-tung's line on army-building, there has prevailed in our army at all times a high level of proletarian political consciousness, an atmosphere of keenness to study the thought of Mao Tse-tung, an excellent morale, a solid unity and a deep hatred for the enemy, and thus a gigantic moral force has been brought into being. In battle it has feared neither hardships nor death, it has been able to charge or hold its ground as the conditions require. One man can play the role of several, dozens or even hundreds, and miracles can be performed.

All this makes the people's army led by the Chinese Communist Party fundamentally different from any bourgeois army, and from all the armies of the old type which served the exploiting classes and were driven and utilized by a handful of people. The experience of the people's war in China shows that a people's army created in accordance with Comrade Mao Tse-tung's theory of army-building is incomparably strong and invincible.

Engels said, "The emancipation of the proletariat, in its turn, will have its specific expression in military affairs and create its specific, new military method." Engels' profound prediction has been fulfilled in the revolutionary wars waged by the Chinese people under the leadership of the Chinese Communist Party. In the course of protracted armed struggle, we have created a whole range of strategy and tactics of people's war by which we have been able to utilize our strong points to attack the enemy at his weak points.

During the War of Resistance Against Japan, on the basis of his comprehensive analysis of the enemy and ourselves, Comrade Mao Tse-tung laid down the following strategic principle for the Communist-led Eighth Route and New Fourth Armies: "Guerrilla warfare is basic, but lose no chance for mobile warfare under favorable conditions." He raised guerrilla warfare to the level of strategy, because, if they are to defeat a formidable enemy, revolutionary armed forces should not fight with a reckless disregard for the consequences when there is a great disparity between their own strength and the enemy's. If they do, they will suffer serious losses and bring heavy setbacks to the revolution. Guerrilla warfare is the only way to mobilize and apply the whole strength of the people against the enemy, the only way to expand our forces in the course of the war, deplete and weaken the enemy, gradually change the balance of forces between the enemy and ourselves, switch from guerrilla to mobile warfare, and finally defeat the enemy.

In the initial period of the Second Revolutionary Civil War, Comrade Mao Tse-tung enumerated the basic tactics of guerrilla warfare as follows: "The enemy advances, we retreat; the enemy camps, we harass; the enemy tires, we attack; the enemy retreats, we pursue." Guerrilla war tactics were further developed during the War of Resistance Against Japan. In the base areas behind the enemy lines, everybody joined in the fighting—the troops and the civilian population, men and women, old and young; every single village fought. Various ingenious methods of fighting were devised, including "sparrow warfare," land-mine warfare, tunnel warfare, sabotage warfare, and guerrilla warfare on lakes and rivers.

In the later period of the War of Resistance Against Japan and during the Third Revolutionary Civil War, we switched our strategy from that of guerrilla warfare as the primary form of fighting to that of mobile warfare in the light of the changes in the balance of forces between the enemy and ourselves. By the middle, and especially the later, period of the Third Revolutionary Civil War, our operations had developed into large-scale mobile warfare, including the storming of big cities. . . .

In order to annihilate the enemy, we must adopt the policy of luring him in deep and abandon some cities and districts of our own accord in a planned way, so as to let him in. It is only after letting the enemy in that the people can take part in the war in various ways and that the power of a people's war can be fully exerted. It is only after letting the enemy in that he can be compelled to divide up his forces, take on heavy burdens and commit mistakes. In other words, we must let the enemy become elated, stretch out all his ten fingers and become hopelessly bogged down. Thus, we can concentrate superior forces to destroy the enemy forces one by one, to eat them up mouthful by mouthful. Only by wiping out the enemy's effective strength can cities and localities be finally held or seized. We are firmly against dividing up our forces to defend all positions and putting up resistance at every place for fear that our territory might be lost and our pots and pans smashed, since this can neither wipe out the enemy forces nor hold cities or localities.

Comrade Mao Tse-tung has provided a masterly summary of the strategy and tactics of people's war: You fight in your way and we fight in ours; we fight when we can win and move away when we can't.

In other words, you rely on modern weapons and we rely on highly conscious revolutionary people; you give full play to your superiority and we give full play to ours; you have your way of fighting and we have ours. When you want to fight us, we don't let you and you can't even find us. But when we want to fight you, we make sure that you can't get away and we hit you squarely on the chin and wipe you out. When we are able to wipe you out, we do so with a vengeance; when we can't, we see to it that you don't wipe us out. It is opportunism if one won't fight when one can win. It is adventurism if one insists on fighting when one can't win. Fighting is the pivot of all our strategy and tactics. It is because of the necessity of fighting that we admit the necessity of moving away. The sole purpose of moving away is to fight and bring about the final and complete destruction of the enemy. This strategy and these tactics can be applied only when one relies on the broad masses of the people, and such application brings the superiority of people's war into full play. However superior he may be in technical equipment and whatever tricks he may resort to, the enemy will find himself in the passive position of having to receive blows, and the initiative will always be in our hands.

We grew from a small and weak to a large and strong force and finally defeated formidable enemies at home and abroad because we carried out the strategy and tactics of people's war. During the eight years of the War of Resistance Against Japan, the people's army led by the Chinese Communist Party fought more than 125,000 engagements with the enemy and put out of action more than 1.7 million Japanese and puppet troops. In the three years of the War of Liberation, we put eight million of the Kuomintang's reactionary troops out of action and won the great victory of the people's revolution. . . .

The Chinese people enjoyed the support of other peoples in winning both the War of Resistance Against Japan and the People's Liberation War, and yet victory was mainly the result of the Chinese people's own efforts. Certain people assert that China's victory in the War of Resistance was due entirely to foreign assistance. This absurd assertion is in tune with that of the Japanese militarists.

The liberation of the masses is accomplished by the masses themselves—this is a basic principle of Marxism-Leninism. Revolution or people's war in any country is the business of the masses in that country and should be carried out primarily by their own efforts; there is no other way.

During the War of Resistance Against Japan, our Party maintained that China should rely mainly on her own strength while at the same time trying to get as much foreign assistance as possible. We firmly opposed the Kuomintang ruling clique's policy of exclusive reliance on foreign aid. In the eyes of the Kuomintang and Chiang Kai-shek, China's industry and agriculture were no good, her weapons and equipment were no good, nothing in China was any good, so that if she wanted to defeat Japan, she had to depend on other countries, and particularly on the U.S.-British imperialists. This was completely slavish thinking. Our policy was diametrically opposed to that of the Kuomintang. Our Party held that it was possible to exploit the contradictions between U.S.-British imperialism and Japanese imperialism, but that no reliance could be placed on the former. In fact, the U.S.-British imperialists repeatedly plotted to bring about a "Far Eastern Munich" in order to arrive at a compromise with Japanese imperialism at China's expense, and for a considerable period of time they provided the Japanese aggressors with war matériel. In helping China during that period, the U.S. imperialists harbored the sinister design of turning China into a colony of their own.

Comrade Mao Tse-tung said: "China has to rely mainly on her own efforts in the War of Resistance." He added, "We hope for foreign aid but cannot be dependent on it; we depend on our own efforts, on the creative power of the whole army and the entire people."

Self-reliance was especially important for the people's armed forces and the Liberated Areas led by our Party. . . .

The problem of military equipment was solved mainly by relying on the capture of arms from the enemy, though we did turn out some weapons too. Chiang Kai-shek, the Japanese imperialists and the U.S. imperialists have all been our "chiefs of transportation corps." The arsenals of the imperialists always provide the oppressed peoples and nations with arms.

The people's armed forces led by our Party independently waged people's war on a large scale and won great victories without any material aid from outside, both during the more than eight years of the anti-Japanese war and during the more than three years of the People's War of Liberation.

Comrade Mao Tse-tung has said that our fundamental policy should rest on the foundation of our own strength. Only by relying on our own efforts can we in all circumstances remain invincible.

The peoples of the world invariably support each other in their struggles against imperialism and its lackeys. Those countries which have won victory are duty bound to support and aid the peoples who have not yet done so. Nevertheless, foreign aid can only play a supplementary role.

In order to make a revolution and to fight a people's war and be victorious, it is imperative to adhere to the policy of self-reliance, rely on the strength of the masses in one's own country and prepare to carry on the fight independently even when all material aid from outside is cut off. If one does not operate by one's own efforts, does not independently ponder and solve the problems of the revolution in one's own country and does not rely on the strength of the masses, but leans wholly on foreign aid—even though this be aid from socialist countries which persist in revolution—no victory can be won, or be consolidated even if it is won. . . .

In the world today, all the imperialists headed by the United States and their lackeys, without exception, are strengthening their state machinery, and especially their armed forces. U.S. imperialism, in particular, is carrying out armed aggression and suppression everywhere.

What should the oppressed nations and the oppressed people do in the face of wars of aggression and armed suppression by the imperialists and their lackeys? Should they submit and remain slaves in perpetuity? Or should they rise in resistance and fight for their liberation?

Comrade Mao Tse-tung answered this question in vivid terms. He said that after long investigation and study the Chinese people discovered that all the imperialists and their lackeys "have swords in their hands and are out to kill. The people have come to understand this and so act after the same fashion." This is called doing unto them what they do unto us.

In the last analysis, whether one dares to wage a tit-for-tat struggle against armed aggression and suppression by the imperialists and their lackeys, whether one dares to fight a people's war against them, is tantamount to whether one dares to embark on revolution. This is the most effective touchstone for distinguishing genuine from fake revolutionaries and Marxist-Leninists.

In view of the fact that some people were afflicted with the fear of the imperialists and reactionaries, Comrade Mao Tse-tung put forward his famous thesis that "the imperialists and all reactionaries are paper tigers." He said,

> *All reactionaries are paper tigers. In appearance, the reactionaries are terrifying, but in reality they are not so powerful. From a long-term point of view, it is not the reactionaries but the people who are really powerful.*

The history of people's war in China and other countries provides conclusive evidence that the growth of the people's revolutionary forces from weak and small beginnings into strong and large forces is a universal law of development of class struggle, a universal law of development of people's war. A people's war inevitably meets with many difficulties, with ups and downs and setbacks in the course of its development, but no force can alter its general trend towards inevitable triumph.

Comrade Mao Tse-tung points out that we must despise the enemy strategically and take full account of him tactically.

To despise the enemy strategically is an elementary requirement for a revolutionary. Without the courage to despise the enemy and without daring to win, it will be simply impossible to make revolution and wage a people's war, let alone to achieve victory.

It is also very important for revolutionaries to take full account of the enemy tactically. It is likewise impossible to win victory in a people's war without taking full account of the enemy tactically, and without examining the concrete conditions, without being prudent and giving great attention to the study of the art of struggle, and without adopting appropriate forms of struggle in the concrete practice of the revolution in each country and with regard to each concrete problem of struggle.

Dialectical and historical materialism teaches us that what is important primarily is not that which at the given moment seems to be durable and yet is already beginning to die away, but that which is arising and developing, even though at the given moment it may not appear to be durable, for only that which is arising and developing is invincible.

Why can the apparently weak new-born forces always triumph over the decadent forces which appear so powerful? The reason is that truth is on their side and that the masses are on their side, while the reactionary classes are always divorced from the masses and set themselves against the masses. . . .

It must be emphasized that Comrade Mao Tse-tung's theory of the establishment of rural revolutionary base areas and the encirclement of the cities from the countryside is of outstanding and universal practical importance for the present revolutionary struggles of all the oppressed nations and peoples, and particularly for the revolutionary struggles of the oppressed nations and peoples in Asia, Africa and Latin America against imperialism and its lackeys.

Many countries and peoples in Asia, Africa and Latin America are now being subjected to aggression and enslavement on a serious scale by the imperialists headed by the United States and their lackeys. The basic political and economic conditions in many of these countries have many similarities to those that prevailed in old China. As in China, the peasant question is extremely important in these regions. The peasants constitute the main force of the national-democratic revolution against the imperialists and their lackeys. In committing aggression against these countries, the imperialists usually begin by seizing the big cities and the main lines of communication, but they are unable to bring the vast countryside completely under their control. The countryside, and the countryside alone, can provide the broad areas in which the revolutionaries can maneuver freely. The countryside, and the countryside alone, can provide the revolutionary bases from which the revolutionaries can go forward to final victory. Precisely for this reason, Comrade Mao Tse-tung's theory of establishing revolutionary base areas in the rural districts and encircling the cities from the countryside is attracting more and more attention among the people in these regions.

Taking the entire globe, if North America and Western Europe can be called "the cities of the world," then Asia, Africa and Latin America constitute "the rural areas of the world." Since World War II, the proletarian revolutionary movement has for various reasons been temporarily held back in the North American and West European capitalist countries, while the people's revolutionary movement in Asia, Africa and Latin America has been growing vigorously. In a sense, the contemporary world revolution also presents a picture of the encirclement of cities by the rural areas. In the final analysis, the whole cause of world revolution hinges on the revolutionary struggles of the Asian, African and Latin American peoples who make up the overwhelming majority of the world's population. The socialist countries should regard it as their internationalist duty to support the people's revolutionary struggles in Asia, Africa and Latin America.

The October Revolution opened up a new era in the revolution of the oppressed nations. The victory of the October Revolution built a bridge between the socialist revolution of the proletariat of the West and the national-democratic revolution of the colonial and semi-colonial countries of the East. The Chinese revolution has successfully solved the problem of how to link up the national-democratic with the socialist revolution in the colonial and semi-colonial countries. . . .

Ours is the epoch in which world capitalism and imperialism are heading for their doom and socialism and communism are marching to victory. Comrade Mao Tse-tung's theory of people's war is not only a product of the Chinese revolution, but has also the characteristics of our epoch. The new experience gained in the people's revolutionary struggles in various countries since World War II has provided continuous evidence that Mao Tse-tung's thought is a common asset of the revolutionary people of the whole world. This is the great international significance of the thought of Mao Tse-tung. . . .

At present, the main battlefield of the fierce struggle between the people of the world on the one side and U.S. imperialism and its lackeys on the other is the vast area of Asia, Africa and Latin America. In the world as a whole, this is the area where the people suffer worst from imperialist oppression and where imperialist rule is most vulnerable. Since World War II, revolutionary storms have been rising in this area, and today they have become the most important force directly pounding U.S. imperialism. The contradiction between the revolutionary peoples of Asia, Africa and Latin America and the imperialists headed by the United States is the principal contradiction in the contemporary world. The development of this contradiction is promoting the struggle of the people of the whole world against U.S. imperialism and its lackeys.

Since World War II, people's war has increasingly demonstrated its power in Asia, Africa and Latin America. The peoples of China,

Korea, Vietnam, Laos, Cuba, Indonesia, Algeria and other countries have waged people's wars against the imperialists and their lackeys and won great victories. The classes leading these people's wars may vary, and so may the breadth and depth of mass mobilization and the extent of victory, but the victories in these people's wars have very much weakened and pinned down the forces of imperialism, upset the U.S. imperialist plan to launch a world war, and become mighty factors defending a world peace.

Today, the conditions are more favorable than ever before for the waging of people's wars by the revolutionary peoples of Asia, Africa and Latin America against U.S. imperialism and its lackeys.

Since World War II and the succeeding years of revolutionary upsurge, there has been a great rise in the level of political consciousness and the degree of organization of the people in all countries, and the resources available to them for mutual support and aid have greatly increased. The whole capitalist-imperialist system has become drastically weaker and is in the process of increasing convulsion and disintegration. After World War I, the imperialists lacked the power to destroy the new-born socialist Soviet state, but they were still able to suppress the people's revolutionary movements in some countries in the parts of the world under their own rule and so maintain a short period of comparative stability. Since World War II, however, not only have they been unable to stop a number of countries from taking the socialist road, but they are no longer capable of holding back the surging tide of the people's revolutionary movements in the areas under their own rule.

U.S. imperialism is stronger, but also more vulnerable, than any imperialism of the past. It sets itself against the people of the whole world, including the people of the United States. Its human, military, material and financial resources are far from sufficient for the realization of its ambition of dominating the whole world. U.S. imperialism has further weakened itself by occupying so many places in the world, overreaching itself, stretching its fingers out wide and dispersing its strength, with its rear so far away and its supply lines so long. As Comrade Mao Tse-tung has said, "Wherever it commits aggression, it puts a new noose around its neck. It is besieged ring upon ring by the people of the whole world."

When committing aggression in a foreign country, U.S. imperialism can only employ part of its forces, which are sent to fight an unjust war far from their native land and therefore have a low morale, and so U.S. imperialism is beset with great difficulties. The people subjected to its aggression are having a trial of strength with U.S. imperialism neither in Washington nor New York, neither in Honolulu nor Florida, but are fighting for independence and freedom on their own soil. Once they are mobilized on a broad scale, they will have inexhaustible strength. Thus superiority will belong not to the United States but to the people subjected to its aggression. The latter, though apparently weak and small are really more powerful than U.S. imperialism.

The struggles waged by the different peoples against U.S. imperialism reinforce each other and merge into a torrential worldwide tide of opposition to U.S. imperialism. The more successful the development of people's war in a given region, the larger the number of U.S. imperialist forces that can be pinned down and depleted there. When the U.S. aggressors are hard pressed in one place, they have no alternative but to loosen their grip on others. Therefore, the conditions become more favorable for the people elsewhere to wage struggles against U.S. imperialism and its lackeys.

Everything is divisible. And so is this colossus of U.S. imperialism. It can be split up and defeated. The peoples of Asia, Africa, Latin America and other regions can destroy it piece by piece, some striking at its head and others at its feet. That is why the greatest fear of U.S. imperialism is that people's wars will be launched in different parts of the world, and particularly in Asia, Africa and Latin America, and why it regards people's war as a mortal danger.

U.S. imperialism relies solely on its nuclear weapons to intimidate people. But these weapons cannot save U.S. imperialism from its doom. Nuclear weapons cannot be used lightly. U.S. imperialism has been condemned by the people of the whole world for its towering crime of dropping two atom bombs on Japan. If it uses nuclear weapons again, it will become isolated in the extreme. Moreover, the U.S. monopoly of nuclear weapons has long been broken; U.S. imperialism has these weapons, but others have them too. If it threatens other countries with nuclear weapons, U.S. imperialism will expose its own country to the same threat. For this reason, it will meet with strong opposition not only from the people elsewhere but also inevitably from the people in its own country. Even if U.S. imperialism brazenly uses nuclear weapons, it cannot conquer the people, who are indomitable.

However highly developed modern weapons and technical equipment may be and however complicated the methods of modern warfare, in the final analysis the outcome of a war will be decided by the sustained fighting of the ground forces, by the fighting at close quarters on battlefields, by the political consciousness of the men, by their courage and spirit of sacrifice. Here the weak points of U.S. imperialism will be completely laid bare, while the superiority of the revolutionary people will be brought into full play. The reactionary troops of U.S. imperialism cannot possibly be endowed with the courage and the spirit of sacrifice possessed by the revolutionary people. The spiritual atom bomb which the revolutionary people possess is a far more powerful and useful weapon than the physical atom bomb.

Vietnam is the most convincing current example of a victim of aggression defeating U.S. imperialism by a people's war. The United States has made South Vietnam a testing ground for the suppression of people's war. It has carried on this experiment for many years, and everybody can now see that the U.S. aggressors are unable to find a way of coping with people's war. On the other hand, the Vietnamese people have brought the power of people's war into full play in their struggle against the U.S. aggressors. The U.S. aggressors are in danger of being swamped in the people's war in Vietnam. They are deeply worried that their defeat in Vietnam will lead to a chain reaction. They are expanding the war in an attempt to save themselves from defeat. But the more they expand the war, the greater will be the chain reaction. The more they escalate the war, the heavier will be their fall and the more disastrous their defeat. The people in other parts of the world will see still more clearly that U.S. imperialism can be defeated, and that what the Vietnamese people can do, they can do too. . . .

The fundamental reason why the Khrushchev revisionists are opposed to people's war is that they have no faith in the masses and are afraid of U.S. imperialism, of war and of revolution. Like all other opportunists, they are blind to the power of the masses and do not believe that the revolutionary people are capable of defeating imperialism. They submit to the nuclear blackmail of the U.S. imperialists and are afraid that, if the oppressed peoples and nations rise up to fight people's wars or the people of socialist countries repulse U.S. imperialist aggression, U.S. imperialism will become incensed, they themselves will become involved and their fond dream of Soviet-U.S. cooperation to dominate the world will be spoiled. . . .

The Khrushchev revisionists assert that nuclear weapons and strategic rocket units are decisive while conventional forces are insignificant, and that a militia is just a heap of human flesh. For ridiculous reasons such as these, they oppose the mobilization of and reliance on the masses in the socialist countries to get prepared to use people's war against imperialist aggression. They have staked the whole future of their country on nuclear weapons and are engaged in a nuclear gamble with U.S. imperialism, with which they are trying to strike a political deal. Their theory of military strategy is the theory that nuclear weapons decide everything. Their line in army-building is the bourgeois line which ignores the human factor and sees only the material factor and which regards technique as everything and politics as nothing.

The Khrushchev revisionists maintain that a single spark in any part of the globe may touch off a world nuclear conflagration and bring destruction to mankind. If this were true, our planet would have been destroyed time and time again. There have been wars of national liberation throughout the twenty years since World War II. But has any single one of them developed into a world war? Isn't it true that the U.S. imperialists' plans for a world war have been upset precisely thanks to the wars of national liberation in Asia, Africa and Latin America? By contrast, those who have done their utmost to stamp out the "sparks" of people's war have in fact encouraged U.S. imperialism in its aggressions and wars.

The Khrushchev revisionists claim that if their general line of "peaceful coexistence, peaceful transition and peaceful competition" is followed, the oppressed will be liberated and "a world without weapons, without armed forces and without wars" will come into being. But the inexorable fact is that imperialism and reaction headed by the United States are zealously priming their war machine and are daily engaged in sanguinary suppression of the revolutionary peoples and in the threat and use of armed force against independent countries. The kind of rubbish peddled by the Khrushchev revisionists has already taken a great toll of lives in a number of countries. Are these painful lessons, paid for in blood, still insufficient? The essence of the general line of the Khrushchev revisionists is nothing other than the demand that all the oppressed peoples and nations and all the countries which have won independence should lay down their arms and place themselves at the mercy of the U.S. imperialists and their lackeys who are armed to the teeth. . . .

We know that war brings destruction, sacrifice and suffering on the people. But the destruction, sacrifice and suffering will be much greater if no resistance is offered to imperialist armed aggression and the people become willing slaves. The sacrifice of a small number of people in revolutionary wars is repaid by security for whole nations, whole countries and even the whole of mankind; temporary suffering is repaid by lasting or even perpetual peace and happiness. War can temper the people and push history forward. In this sense, war is a great school. . . .

In diametrical opposition to the Khrushchev revisionists, the Marxist-Leninists and revolutionary people never take a gloomy view of war. Our attitude towards imperialist wars of aggression has always been clear-cut. First, we are against them, and secondly, we are not afraid of them. We will destroy whoever attacks us. As for revolutionary wars waged by the oppressed nations and peoples, so far from opposing them, we invariably give them firm support and active aid. It has been so in the past, it remains so in the present and, when we grow in strength as time goes on, we will give them still more support and aid in the future. It is sheer day-dreaming for anyone to think that, since our revolution has been victorious, our national construction is forging ahead, our national wealth is increasing and our living conditions are improving, we too will lose our revolutionary fighting will, abandon the cause of world revolution and discard Marxism-Leninism and proletarian internationalism. Of course, every revolution in a country stems from the demands of its own people. Only when the people in a country are awakened, mobilized, organized and armed can they overthrow the reactionary rule of imperialism and its lackeys through struggle; their role cannot be replaced or taken over by any people from outside. In this sense, revolution cannot be imported. But this does not exclude mutual sympathy and support on the part of revolutionary peoples in their struggles against the imperialists and their lackeys. Our support and aid to other revolutionary peoples serves precisely to help their self-reliant struggle. . . .

When Japanese imperialism launched its war of aggression against China, the Chinese people had only a very small people's army and a very small revolutionary base area, and they were up against the biggest military despot of the East. Yet even then, Comrade Mao Tse-tung said that the Chinese people's war could be won and that Japanese imperialism could be defeated. Today, the revolutionary base areas of the peoples of the world have grown to unprecedented proportions, their revolutionary movement is surging as never before, imperialism is weaker than ever, and U.S. imperialism, the chieftain of world imperialism, is suffering one defeat after another. We can say with even greater confidence that the people's wars can be won and U.S. imperialism can be defeated in all countries.

The peoples of the world now have the lessons of the October Revolution, the Anti-Fascist War, the Chinese people's War of Resis-tance and War of Liberation, the Korean people's War of Resistance to U.S. Aggression, the Vietnamese people's War of Liberation and their War of Resistance to U.S. Aggression, and the people's revolutionary armed struggles in many other countries. Provided each people studies these lessons well and creatively integrates them with the concrete practice of revolution in their own country, there is no doubt that the revolutionary peoples of the world will stage still more powerful and splendid dramas in the theater of people's war in their countries and that they will wipe off the earth once and for all the common enemy of all the peoples, U.S. imperialism, and its lackeys. . . .

We are optimistic about the future of the world. We are confident that the people will bring to an end the epoch of wars in human history. Comrade Mao Tse-tung pointed out long ago that war, this monster, "will be finally eliminated by the progress of human society, and in the not too distant future too. But there is only one way to eliminate it and that is to oppose war with war, to oppose counter-revolutionary war with revolutionary war."

All peoples suffering from U.S. imperialist aggression, oppression and plunder, unite! Hold aloft the just banner of people's war and fight for the cause of world peace, national liberation, people's democracy and socialism! Victory will certainly go to the people of the world!

Long live the victory of people's war!

Franz Michael

CHINA'S DESIGN FOR AGGRESSION

Franz Michael, director of the Sino-Soviet Institute at George Washington University, Washington, D.C., represents those scholars who viewed China as a dangerously expansive state. To him China was not expansionist in any traditional sense, but, as Lin Piao insisted, as a revolutionary force. China, believed Michael, was the world's leading exponent of Lenin's strategy of promoting "national wars of liberation." The author argued that Chinese intentions, as embodied in official Chinese statements, were a proper cause for alarm. He asserted also that the absence of a Communist monolith did not necessarily reduce the Communist menace. But if the Sino-Soviet split made possible two tactical approaches, Michael doubted that the division served the Communist world. Instead, he assumed a close relationship between a Soviet-Chinese agreement on dogma and the state of relations between the two Communist giants. He believed that the relationship, so bitter in the 1960s and so disruptive of Communist unity, was moving into a period of greater cooperation. Thus for Michael communism, not nationalism, remained the perennial threat to the stability of Asia.

Commentators who talk about Communist Chinese "expansionism" tend to approach the subject in terms of the nineteenth- or early twentieth-century concept of the game of international power politics played among nation-states. "What will *China* do next?" is the issue often posed, as if in our time international relations could still be described in terms of the actions taken by individual states. Too little attention is paid to the fact that since the establishment of Communist power in the Soviet Union in 1917, a new dimension has been added to world politics—a unique Communist policy, known in doctrinal terminology as "socialist internationalism." After the Com-

Reprinted by permission from "A Design for Aggression," *Problems of Communism* 20 (January–April 1971): 62–68.

munist seizure of power in China in 1949, this new dimension, related as it is to the drive for a worldwide Communist revolution, became an integral factor in Chinese Communist foreign policy. In the writer's view, it promises to assume an even larger role in the aftermath of the GPCR—China's Great Proletarian Cultural Revolution of 1966–67.

This ideological dimension is of major importance in the foreign policy of all Communist countries. When the Union of Soviet Socialist Republics was first founded, Lenin and his colleagues envisioned the new polity as the nucleus of a world structure, to be joined by "soviets"—that is, victorious revolutionary governments—from all continents of the globe. The first military force in the U.S.S.R. was recruited not only among Russians but from German and Austrian prisoners of war and other nationalities; it was meant to be a truly international army, fighting for the goal of world revolution.

That phase ended within a year, when the Treaty of Brest-Litovsk forced the revolutionary movement to assume the functions of a state and introduced Leninist communism to the rules of international conduct which had evolved among nation-states over several centuries. When other Communist governments were formed after World War II, they too took their place in the traditional state system.

However, the principal aspect of communism—its identity as an international movement—was not abandoned. Rather, it formed the basis for a new type of international system in which all Communist parties participated then and still participate today. The initial institutional form of this Communist internationalism, Lenin's Comintern, was abandoned in 1943; its lesser successor, Stalin's Cominform of 1947, was dissolved in its turn in 1956. Since that time, the formal instrument for coordinating Communist strategy and formulating the international party line has been the occasional interparty conference, in which allegedly equal and independent Communist parties have participated. In the conflicts arising within the Communist movement, such conferences themselves have become a subject of argument.

Despite the several shifts in—and progressive weakening of—the institutional forms, the basic conceptual approach to international affairs has remained the same among all Communist parties. This approach distinguishes between traditional interstate relations and a modern form of international relations expressed in the broad interaction of Communist parties, revolutionary movements, classes, and social groups as interpreted by Communist doctrine. The doctrine thus serves as a framework in which all international development is to be understood and utilized. The clearest expression of this world view can be found in discussions of the two forms of international law—the "capitalist" and the Communist. In both Chinese and Soviet writings, the thesis has been advanced that a gradual transformation of traditional "capitalist" international law into new forms of Communist law is taking place. While "capitalist" law is still in use—and will be as long as the world order contains "capitalist" states—Communist international law is claimed to be in the ascendancy. The latter represents the rules of "socialist internationalism" and covers relations within the Communist movement as well as within the Communist commonwealth. It also applies to relationships between the Communists and disaffected groups in any society, supplying justification for the support of revolution in non-Communist countries and in particular for the support of "national liberation movements." Thus, in law as in fact, Communist foreign policies are conducted on two levels—traditional state-to-state relations, and direct contact with and backing of militant movements and social groups, revolutionary actions, and "national liberation wars." When we speak of Communist aggressiveness we must therefore think not only in terms of traditional state relations and traditional military attacks, but also—and primarily—in terms of Communist revolutionary strategy, backed by military power.

In terms of the traditional concepts of what constitutes aggressive international behavior, it can be argued that Communist China is *not* an expansionist power. In the writer's view, the Chinese Communist regime has demonstrated no territorial ambitions beyond its present borders—though within the latter it does, of course, lay claim to the lands of certain non-Chinese peoples who were part of the former Chinese empire. The maltreatment of minority groups within China proper, the swamping of the Turki tribes in Sinkiang by government-enforced migration of ethnic Chinese into that province, the genocide committed by the Communist Chinese in Tibet—all can be explained within the framework of a ruthless internal communization and Sinification policy which does not respect ethnic or cultural autonomy. But—with the exception, perhaps, of Chinese action in the Himalayas—this policy stops at the present border. The Chinese

Communists' military aid to North Korea in 1950 and more recent assistance to North Vietnam help to demonstrate the nature of Peking's objectives—which are confined to support of Communist policies or regimes and pursuit of certain limited frontier goals, stopping short of any attempt to conquer new colonies or to extend Chinese rule over new peoples.

Peking's disinterest in old-style empire-building has deflected Western attention from the far more important form of "expansionism" that it practices—the spread of Communist world revolution. Comprehension of this phenomenon is crucial since we live in a revolutionary epoch and since today, more than ever, Communist China plays a special part in Communist revolutionary strategy.

Briefly described, Chinese communism has been both the test case and the proclaimed model for the strategy of creating "national liberation movements" and promoting "national wars of liberation." This strategy was originally conceived and directed by Lenin and his Soviet successors. Following the initial heady months of the Bolsheviks' seizure of power in 1917, after the Communists lost hope that the wave of revolution would spill over into Central Europe, Lenin began to look eastward. The new strategy he developed called for the formation of national liberation movements based on an alliance, or "united front," of Communists and "bourgeois nationalists" in the colonial world of Asia, with the aim of promoting anti-imperialist revolution as part of the Communist world revolution. This second strategy was to tie in with strategy number one, the promotion of "proletarian revolution" in the industrial countries of the world. Whether strategy number two was to play a secondary, equal, or even a primary role in world Communist revolution remained a moot point. What differentiated the strategy of "national liberation movements" from the strategy of proletarian revolution was its military character. In place of urban uprisings, the general strike, and conspiratorial and open activities of Communist parties, the new Communist strategy assigned a special role to revolutionary armies. In fact, Mao's slogan that "power grows out of the barrel of a gun" specifically derived from a reference made by Stalin in 1925 to the Chinese "revolutionary army's" special role in contrast to civilian uprisings elsewhere. Prolonged warfare and a party-army structure distinguished this type of Communist strategy from that developed in the Soviet system.

In the institutional structure that emerged under Chinese communism, the relationship of party to army differed from that in the Soviet Union or in other Communist countries. The Soviet Red Army, which was Leon Trotsky's personal creation, was established *after* the Bolsheviks' seizure of power. It remained under the control of civilian party leaders, and its professional military generals, with one exception, never rose to the top level of political leadership. By contrast, the protracted civil war in China led to the virtual fusion of the Communist political and military leadership; the party was in effect imbedded in the army. Mao started his career as political commissar in the Chu-Mao forces in the Chingkang mountains and rose to a leading position in the party through military backing. Military commanders and commissars were all part of the party leadership and were vitally concerned with overall policy as well as with military matters.

The party-army structure prevailed through the early phase of civil war in the mid-1920s, the Kiangsi and Yenan periods, the war with Japan, the 1945–49 period, and the first years after the Communist victory in 1949. In all these stages of Chinese communism the military was the dominant factor; whatever party and administrative structure existed was attached to the military. The military, however, had its own political infrastructure; in stating that "the party controls the gun," Mao made it clear that the party element within the army had authority over the military command.

Although the fusion of party and army was designed for the conduct of the civil war, it continued to have an impact on the political structure after the Chinese Communists' conquest of power. When separate party and government structures were formed in 1953 in a trend towards civilian control, the Chinese military man remained much more influential in the party and government structure than was his counterpart in the Soviet Union. The trend was in any event reversed after 1959, when Mao, with the support of the newly appointed Minister of Defense, Lin Piao, began to use the People's Liberation Army (PLA) to buttress his power and propagate his cult.

During the Great Proletarian Cultural Revolution, the military provided the logistics for the Red Guard rallies in Peking, supported the Maoist "Left" in its drive against the party leadership in the provinces, and helped promote the so-called "seizure of power" by the Maoists. When the "revolutionary rebels" were in turn discarded, the military itself assumed ruling authority. As a result of the Cultural Revolution, the military has thus come to resume its civil war role and once more predominates in the reorganized government structure and in the new party apparatus.

Over the years the Chinese "model" for revolution has been widely heralded in Communist propaganda and its importance keenly debated in the West. Mao's writings on guerrilla warfare have been used as texts for this kind of strategy by many aspirants to revolutionary leadership from insurgents in a number of Asian and African countries to Che Guevara and other insurrectionists on the Latin American continent.

In the writer's view, however, the essence of Mao's revolutionary strategy has been misunderstood by its imitators and its adversaries alike, leading to classical failures like Che's fiasco in Bolivia. Where the strategy has had success, the explanation has lain not so much in the alleged utilization of popular issues or in the application of phased stages of warfare—which in fact proved counterproductive in the case of the 1968 Tet offensive in Vietnam (although highly successful as a propaganda issued in the United States)—but rather in its reliance on special institutionalized methods of attack and on the weapons of terror and intimidation. What has emerged is a new kind of organized warfare in which, conceptually and practically, a Communist infrastructure, combining military with political leadership and planning, plays a crucial part.

If the importance of this institutional factor has escaped the Guevaras, it is no wonder that the new warfare is also little understood in the West. Some of the debates in the United States about Vietnam and Cambodia have concentrated on the problem of the constitutionality of an undeclared war; yet to pose the issue in these terms is to apply to the present military action a conceptual approach that was designed for conventional wars between states. This tradition-bound thinking is simply inapplicable to the problem of aggression as it is waged by today's insurgent forces, backed up by the supportive efforts of the Communist epicenters.

As the major adaptor of the new revolutionary strategy, the Chinese Communist regime has assumed a special role in championing "wars of liberation." Even at the height of the Cultural Revolution, when the regime's attention was primarily focused inward, it did not abandon its support of insurrectionary activity abroad. And lately, it has become increasingly clear that Peking intends to adopt a more activist role in the international arena.

In recent moves initiated by the Communist leader Chou En-lai, China has clearly broken away from its relative isolation in the years of the Cultural Revolution. Under the new policy, the Communist leadership in Peking not only has renewed diplomatic relations with certain countries in the noncommitted world and in the West but—more significantly—has resumed an active part in promoting Communist advances in Asia.

This new militancy has been embodied in what the Chinese Communists call their Asian United Front. The major targets at present are South Korea and the countries of Indochina. During a visit to Pyongyang by Chou En-lai in early 1970, the unity of the Korean and Chinese Communist leaderships was proclaimed in statements resorting to the most bitter and strident language used in years to attack "American imperialism" as the main enemy, along with the United States' "lackeys" in Japan, South Korea, Taiwan, Indochina and Israel. Chou's visit was followed by an exchange of visits between Chinese Communist and North Korean chiefs of staff and top military leaders, resulting in prolonged discussions whose contents at this time can only be surmised. A similar indication of a more aggressive approach on China's southern flank was provided by Chou's participation in the Indochina Conference, held somewhere in South China in late April 1970, resulting in pledges of support for Sihanouk's attempt to reestablish his rule over Cambodia with the aid of Hanoi's troops.

The militancy recently displayed by Peking is obviously related to Peking's acquisition of a nuclear deterrent. Its new position as a nuclear power—albeit a lesser power—has clearly played a part in Peking's decision to engage in more vigorous sponsorship and support of "wars of liberation" in Asia. The statements and agreements between Peking and her North Korean and Indochinese allies underscore this point in advertising China's position as a "reliable rear area" for such wars. Backing up their words, the Chinese Communists have made disproportionately heavy investments in the field of nuclear weapons and missiles as compared to other economic and military expenditures.

This enunciation of a policy of aggression makes it necessary to take new stock of Chinese aims, techniques and tactics, and to find ways to counter them. The clear intent of current Chinese policy is to promote, foster and support Communist revolutions. In this respect there is no reason why we should not accept the words and actions of the Chinese Communist leaders at face value—yet it has been fashionable for some time to refuse to do just that. A good deal has been written in the pages of this journal and elsewhere about the myth, now almost universally repudiated, that communism in the Stalin era represented a monolithic system. As much has been written about the more recent, reverse tendency to assume that since communism is *not* monolithic but in fact defines and embraces various conflicting trends, it does not constitute either a real movement or a real menace to the non-Communist world. This, too, is a myth—but all too often the fact is not recognized. Indeed, multi-centered communism can be perceived as a vastly more effective entity than a monolithic system, insofar as it existed, ever was.

Quarrels within the Communist movement can, of course, hamper the effectiveness of the overall strategy to enhance Communist power. Obviously the most important issue in this regard has been the Sino-Soviet conflict. For several years this conflict has been a crucially divisive factor in the Communist world with respect to a whole range of issues involving strategy, ideology and leadership.

Just how seriously the Sino-Soviet conflict has handicapped the promotion of broad Communist aims could, however, be made a matter of argument. A strategy directed from two centers, each of which must concentrate part of its propaganda and its military force against the other, obviously weakens efforts toward the common goal of spreading communism. The Sino-Soviet conflict has thus reduced the pressure which both contenders might apply to the outside world. On the other hand, it has also made possible the simultaneous pursuit of the overall goal by two different tactical approaches, permitting the use of soporific propaganda under the strategy of peaceful coexistence, and the use of force and terror under the strategy of revolutionary warfare. In light of Peking's militant pronouncements supporting "national liberation movements" and revolutionary violence, Moscow has appeared peaceful indeed, while to young radicals the Maoist image has become a revolutionary idol far more attractive than Moscow's "revisionist" policy, believed to be outdated and futile. The practical effect of promoting Communist policy with two differing accents, respectively articulated by Moscow and Peking, has been well defined by a Chinese military leader, the former chief-of-staff Lo Jui-ch'ing, in comments on what he called the "debate" between Moscow and Peking. In Lo's words:

> One aspect of the historic significance of the debate of the last few years between the two lines in the international Communist movement is that it has enabled Marxism-Leninism to spread on an unprecedented scale and has promoted the integration of the universal truth of Marxism-Leninism with the concrete practice of the people's revolution in every country.

There has been no clearer statement describing the advantage to communism of applying simultaneously two differing strategies from two world centers.

While quite a case could be made in support of this point of view, it is the writer's judgment that on balance the Sino-Soviet conflict has been detrimental to the Communist cause. Thus it seems clear that the effectiveness of Peking's, as well as Moscow's, policies for advancing the Communist cause may well depend on the future course of Sino-Soviet relations.

During 1969 the Sino-Soviet conflict reached its maximum danger point. The buildup of massive Soviet forces of well over 30 divisions along the border of Manchuria, in Outer Mongolia, and along the Sinkiang border indicated the serious possibility of Soviet military action against the maverick Chinese Communists. The example of the Soviet occupation of Czechoslovakia and the ominous implications of the "Brezhnev Doctrine" similarly shook the Chinese leadership, which had felt previously that it could safely insult the Soviet leaders and with impunity conduct frontier probes in a war of nerves and propaganda. The great shift launched under Chou En-lai's direction, initiating a new phase of Chinese foreign policy, was obviously related to this Soviet threat. In brief, it combined a defusing of the Sino-Soviet conflict with a new aggressiveness towards the West. This policy constituted *"eine Flucht nach vorne"*—a flight forward, to use a German idiom, rushing away from the Sino-Soviet conflict into a new course of militancy against the United States and its allies.

A number of factors can be cited as indications that the issues and manifestations of the Sino-Soviet conflict have lost a good deal of their acerbity. Since April 1970 no frontier clashes have occurred, a navigation agreement has been reached, a new Soviet ambassador has arrived in Peking, a new Chinese ambassador has been sent to Moscow, and Sino-Soviet negotiations continue in Peking.

The recent trend toward closer Chinese cooperation with North Korea and North Vietnam could be interpreted as a policy designed to break out of Soviet containment; but since neither Pyongyang nor Hanoi has permitted a decline in its relations with Moscow as a result of negotiations with Peking, another interpretation of the new Chinese moves suggests itself: once, in the earlier stages of their conflict, Moscow and Peking attacked one another by proxy, through Yugoslavia and Albania. Now, one could contemplate a Sino-Soviet rapprochement by proxy. At the very least, the sharp lines of controversy have been blurred.

More important still, the cult of Mao has clearly declined; and so has the challenge to the Soviet Union formerly implied in the claim of Mao's personal leadership of the world revolution. For instance, in recent statements containing an exchange of felicitations between North Korea and Peking, Mao, as leader of the Chinese people and Chairman of the Chinese Communist Party, shared equal status with Kim Il-song, as leader of the North Korean people and Chairman of the Korean Workers' Party. Such hints of new "ideological modesty," as it were, on the part of Peking are of greater import than might be apparent to a reader uninitiated in the sign language of the Communists.

At the same time, there has been an obvious decline of Sino-Soviet name-calling since April of last year. It may well be that Peking now speaks with more than one voice. The crucial point here, however, is that reciprocal accusations have been reduced to a level that both sides appear able to tolerate. If the newly emerging political-military structure in China is acceptable within a Communist order directed, though not dominated, by Moscow, the possibility of a withering away of the conflict—through the adoption of parallel policies or even genuine rapprochement—must certainly be taken into consideration. Such a shift in intra-Communist relations would vitally affect the potential threat and aggressiveness of either Communist center vis-à-vis the non-Communist world. Even without full reconciliation, a lessening of the conflict would strengthen the effectiveness of Chinese pressure in Asia.

Those in the United States who belittle the danger of Communist victories in the small countries of Southeast Asia and who favor a U.S. retreat from Asia often argue that the U.S. mainland is itself safe from attack. Such views are based on the concept of a half-world centered around Europe and America and isolated from outside pressure; they ignore the effect that a shrinking of the area occupied by free nation-states outside the Communist orbit would have not only on power relations in Asia but on the security of the whole pluralist world system, including the United States—in short, they disregard the global scope of the strategic problems posed by communism. To deny the importance of the Indochinese peninsula—which, as has already been pointed out, is one of the two main targets of Peking's current policy to promote political-military warfare—is to forget some lessons of the past. In World War II, when the Japanese penetrated Indochina, the defense of that area became a crucial issue in the final confrontation between Japan and the United States. A frequent topic of discussion at that time linked the Nazi movement against the Suez Canal and the Japanese strike against India as two arms of a global threat. Today, Moscow's attempts to gain the use of the Suez Canal as a channel for the Soviet fleet (which is already in the Indian Ocean), the respective tactics of Communist China and the U.S.S.R. to secure footholds on the African Coast, on the Arab peninsula, in Ceylon, and in Singapore, and finally the support given by both Communist powers to guerrilla wars in Southeast Asia, combine to represent a global potential reminiscent of the past. The wars in Indochina are a part of this global strategy.

The methods used to support these wars of subversion are multi-faceted. On Peking's part, in addition to the protection provided by the Chinese nuclear deterrent (supplemented, of course, by the Soviet deterrent), direct aid is offered in the form of equipment, manpower, and technical know-how. Peking also helps to train cadres in the skills of guerrilla warfare. A division of labor between China and North Vietnam appears to have assigned the training of cadres for South Vietnam, Laos and Cambodia to Hanoi, while Peking conducts insurgency schools for revolutionaries from Malaysia, Burma and Thailand. In the area of manpower, the Chinese have contributed large numbers of soldiers and laborers to perform production and defense tasks in North Vietnam; while at present it seems unlikely, the possibility cannot be precluded that under certain conditions Peking might some day send "volunteers" to engage in direct fighting in Indochina, as it did in North Korea.

Perhaps the most crucial supportive service provided by Peking lies in the area of psychological warfare. The success of insurrections carried out by revolutionary infrastructures depends not only on the weakening of the target country by tactics of terror and intimidation but also on the waging of psychological warfare to create an impact on the rest of the world. Thus the strategy of "national wars of liberation" relies heavily on an intensive propaganda effort to characterize the goals, motivations and techniques of the revolutionary as highly moral, not only in terms of Communist values but also in terms of Western ethics and ideals of social justice. At the same time, a constant attempt is made to discredit the side of the defenders. The making and breaking of images is one of the most vital functions involved in the conduct of "wars of national liberation." The defamation of antirevolutionary regimes, the exploitation of their structural weaknesses, and the sowing of suspicion between them and their allies constitute very effective means of undermining resistance. Such propaganda operations are not restricted to the issues involved in the "liberation" struggle but rather attempt to undercut general morale in any way possible.

In the conduct of psychological warfare, the Chinese Communists issue an incessant barrage of political propaganda which is the more dangerous in that it often sounds crude and obvious to non-Communist ears, obscuring the fact that it is highly effective in advancing Peking's objectives. Depending on the audience, China's propagandists are quite able to pursue a militant line supporting revolutionary activity in neighboring countries while simultaneously endorsing the principles of peaceful coexistence and noninterference in other nations' affairs.

In short, Peking's is an elastic stance that pushes as far as opportunity permits. It is in this sense unremittingly "expansionist"—and any real or imagined weakness on the side of the free world tempts the Communists to respond with pressure. In the mix of military and political tactics that make up this strategy of expansionism, military activity could become the more dominant feature should the Communists' chances of effective aggression seem to increase. The credibility of the United States' commitments in Asia thus becomes a major factor in the current phase of psychological warfare, and U.S. efforts aimed at building up the strength of its allies to defend themselves must be meticulously defined in terms that will avoid the impression that Washington is veering toward isolationism. It is one thing to talk with Peking; it would be another to assist Peking in its political warfare by propounding policies which could be exploited in hostile propaganda as a sign of weakness.

In the writer's view, it is vital that more be done to define and publicize the nature of the psychological warfare being waged not only by Communist China but also by the U.S.S.R. In particular, representatives of the communications media should be alert to expose the goals and methods of hostile propaganda and to transmit to their audiences a clearer understanding of the Communists' psychological offensive. Most important, the United States and its allies must develop more effective psychological operations of their own. The world is moving into a phase in which the term "cold war" may well yield to the term "psywar," and non-Communist societies have yet to shape the tools they need to give force to their beliefs in an age of revolution.

Oliver M. Lee

THE MYTH OF CHINESE AGGRESSION

Unlike Franz Michael, Oliver M. Lee judged Chinese foreign policy by traditional standards and found it moderate and scarcely expansionist. He rejected the official view of China as a "deepening shadow across Asia." The Lyndon Johnson administration, he charged, found Lin Piao's article useful because it served to rationalize established American attitudes toward China as well as the United States involvement in Vietnam. Thereafter Lee sought to demonstrate that not one episode in China's alleged record of aggression could be termed aggression under international law. For 250 years no government had recognized Tibet as an independent nation. In Korea, wrote Lee, the Chinese attempted to defend a buffer region from elimination by the world's most powerful nation. The author doubted that mainland ambitions

Reprinted by permission of the publisher from *The Nation*, November 6, 1967, pp. 459–463.

toward Taiwan defied any principle or law. Again he argued that Chinese "aggression" along the disputed Indian border in 1962 was hardly an assault on all Asia, as some Americans insisted. Lee could find no evidence that the Chinese notion of inevitable war had any effect on Chinese policy. The image of an aggressive China, Lee concluded, merely sustained American military commitments in Asia. China, for Lee, was a nation among nations, behaving according to historic rules.

Unable to defeat the incredibly tenacious guerrillas in South Vietnam, the Johnson Administration in February, 1965, carried the war to North Vietnam through systematic air attacks, on the pretext that the Vietcong were controlled by Hanoi, which therefore was more truly the enemy to be subjugated. But even this enemy's "aggression" was viewed as only the surface manifestation of a much more powerful menace. Specifically, President Johnson in his 1965 Johns Hopkins speech claimed to perceive, hovering over the Vietnamese War and all of Asia, "another reality: the deepening shadow of Communist China." More recently, of course, Secretary of State Dean Rusk has taken the same line.

The image of a ruthless, irrational and aggressive Chinese Communist regime had been peddled in the United States from the beginning, mostly by private and Congressional sources rather than by the Administration. But by 1965, the Administration itself deemed it necessary to fan the flames of anti-Chinese Communist hysteria. The identification of China as the main enemy now serves the same function in the Vietnamese War as our allegations of North Vietnamese aggression had done earlier. In each case the alleged existence of a newer, larger, more real enemy provides an excuse for our inability to crush the initial, smaller enemy. In each case, furthermore, the increasing villainy of the "real" enemy provides a justification for turning our wrath and firepower upon him. In the case of North Vietnam, this has already been done; in the case of China, only time will tell whether the United States will choose that terrifying option.

The specter of the yellow peril, in Red garb, being deemed useful by the Johnson Administration, the publication in September, 1965, of an article by China's Defense Minister Lin Piao titled "Long Live the Victory of the People's War!" was most opportune. Although most of his points had been made by Peking often before, this was the first major foreign policy statement by Lin Piao in his six years as

Defense Minister. The article was vitriolic in its condemnation of U.S. imperialism. It repeated some of Mao Tse-tung's vivid phrases, such as "political power grows out of the barrel of a gun" and "all reactionaries are paper tigers," and vigorously encouraged resort to revolutionary violence, people's war, and even world revolution.

It so happens that all of Lin Piao's references to justifiable violence dealt with autonomous and self-reliant revolutionary movements within nations, particularly in Asia, Africa and Latin America. Not a single sentence by Lin Piao can be construed as threatening Chinese military action aimed at the "liberation" of the people of another country. But the American Government was not to be denied its opportunity to hang a picture of an expansionist China on the slender pegs of militant Chinese words twisted and taken out of context. Thus McNamara smeared Lin Piao's article by crisply declaring: "It is a program of aggression. It is a speech that ranks with Hitler's *Mein Kampf*." Dean Rusk chimed in by allowing that Lin's article "is as candid as Hitler's *Mein Kampf*." Not content with linking China with the horrors of Nazi aggression in Europe, McNamara went so far as to warn the European members of NATO that "they should plan now to meet a Chinese Communist threat to their own security within five years."

True, some U.S. officials will concede that China's militancy is in support of indigenous revolutions in the underdeveloped world rather than a threat of military invasion. Assistant Secretary of State William Bundy, contradicting his superior, said that "to describe these objectives as deeply expansionist is by no means to paint the picture of another Hitler." Rather, he held, Peking aims at "the instigation and support of movements that can be represented as local movements, designed to subvert and overthrow existing governments." Yet Bundy could not resist prognosticating that China would use conventional military forces in its expansionist efforts "if it were required," and he reminded his audience of China's "threat" against India. He thereby conveyed the idea that old-fashioned military aggression, though not the preferred method, is nonetheless one of the instruments of Chinese foreign policy.

"Aggressive statements" by the Peking leaders, then, are one of Washington's main justifications for expressing concern about the possibility of future Chinese aggression, and for maintaining a policy of containment. "We should take the Chinese Communists at their word," admonishes McNamara. A Defense Department pamphlet for "information and education" puts it in zoological terms: "We would not ignore the buzz of a rattlesnake! . . . We must not ignore the roar of the dragon!" I shall take up in a moment the content of Peking's militant propaganda.

Another major reason for American fear of the yellow hordes is an alleged record of actual Chinese Communist aggression over the past eighteen years. Specific cases usually cited are those involving military action against Tibet, Korea and the Sino-Indian border, and threatened action against Taiwan. Such extrapolation from a series of past aggressions is sound in principle, but it becomes worthless if the premise of past aggressions is false, which is demonstrably the case.

The truth is that if aggression be defined as the initiation of military attack by one sovereign state against the territorial integrity of another sovereign state, Communist China did not commit aggression or plan aggression in any of the cases just mentioned. I make this assertion on the basis of evidence available but little known in the United States, and by the application of fundamental principles of international law. Following is a brief analysis of each actual or potential crisis.

Tibet. This vast plateau came under Chinese suzerainty in 1720, and in terms of international law has been part of China from that time to the present. This is true despite the fact that between 1911 and 1950 successive Chinese central governments were too weak actually to control Tibet; during those years, it should be recalled, many other regions of China were ruled by warlords who were also independent of the central government. For 250 years, no government in the world has recognized Tibet as an independent nation. As for the United States, in 1943 the State Department succinctly reminded the British that "The Government of the United States has borne in mind the fact that the Chinese government has long claimed suzerainty over Tibet and that the Chinese constitution lists Tibet among the areas constituting the territory of the Republic of China. This Government has at no time raised a question regarding either of these claims." Even India, the one nation which, besides China, has the greatest reason to be interested in the legal status of Tibet, in 1954 concluded a treaty with Peking on "Trade and Intercourse Between Tibet Region of China and India." It might be added that our Nationalist allies on Taiwan are every bit as adamant as the Communists about China's title to Tibet.

The People's Liberation Army did enter Tibet in 1950 and did use force to put down sporadic rebellion there. There is no doubt that the Peking government has drastically uprooted the feudalistic social and economic structure of Tibet, replacing it with the Socialist system that prevails in the rest of China. Social revolution of such intensity inevitably brings about much dislocation and suffering, and one's judgment of whether such revolution represents progress or whether the progress is worth the price depends on one's value system. But a negative judgment of the revolution does not entitle one to label as military aggression the advent of the Chinese Revolution in a region that has long been internationally recognized as an integral part of China. Federal troops enforcing the Constitution in Mississippi must similarly be absolved from any charge of aggression.

Korea. Five months after the outbreak of the Korean War in 1950, as the United Nations forces under General MacArthur's command were approaching the Chinese border at the Yalu River, 300,000 Chinese troops astounded the world by entering the war. They smashed through the center of MacArthur's line, and in a matter of weeks pushed the U.N. forces out of North Korea and south of the 38th Parallel. Thereupon the General Assembly, by overwhelming majority vote, declared Communist China an aggressor.

From the legal standpoint, this charge of Chinese aggression would be well founded if—but only if—it could be established that North Korea, the recipient of Chinese assistance, had committed aggression in the first place. This cannot be done. The proposition that North Korea initiated the military action resulting in the Korean War has been widely accepted in the non-Communist world on the assumption that an impartial United Nations commission happened to be on the scene and witnessed the outbreak of the war. In reality, the U.N. field observers had traveled along the 38th Parallel from June 9 to June 24, returning to the capital one day before the alleged North Korean aggression, which they therefore did not witness. The initial cable from the commission, reporting an attack by North Korean forces, was based purely on allegations by the South Korean government.

In view of South Korean President Syngman Rhee's frequent threats to unify Korea by war, and MacArthur's promise to him in 1949 to "defend South Korea as I would defend the shores of my own native land," the alternative hypothesis of a South Korean military attack with the aim of provoking a strong counterattack is plausible. And what are we to think of John Gunther's report that at MacArthur's headquarters the first words on the war, uttered by an "important" official, had been: "A big story has just broken. The South Koreans have attacked North Korea!"?

Another problem lies in the fact that North and South Korea were legally one nation rather than two, and that therefore any military action between them, initiated by whomever, constituted civil war, to which the concept of international aggression is not applicable. Korea is one nation not only in historic, cultural and ethnic terms but in 1950 was viewed as one nation even by the two Korean regimes and the two postwar military occupation powers (the United States and Russia), and by the U.N. General Assembly. Each Korean government has claimed to be the government of all Korea, the Southern claim being reflected in the fact that in the May, 1950, legislative election in South Korea, one-third of the seats were kept vacant, to be filled by future delegates from the North.

If North Korea cannot be shown to have committed aggression, it follows that China was not an accomplice thereto. But even assuming, for the sake of discussion, that Peking did commit aggression in this case, I submit that the circumstances were such that China was acting to avert a serious threat to its national security, and that such action proves absolutely nothing about the existence of territorial ambitions or other expansionist aims.

No government worthy of the name would, under similar circumstances, have failed to come to the rescue of a friendly buffer region that was in the process of being eliminated by the most powerful nation on earth—a nation which also contained influential factions extremely hostile toward the government in question. The depth of such hostility in the United States was revealed when Secretary of the Navy Francis Matthews, on August 25, 1950, advocated "instituting a war to compel cooperation for peace. . . . We would become the first aggressors for peace." *The New York Times'* military analyst reported that Matthews' speech was a "trial balloon" backed by Secretary of Defense Louis Johnson, "who has been selling the same doctrine of preventive war in private conversations around Washington.''

It is true that Johnson resigned soon after this report, and that Truman exerted strong influence, both before and after China's crossing of the Yalu, against expanding the war into China. But Peking had no guarantee that in the power struggle in Washington the "hawks" like MacArthur, Dulles and Louis Johnson would not gain control. A Korea unified through American military power, with the supine acquiescence of China, would have constituted a powerful link in the chain of encirclement the United States was engaged in forging against China.

Taiwan. Here the problem is not the waging of actual warfare but Communist China's implied assertion that it has the right to use force to gain control of Taiwan. ''By all suitable means at a suitable time'' is Peking's way of putting it.

Taiwan had been part of China from 1683 to 1895, when it was ceded to Japan by the defeated and tottering Manchu dynasty. Decades later, at the Cairo Conference of 1943, Roosevelt, Churchill and Chiang Kai-shek agreed that ''all the territories Japan has stolen from the Chinese, such as Manchuria, Formosa and the Pescadores, shall be restored to the Republic of China.''

In practice, the island was returned to the Middle Kingdom when Chinese Nationalist troops accepted the surrender of the Japanese garrison, so that in 1950 Secretary of State Dean Acheson was able to report: ''The Chinese have administered Formosa for four years. Neither the United States nor any other ally ever questioned that authority and that occupation.'' The U.S. officially continues to regard Taiwan as part of China, as does the Chiang Kai-shek government in its vain attempt to play the role of the government of China and the protector of its territorial integrity.

If Taiwan is acknowledged to be part of China, it follows that the government of China, on the basis of the principles of national sovereignty and territorial integrity, has the legal right to use force to reunify Taiwan with the mainland; whether Peking will actually do so remains an open question. As for those, like the United States Government, who refuse to accept the legitimacy of the Peking government, the only alternative to such acceptance is to regard the Chinese Communists as a rebellious faction trying to replace the legitimate ''national'' government located on Taiwan. And even such an interpretation cannot be used to bolster a charge of aggression, as there is nothing in international law which prohibits rebellion or revolution forceful or otherwise.

The Sino-Indian Border. Twenty thousand Chinese troops in October, 1962, poured southward through the Himalayan Mountain passes, and within thirty days penetrated 85 miles behind Indian front-line positions. *The Washington Post*, in an editorial titled "World War III?," ventured that "perhaps no aggression since World War II holds so large a threat to the peace, safety, independence and security of other lands." *The New York Times* feared that the Chinese action "could engulf India and menace all Asia and the world."

Before the ink was dry on that editorial, Peking announced a unilateral cease-fire and promised to pull its troops back to their original positions north of the Himalayan crest. *The New York Times* found this "startling and puzzling in the extreme," as well it might, having twenty-four hours earlier reminded its readers that India was once conquered by Mogul emperors descended from Genghis Khan and Tamerlane, and asserted that "any Communist rule would be far more brutal than theirs."

Did the Chinese military action, temporary though it was, constitute a "brutal invasion," as Nehru cried? A "naked and large-scale aggression," as Defense Minister Krishna Menon asserted? To answer these questions requires some background in the diplomatic history of the border dispute.

The respective claims to the border areas between China and India are of mixed validity. On the basis of old maps, old treaties, administrative history and other technical aspects, the disputed areas do not clearly belong to either India or China; but China's claims are at least as good as those of India. To cite just one type of evidence favoring the Middle Kingdom: all official British maps of British India, prior to 1914, show the presently disputed Himalayan region to be within China. Britain in 1914 unilaterally claimed that region, but not until 1937 did it have the audacity to change its maps accordingly.

Peking's basic position has been that no valid treaties exist for defining the boundaries between the two countries, and that therefore a treaty should be negotiated. U.S. Secretary of State Christian Herter in 1959 tended to support the Chinese in this by saying: "The border, as you know, has been for many years pretty ill defined." India's attitude, in contrast, was that it knew exactly where the boundaries were, that no negotiations were necessary, and that Chinese troops were sitting on part of Indian soil and should remove themselves.

Since the Chinese considered that same area to be theirs, they saw no need to leave, unless as a result of a negotiated border treaty. India thereupon embarked on a prolonged military campaign, in which it boasted to having "reclaimed" 2,500 square miles from the Chinese north of the Karakoram Range. The Indian troops accomplished this by means of marching up to the Chinese frontier posts and occupying them after Mao Tse-tung's troops, in every single case, pulled back without a fight.

It is these facts which led Congressman Sikes of Florida to ask General Maxwell Taylor, then chairman of the Joint Chiefs of Staff, in a Congressional hearing in February, 1963: "Let me talk about the Red China and the Indian operation. Did the Indians actually start this military operation?" To which Taylor replied: "They were edging forward in the disputed area; yes, sir." At this point the testimony was censored out of the public transcript.

The "edging forward" by Indian troops occurred not only in the western corner of India's frontier with China but also in the eastern corner where the New Delhi government asserted the validity of the McMahon Line. Peking, while denying its validity, was willing to respect that line provisionally, pending a negotiated settlement. But Indian troops, in places, penetrated even to the north of *that*, on the ground that "blind adherence" to the McMahon Line was not as proper as seeking out a border conforming to the "principles" that Sir Arthur Henry McMahon had had in mind when drawing the line in 1914. These two types of penetration, backed up by Nehru's order of October 12 to push the Chinese out of all "Indian territory," constituted the provocations against which China retaliated.

Such, then, has been Communist China's behavior in terms of major military action carried out or contemplated. Its behavior in the propaganda realm, which is also used in an effort to prove Chinese Communist expansion, has likewise been grossly distorted in the non-Communist world, and even in the Soviet orbit.

To revert to Lin Piao's 1965 article, for example, while it is true that he urged the violent overthrow, through "people's war," of exploitative systems in Asia, Africa and Latin America, he did not threaten to use Chinese troops to this end. On the contrary he has a section, titled "Adhere to the Policy of Self-Reliance," in which he points out: "The liberation of the masses is accomplished by the masses themselves—this is a basic principle of Marxism-Leninism. Revolution or people's war in any country is the business of the masses in that country and should be carried out primarily by their own efforts; there is no other way." Interestingly enough, McNamara, in his 1966 testimony before the Senate Armed Services Committee, inserted three pages of excerpts from Lin Piao's article, but omitted any reference to this self-restricting aspect of Peking's foreign policy.

It is often asserted in the West that the Chinese Communists regard world war to be inevitable. From this it is inferred that Peking is dangerous because it thereby acquires an incentive to choose the right circumstances to set off a world conflagration. The truth is that Peking agrees with Moscow that "the Communists must work untiringly among the masses to prevent underestimation of the possibility of averting a world war." Do the Chinese Communists desire world war, as it is often asserted? Peking says, "No Marxist-Leninist has ever held or ever will hold that revolution must be made through world war."

But, it may be asked, is it not a fact that the Chinese Communists have said in so many words that "wars are inevitable"? So they have, but not world war. What about lesser wars between nations? Peking again agrees with Moscow that "it is possible to combat effectively the local wars started by the imperialists and to stamp out successfully the hotbeds of such wars." But what they do regard as inevitable are revolutionary and counterrevolutionary wars, anti-colonial wars and "imperialist wars of suppression against colonies and semi-colonies," as long as capitalism exists. Among these types of wars, Mao and his colleagues of course favor revolutionary and anti-colonial wars, but this in no way represents an announced Chinese policy to expand, to invade, to conquer, to rule or to dominate, either before or after a successful revolutionary or anti-colonial war. What they have announced, instead, with regard to about forty non-Communist nations, is that "it is absolutely impermissible and impossible for countries practicing peaceful coexistence to touch even a hair of each other's social system." With many of these, particularly with the neutralist nations, closest to China, and therefore the most easily "dominated," such as Afghanistan, Pakistan, Nepal, Burma and Cambodia, Peking has in fact signed treaties incorporating the "five principles of peaceful coexistence," thereby committing itself not to interfere with the territorial integrity and sovereignty of the smaller nation. Treaty commitments do not necessarily reflect actual behavior, and Prince Sihanouk's recent charge of "extraordinary interference" by Communist China in Cambodia's affairs bears watching in this regard. But we are dealing here with the allegations that Peking, in a manner as frank as that of Hitler, has announced a program of aggression, domination, etc. Demonstrably it has not.

One final canard is the charge that rulers of China regard nuclear war as inevitable and indeed desirable, and that they are ignorant of the destructive power of nuclear weapons. What Peking actually says is that "the complete banning and destruction of nuclear weapons is an important task in the struggle to defend world peace." They acknowledge that "nuclear weapons are unprecedentedly destructive." And we have it on the authority of Morton H. Halperin, a foremost American expert on Chinese nuclear strategy, writing in *China and the Bomb*, that "the Chinese have never claimed that nuclear war is inevitable."

Though regarding such a war as avoidable and as highly destructive, have not the Maoists nevertheless boasted of a readiness to start a nuclear war on the ground that, on balance, capitalism would be damaged more than communism? The answer is, again, No. On the occasion of China's first nuclear explosion, in October, 1964, Peking sent a letter to all governments in the world, stating: "The Chinese Government solemnly declares that at no time and in no circumstances will China be the first to use nuclear weapons." Washington, in contrast, has persistently refused to make a similar pledge, and has rejected Peking's call for prohibition of nuclear weapons as a "smoke screen."

In the absence of Chinese Communist threats to use either conventional or nuclear power to impose its domination on any other country, it is nonsense for the Defense Department to invoke the image of "the buzz of a rattlesnake." With the Chinese leaning backward to make legal and political commitments, on a reciprocal basis, to respect the sovereignty and territorial integrity of other nations, conjuring up the image of a roaring dragon is simply another Establishment attempt to brainwash George Romney along with the rest of the American people.

James C. Thomson, Jr.

CHINA'S NEW DIPLOMACY

James C. Thomson, Jr., a member of the East Asian Research Center at Harvard and the National Security Council staff under Presidents Kennedy and Johnson, attempts, in the following essay, to explain China's new outlook which encouraged that nation to seek and accept better relations with the United States. The editors of Problems of Communism *had posed the question: What domestic and foreign factors prompted the Chinese leadership to initiate their 1971 foreign policy overtures to the United States? Thomson, as his essay begins, discovered the pressures for change in China's external world. The dangers of Russia and Japan, added to the American withdrawal from the Far East, suggested the need for a better Sino-American relationship. Thomson acknowledged the existence of China's revolutionary visions, but doubted that they would have much influence on China's foreign policies. Thomson, like Lee, viewed China in traditional terms as a large, but generally weak country, too often the victim of more powerful neighbors.*

Peering at China through a glass darkly, I would give heaviest weight to foreign factors in producing Peking's new diplomatic excursions. Domestic factors—e.g., the restoration of relative order after the Cultural Revolution—have mainly provided the milieu in which cartographic imperatives can begin to shape foreign policy. By cartographic imperatives I mean the world map as viewed from Peking. Its two central features, as China moves into the 1970s, are the very long frontier shared with a hostile Soviet superpower and the awesome unleashed energy of the Japanese archipelago. Moscow combines ideological heresy (or, at the least, schism) with territorial imperialism, nuclear power, and the Czech example of the Brezhnev Doctrine in action. Tokyo combines dazzling economic power with an as yet unfocused nationalism, a recent imperialist past, and a potential nuclear future.

Counterposed against these not imaginary threats is the fact, as Peking seems to see it, of American withdrawal from Pacific overextension—a withdrawal dictated both by non-success in Indochina and by disarray back home. Once the Laos "incursion" collapsed and Nixon did not respond by going nuclear, the

Reprinted by permission from *Problems of Communism* 21 (January–February 1972): 48–51.

Chinese—or so recent visitors have told us—decided that events as well as intentions would force some real substance into the so-called Nixon Doctrine. America, if still an enemy, was a receding threat. But not so the two other threats.

The principle of using barbarians to control other barbarians is hardly new to Chinese geopolitics. So it seems reasonable for Peking to begin to patch things up with Washington as a balance against both Moscow and Tokyo. All that was needed was evidence that Washington meant business about winding down the war and that Washington was serious about a Sino-American thaw—indeed, that President Nixon, for multifarious reasons, needed such a thaw. Laos provided such evidence; and so has the administration's behavior on both the Kissinger and United Nations tracks (actually two eventually competing tracks)—a successful experiment in the diplomacy of multiplicity.

These developments, now capped by Peking's entry into the United Nations, foretell a not-so-new Chinese return to international involvement as a great-but-not-superpower spokesman for (a) Chinese national interests, and (b) "Third World" interests. Sometimes the two will clash, as in East Pakistan; and one can probably assume that—at least close to home—Chinese national interests, as judged from Peking, will prevail.

To put the matter simply, China has returned to the diplomacy of Bundung and Geneva. But the world, of course, has changed; and in the changed context China emerges as a permanently accepted, adult power, thanks to new recognitions by other governments and the U.N. vote. From here on, club membership can work two ways: it can bring some altered ground rules to the club itself, forced by the new member in league with others; but it can also affect the new member's world view, inducing adjustment and compromise lest he find himself standing entirely alone looking foolish and impotent.

It is no new thing for Peking to have to let state-to-state relations co-exist with revolutionary aspirations. But it is a new thing to have to do so on such a grand and complex scale. China's revolutionary aims and visions will not soon change—indeed, they will be regularly reemphasized in Chinese rhetoric; but China's actual behavior, long constrained by do-it-yourself caveats about the export of revolution (as well as by military realism), will be further constrained by the processes of international bureaucratic engagement. Add to such constraints traditional Chinese adroitness at accommodation where vital national interests are not involved, and the Chinese may soon be behaving, if not sounding, like a senior club member rather than a new boy.

It is a truism that China's paramount external interest is the security of China's frontiers—and, by extension, the maintenance of nonhostile neighbors on those frontiers. China's borders have seemed threatened in recent years by both the United States and the Soviet Union. But the U.S. presence in Asia is receding, and soon Japan may feel some itch to fill the vacuum through its economic involvement in South Korea, Taiwan, and Southeast Asia.

China's primary territorial aspiration is the recovery of Taiwan. Yet such is Peking's confidence about the ultimate outcome that it may well be willing to bypass the Taiwan issue in its relations with some states. This is clearly one meaning of the Chinese leader's readiness to receive the President in spite of Washington's dual-representation effort at the U.N. and the U.S. defense treaty with the Chinese Nationalists. Peking seems to be choosing, with good reason, to put its faith in time and mortality · Hong Kong, that foreign enclave on Chinese soil, is a mutually profitable anomaly that will probably rejoin the mainland at the end of the century when the relevant British lease expires. Chinese ingenuity and patience on both sides of the Taiwan Straits could make of Formosa—once Chiang Kai-shek and Mao depart the scene—another Hong Kong, temporarily independent for years to come, sustained by ambiguity and by mutual economic advantage, but perhaps eventually becoming part of China on terms acceptable to both sides. In the meantime, all that Peking may actually require, for face-saving purposes, is the withdrawal of U.S. military forces from Taiwan but not abrogation of the defense treaty—a withdrawal that will still leave the island entirely capable of its own defense.

Beyond its frontiers and Taiwan, Peking's central long-term concern in Asia is, as indicated earlier, the evolving role of Japan. Here the Peking-Washington relationship can be used by the Chinese to press Prime Minister Sato—or, more likely, his successor—into more rapid accommodation with China. Peking's leverage in Japanese politics has increased as a result, *inter alia*, of the rather harsh diplomacy that Washington has employed vis-à-vis Tokyo. This volatile trilateral relationship is, however, one that Peking must play upon with care. Complete alienation between Tokyo and its American nuclear protector could produce a free-floating, insecure, nationalist Japan that might move once again into the path of military adventurism.

Those unresolved conflicts in Asia, namely Korea and Indochina, will continue to rank high in terms of Chinese rhetoric. But the status quo in Korea seems unchangeable and relatively unthreatening, hence tolerable to Peking for the foreseeable future. And Peking may well calculate that the Indochina conflict, posing no further threat to China, will probably be resolved in favor of local Communist forces (or at the least "neutralists") in the next several years.

In general, it can be assumed that Peking will continue to cheer on Asian revolutionary movements where they stand a good chance of success, but to subordinate such cheering to correct state-to-state relations in the majority of cases.

A central spur to both American and Chinese initiatives that led to the thaw of 1971 has been each nation's relationship with the U.S.S.R. For two decades now Sino-American hostility has been a great boon to Moscow; Russian leaders could act as they chose toward each party without having to calculate the consequences on the third side of the triangle. That luxury has now been terminated—with consequences far less disturbing to the Soviet-American relationship than Washington's Soviet experts had predicted through much of the 1960s.

Chinese and American initiatives have certainly made the Russians uncomfortable. But the longer-term consequence should be precisely what Washington and Peking had in mind: the addition of new constraints to Soviet foreign policy. Such constraints may well push Moscow toward greater accommodation with Peking as well as with Peking's rivals (Japan, the U.S., perhaps even Taiwan). The outcome, however, will not be warm rapprochement between Moscow and Peking. There is too much at issue—in both the ideological and state realms—to permit such a result in the new quadrilateral world of East Asia.

Peking seeks, first and foremost, a relationship of equality with the U.S. and other Western nations. Relations in the past have been strikingly unequal. Under the doctrine of containment and isolation, American military forces spread out to fill the Asian power vacuum left by Japan's World War II defeat. Regardless of the validity of

Washington's various rationales, such moves looked to Peking like a
clear and present threat: a quest for American hegemony by force of
arms.

America's Indochina intervention seemed to Peking the last great
effort to achieve such hegemony. But now that an incumbent President can call that intervention a "mistake" and can seek to
withdraw—however slowly and however destructively in terms of the
war's elevation from ground to air—Peking is fairly sure that the old
inequality is being corrected. In the fluid new circumstances of the
early 1970s, a reemerging China can begin to discuss with a receding
America some alternative structure—some new ground rules—for
peace in Asia. It is important to the Chinese to enter such discussions before the new Japan moves in, with or without American
encouragement, to fill the gap.

In this context, Peking stands a fairly good chance of moving
gradually toward satisfactory one-to-one relationships with the U.S.
and other Western powers. The primary content of such relationships
will be verbal: i.e., discussions at all levels, long and difficult negotiations groping toward mutually acceptable formulas of disengage-
ment, and perhaps, in time, even formal treaties of nonaggression.
But at the same time, such primary content will probably be gradually
expanded to include scientific and cultural exchanges and also trade.
In the area of trade, Sino-American relations are likely to proceed
especially slowly as a result of the Taiwan obstacle, China's dedication to economic "self-reliance," and the fact that much that America
might offer in goods can be obtained more cheaply elsewhere.

Suggestions for Additional Reading

United States-Asian relations since World War II have created a unique intellectual challenge. All literary efforts at analysis have sought necessarily to establish not only the relative strength of nationalism and communism in Asia but the nature of Asian communism as well. At no time during the three decades of the Cold War have writers agreed on the significance of communism as a revolutionary force to either the Asians themselves or the nations of the Western World. Some scholars have insisted that communism was no more than a radicalized nationalism, gaining its support from the twin drives of nationalism and reform. But another impressive group of scholars has argued—and continues to argue—that communism in Asia remains an international force which places Asian Communists under the direction of an international conspiracy. Fortunately the writings on Asian nationalism and communism fall into a series of clearly defined schools of thought, all of which existed as early as mid-century.

Nationalism has created no major problem in perception, for its intellectual and emotional foundations have been demonstrated throughout the present century. Vera Micheles Dean, in her book *The Nature of the Non-Western World* (New York, 1957), discusses with remarkable lucidity the strength and purposes of Asian nationalism as it developed through the present century. Jan Romein, in *The Asian Century: A History of Modern Nationalism in Asia* (London, 1962), adds detail but little more. For a thoughtful analysis of nationalism as a nondemocratic force in Asia, see M. N. Roy, "Democracy and Nationalism in Asia," *Pacific Affairs* 25 (June 1952): 140–146. A more general discussion can be found in C. J. Chancellor, "Nationalism in Asia: The Eleventh Conference of the Institute of Pacific Relations," *International Affairs* 27 (April 1951): 184–191. Two more specific studies are Karan Singh, *Prophet of Indian Nationalism: A Study of the Political Thought of Sri Aurobindo Gosh, 1893–1910* (London, 1963), and Steven Runciman, *The White Rajahs: A History of Sarawak from 1841 to 1946* (Cambridge, Eng., 1960).

Communism in Asia raises questions regarding both its appeal and its relationship to external forces. Jean Lacouture's *Ho Chi Minh: A Political Biography* (New York, 1968) views Ho as primarily an

Indochinese nationalist. On the nature of communism in other Asian countries, see Arnold Brackman, *Indonesian Communism: A History* (New York, 1963); Harry Benda and Ruth McVey, *The Communist Uprisings of 1926-1927 in Indonesia: Key Documents* (Ithaca, N.Y., 1960); Gene Hanrahan, *The Communist Struggle in Malaya* (New York, 1954); M. R. Masani, *The Communist Party of India: A Short History* (New York, 1954); Institute of Pacific Relations, *Indian Communist Party Documents, 1930–1956* (New York, 1957); and David Druhe, *Soviet Russia and Indian Communism* (New York, 1959). Druhe sees in Asian communism the effort of the Soviet Union to gain some form of external control over Asian countries.

Chinese communism has a sizable literature of its own. For a Soviet viewpoint, see David Dallin, *Soviet Russia and the Far East* (New Haven, 1948). See also Robert C. North, *Moscow and the Chinese Communists* (Stanford, Calif., 1953), and Henry Wei, *China and Soviet Russia* (Princeton, N.J., 1956). A more general account is O. Edmund Clubb, *Twentieth-Century China* (New York, 1964). On the rise of Mao Tse-tung to power in China, see Benjamin Schwartz, *Chinese Communism and the Rise of Mao* (Cambridge, Mass., 1951); Han Suyin, *The Morning Deluge: Mao Tse-tung and the Chinese Revolution, 1893–1954* (Boston, 1973); the more critical Edward E. Rice, *Mao's Way* (Berkeley, Calif., 1973); and Stuart R. Schram, "What Makes Mao a Maoist," *The New York Times Magazine,* March 8, 1970, pp. 36–37, 58–82. On the role of the peasantry in China's revolution, see Chalmers A. Johnson, *Peasant Nationalism and Communist Power: The Emergence of Revolutionary China, 1937–1945* (Stanford, Calif., 1962); David Mitrany, *Marx Against the Peasant: A Study in Social Dogmatism* (Chapel Hill, N.C., 1951); and Chao Chao-Kuo, *One Month in Yenan* (Chungking, 1944). Two studies devoted specifically to Chinese communism are Conrad Brandt, Benjamin Schwartz, and John K. Fairbank, *A Documentary History of Chinese Communism* (Cambridge, Mass., 1952), and Allan B. Cole, *Forty Years of Chinese Communism* (Washington, D.C., 1962). The latter volume is a publication of the Service Center for Teachers. General studies of the Chinese Revolution are C. P. Fitzgerald, *Revolution in China* (New York, 1962), and Harold R. Isaacs, *The Tragedy of the Chinese Revolution* (rev. ed., Stanford, Calif., 1951).

For the impact of the Japanese occupation on Asian nationalism, see Willard Elsbree, *Japan's Role in Southeast Asian Nationalist*

Movements, 1940–1945 (Cambridge, Mass., 1953); M. A. Aziz, *Japan's Colonialism and Indonesia* (The Hague, 1955); H. J. van Mook, *The Stakes of Democracy in Southeast Asia* (New York, 1950); and an excellent article by James A. Michener, "Blunt Truths About Asia," *Life*, June 4, 1951, pp. 96–121.

Voluminous writings deal with the status and purpose of Asian nationalism in the postwar world. Quite typical of the early observations are Rupert Emerson, "An Analysis of Nationalism in Southeast Asia," *The Far Eastern Quarterly* 5 (February 1946): 208–215; Robert Payne, "The Challenge of Asia," *Pacific Affairs* 21 (March 1948): 51–58; W. Macmahon Ball, "East Asia and the West," *Behind the Headlines* 10 (January 1951): 1–7; Edgar Ansel Mowrer, "What Asia Wants," *Harper's* 203 (October 1951): 67–72; Guy Wint, "The Aftermath of Imperialism," *Pacific Affairs* 22 (March 1949): 63–70; and Owen Lattimore, *The Situation in Asia* (Boston, 1949). Later studies which continue the same themes are William R. Braisted, "Nationalism in East Asia," *The Journal of Modern History* 26 (December 1954): 356–363; Rupert Emerson, *From Empire to Nation* (Cambridge, Mass., 1960); Steward C. Easton, *The Twilight of European Colonialism: A Political Analysis* (New York, 1960); and Victor Purcell, *The Revolution in Southeast Asia* (London, 1962).

On the nationalist movement in Indonesia, see Justus M. van der Kroef, "The Indonesian Revolution in Retrospect," *World Politics* 3 (April 1951): 369–398; George M. Kahin, *Nationalism and Revolution in Indonesia* (Ithaca, N.Y., 1952); also Kahin, "Indonesian Politics and Nationalism," in William L. Holland, ed., *Asian Nationalism and the West* (New York, 1953). On nationalism in Malaya, see T. H. Silcock, *Towards a Malayan Nation* (Singapore, 1961). Two volumes on nationalism in Japan are Delmer Brown, *Nationalism in Japan* (Berkeley, Calif., 1955), and Ivan Morris, *Nationalism and the Right Wing in Japan: A Study of Post-War Trends* (London, 1960). Richard Butwell analyzes a leading Burmese nationalist in *U Nu of Burma* (Stanford, Calif., 1963).

More specifically on the role of communism in the postwar revolutionary movements are such volumes as Sir Francis Low, *Struggle for Asia* (London, 1955); W. Macmahon Ball, *Nationalism and Communism in East Asia* (New York, 1952); Richard Adloff and Virginia Thompson, *The Left Wing in Southeast Asia* (New York, 1950); M. N. Roy, "The Communist Problem in East Asia: An Asian

View," and W. Macmahon Ball, "The Communist Problem in East Asia: A Western View," *Pacific Affairs* 24 (September 1951): 227–256; and J. H. Brimmell, *Communism in South East Asia: A Political Analysis* (London, 1959). See also Morris Watnick, "The Appeal of Communism to the Underdeveloped Peoples," in Bert F. Hoselitz, ed., *The Progress of Underdeveloped Areas* (Chicago, 1952); W. Gordon Graham, "Communism and South Asia," *Pacific Spectator* 5 (Spring 1951): 215–231; Roy C. Macridis, "Stalinism and the Pattern of Colonial Revolt," *The Western Political Quarterly* 7 (March 1954): 23–35; Bernard H. M. Vlekke, "Communism and Nationalism in Southeast Asia," *International Affairs* 25 (April 1949): 149–156; and Karl A. Wittfogel, "Russia and Asia: Problems of Contemporary Area Studies and International Relations," *World Politics* 2 (January 1950): 445–462.

On Communism in Indochina are Lacouture's *Ho Chi Minh: A Political Biography* (New York, 1968); John T. McAlister, Jr., and Paul Mus, *The Vietnamese and Their Revolution* (New York, 1971); and Harrison E. Salisbury, "Image and Reality in Indochina," *Foreign Affairs* 49 (April 1971): 381–394. These writings see Ho as a nationalist who found his strength largely in the Indochinese villages. Viewing the Communists of Indochina and elsewhere in Southeast Asia as the obedient servants of Moscow and Peking is Frank Trager, ed., *Marxism in Southeast Asia: A Study of Four Countries* (Stanford, Calif., 1960). Joseph M. Siracusa reveals how that notion crept into official American thought in "The United States, Viet Nam, and the Cold War: A Reappraisal," *Journal of Southeast Asian Studies* 5 (March 1974): 82–101.

Representative of writings which comprised the great China debate of 1949 and 1950 are such contributions as John K. Fairbank, "Competition, Not Containment," *Foreign Policy Reports,* (March 15, 1949); C. M. Chang, "Communism and Nationalism in China," *Foreign Affairs* 28 (July 1950): 548–564; Derk Bodde, *Peking Diary: A Year of Revolution* (New York, 1950), which covers portions of the years 1948 and 1949; John F. Melby's similar diary, *The Mandate of Heaven: Record of the Civil War in China, 1945–1949* (Toronto, 1969); Tang Tsou, *America's Failure in China, 1941–1950* (Chicago, 1963); and W. W. Rostow et al., *The Prospects for Communist China* (New York, 1954).

After mid-century the lines in Indochina were sharply drawn, with the literary debate turning on the presumed relationship of Ho Chi Minh to international communism. J. R. Clémentin took up that issue in "The Nationalist Dilemma in Vietnam," *Pacific Affairs* 23 (September 1950): 294–310. Jacques Soustelle's theme is suggested by the title of "Indo-China and Korea: One Front," *Foreign Affairs* 29 (October 1950): 56–66. Seymour Topping sees danger in "Indo-China on the Razor's Edge," ibid. 29 (April 1951): 468–474. A military view of the struggle for Indochina, with political overtones, is Edward L. Katzenbach, Jr., "Indo-China: A Military-Political Appreciation," *World Politics* 4 (January 1952): 186–218. On the Vietcong as a political-military force is George A. Carver, Jr., "The Faceless Viet Cong," *Foreign Affairs* 44 (April 1966): 347–372. Amry Vandenbosch and Richard A. Butwell deal with such issues in *Southeast Asia Among the World Powers* (Lexington, Ky., 1957). Three articles which take a more critical view of the trend toward American involvement in Southeast Asia are John F. Cady, "Challenge of Southeast Asia," *Far Eastern Survey,* February 8, 1950, pp. 21–27; Harold R. Isaacs, "The Prospect in Asia," *The Nation,* December 16, 1950, pp. 552–556; and Lawrence S. Finkelstein, "United States at an Impasse in Southeast Asia," *Far Eastern Survey,* September 27, 1950, pp. 165–172.

Throughout the early and mid-fifties *The New York Times Magazine* published a large number of articles which emphasized the force of nationalism in Asia and warned against the widespread tendency to attribute change to communism. Examples of such articles are Carlos P. Romulo, "The Crucial Battle for Asia," *The New York Times Magazine,* September 11, 1949; Robert Trumbull, "Spokesman of a Troubled Continent (Nehru)," ibid., October 9, 1949; Raymond B. Fosdick, "Asia's Challenge to Us—Ideas, Not Guns," ibid., February 12, 1950; Gerard Swope, "Clues to an Understanding of the Far East," ibid., October 1, 1950; Lionel Fielden, "The Mind That Still Eludes Our Grasp," ibid., November 19, 1950; Harold Callender, "Where We Are Losing the War of Ideas," ibid., December 3, 1950; Barbara Ward, "Recipe for Victory in the Far East," ibid., March 25, 1951; Robert Trumbull, "Nehru's Dilemma—West or East?" ibid., June 10, 1951; Trumbull, "Nehru Answers Some Basic Questions," ibid., November 11, 1951; Peggy Durdin, "On Trial—The White Man in Asia," ibid., June 5, 1955; Barbara Ward, "The Challenge We

Neglect in Asia," ibid., February 13, 1955; and A. M. Rosenthal, "India: A Case History in the 'Cold War,' " ibid., February 5, 1956. Studies which analyze post-Stalinist (1953) policies in Asia are three articles by Alvin Z. Rubinstein, "Soviet Policy in South and Southeast Asia," *Current History* 36 (January 1959): 24–30, "Soviet Policy in South Asia," ibid. 32 (February 1957): 97–104, and "The U.S.S.R., Southeast Asia, and Point Four," ibid. 28 (February 1955): 103–108; Charles Wolf, Jr., "Soviet Economic Aid in Southeast Asia: Threat or Windfall?" *World Politics* 10 (October 1957): 91–101; Harold H. Fisher, "The New Soviet Challenge in Asia," *Pacific Spectator* 10 (Autumn 1956): 317–332; Robert Loring Allen, *Middle Eastern Economic Relations with the Soviet Union, Eastern Europe, and Mainland China* (Charlottesville, Va., 1958); Philip Mosley, "Soviet Policy in the Developing Countries," *Foreign Affairs* 43 (October 1964): 87–98; Guy J. Pauker, "The Soviet Challenge in Indonesia," ibid. 40 (July 1962): 612–626; Henry G. Aubrey, "Sino-Soviet Aid to South and Southeast Asia," *World Politics* 12 (October 1959): 62–70; A. Nove, "The Soviet Model and Under-developed Countries," *International Affairs* 37 (January 1961): 29–38; Ivar Spector, "Soviet Policy in Asia: A Reappraisal," *Current History* 43 (November 1962): 257–262; Elliot R. Goodman, *The Soviet Design for a World State* (New York, 1960); Chiang Kai-shek, *Soviet Russia in China* (New York, 1957); Kurt London, ed., *New Nations in a Divided World* (New York, 1963); Thomas Balogh, "The Challenge of Totalitarian Planning in Asia," *International Affairs* 31 (July 1955): 300–310; Lucian W. Pye, "Communist Strategies and Asian Societies," *World Politics* 11 (October 1958): 118–127; and Donald S. Zagoria, "Communism in Asia," *Commentary* 39 (February 1965): 53–58. For a Russian viewpoint see N. S. Khrushchev, *The National Liberation Movement* (Moscow, 1963).

The impact of post-Stalinist policy on the Moscow-Peking alliance is analyzed in two articles by Franz Borkenau, "The Peking-Moscow Axis and the Western Alliance: How Really Hopeful for Us Are Their Disagreements?" *Commmentary* 18 (December 1954): 513–521, and "World Communism Shifts Its Line: Making Room for Mao and Tito," ibid. 21 (January 1956): 7–16. An important study of Sino-Soviet relations by four authorities is Howard L. Boorman, ed., *Moscow-Peking Axis: Strengths and Strains* (New York, 1957). Other variations on this theme are Edward Crankshaw, "China and Russia," *Atlantic Monthly* (June 1956), pp. 27–31; David J. Dallin, "The Future of the

Sino-Soviet Alliance," *Orbis* 1 (Fall 1957): 315–325; G. F. Hudson, "Mao and Moscow," *Foreign Affairs* 36 (October 1957): 78–90; Hudson, "Moscow and Peiping: Seeds of Conflict?" *Problems of Communism* 5 (November-December 1956): 17–23; Bernard Morris, "Soviet Policy Toward National Communism: The Limits of Diversity," *The American Political Science Review* 53 (March 1959): 128–137; Henry L. Roberts, "The Crisis in the Soviet Empire," *Foreign Affairs* 35 (January 1957): 191–200; and Charles B. McLane, "The Moscow-Peking Alliance: The First Decade," *Current History* 37 (December 1959): 326–332. The most detailed, yet moderate, assessment of the Sino-Soviet conflict is Donald S. Zagoria, *The Sino-Soviet Conflict, 1956–1961* (Princeton, N.J., 1962). A good brief account is William E. Griffith, *World Communism Divided,* Headline Series No. 166, Foreign Policy Association (New York, 1964).

As the postwar world began to stabilize in the 1950s the nations of Asia revealed a more determined independence from Western and Cold-War pressures. The first major assertion of neutralism in regard to the Soviet-Western conflict was the Afro-Asian Bandung Conference of 1955. Three volumes which deal with that conference are George M. Kahin, *The Asian-African Conference, Bandung, 1955* (Ithaca, N.Y., 1956); Carlos P. Romulo, *The Meaning of Bandung* (Chapel Hill, N.C., 1956); and Richard Wright, *The Color Curtain: A Report on the Bandung Conference* (Cleveland, 1956). Other volumes that focus on nationalism and neutralism are Claude A. Buss, *The Arc of Crisis: Nationalism and Neutralism in Asia Today* (New York, 1961); Peter Lyon, *Neutralism* (Leicester, 1963); Habib Bourguiba, "Nationalism: Antidote to Communism," *Foreign Affairs* 35 (July 1957): 646–654; Lucian W. Pye, "Eastern Nationalism and Western Policy," *World Politics* 6 (January 1954): 248–265; Werner Levi, "Asian Nationalism Reconsidered," *Eastern World* 17 (October 1963): 7–10; Guy J. Pauker, "Southeast Asia as a Problem Area in the Next Decade," *World Politics* 11 (April 1959): 325–345; Michael Brecher, *The New States of Asia* (London, 1963); Saul Rose, ed., *Politics in Southern Asia* (London, 1963); Russell A. Fifield, *The Diplomacy of South-East Asia, 1945–1958* (New York, 1958); and Saul Rose, "Asian Nationalism—The Second Phase," *International Affairs* 43 (1967): 282–292. For Rose the purpose of the first phase was independence; the second phase, nation-building—far more complex and divisive.

On the development of United States policy toward Southeast

Asia, see Lord Birdwood, "The Defence of South-East Asia," *International Affairs* (January 1955): 17–25; Max F. Millikan and Donald C. M. Blackmer, *The Emerging Nations: Their Growth and U.S. Policy* (Boston, 1961); Russell A. Fifield, *Southeast Asia in U.S. Policy* (New York, 1963). Three books on United States assistance to Southeast Asia are John D. Montgomery, *The Politics of Foreign Aid: American Experience in South-East Asia* (New York, 1962); Amos Jordan, *Foreign Aid and the Defense of South-East Asia* (New York, 1962); and Charles Wolf, Jr., *Foreign Aid: Theory and Practice in Southeast Asia* (Princeton, N.J., 1960).

Volumes which illuminate the role of nationalism and communism in wartime Indochina, as well as the American response, include Joseph Buttinger, *The Smaller Dragon: A Political History of Vietnam* (New York, 1958); Donald Lancaster, *The Emancipation of French Indochina* (New York, 1961); Bernard Fall, *Street Without Joy: Indochina at War* (Harrisburg, Pa., 1961) and *The Two Vietnams: A Political and Military Analysis* (New York, 1963); Robert Scigliano, *South Vietnam: Nation Under Stress* (Boston, 1961); and Denis Warner, *The Last Confucian* (New York, 1963). The last Confucian was Ngo Dinh Diem who died in 1963. Other highly useful volumes are Robert Shaplen, *The Lost Revolution: The Story of Twenty Years of Neglected Opportunities in Vietnam and of America's Failure to Foster Democracy There* (New York, 1965); General Vo Nguyen Giap, *People's War, People's Army* (New York, 1962)—a North Vietnamese view; William Pfaff, "Vietnam: The Roots of Chaos," *The Commonweal,* November 6, 1964, pp. 183–190; Edward G. Lansdale, "Viet Nam: Do We Understand Revolution?" *Foreign Affairs* 43 (October 1964): 75–86; and Dennis J. Duncanson, *Government and Revolution in Vietnam* (New York, 1968). Duncanson, a British official in Saigon from 1961–1965, views the revolution as a conspiracy, internationally based, that had no interest in the welfare of the Vietnamese people.

China, a large, complex, and ideological country, has posed a major challenge to understanding. That becomes obvious from any examination of the literature on Chinese external policy. Some writings which take a fearful view of China are Michael Lindsay, *China and the Cold War* (Melbourne, 1955); Lindsay, "China, Communism, and the United States," *World Politics* 12 (October 1959): 146–154; Victor Purcell, *The Chinese in Southeast Asia* (London, 1951); Amry Vandenbosch, "Chinese Threat in Southeast Asia," *Current History*

39 (December 1959): 333–338; Frank N. Trager, "Communist China: The New Imperialism," *Current History* 41 (September 1961): 136–140; Lucian W. Pye, *Some Observations on the Political Behavior of Overseas Chinese* (Cambridge, Mass., 1954); N. A. Simoniya, *Overseas Chinese in Southeast Asia: A Russian Study* (Ithaca, N.Y., 1961)—a Russian view; Peter Tang, *Communist China Today* (Washington, D.C., 1961); R. G. Boyd, *Communist China's Foreign Policy* (New York, 1962); Alice Langley Hsieh, *Communist China's Strategy in the Nuclear Age* (Englewood Cliffs, N.J., 1962); Richard L. Walker, *The China Danger* (Chicago, 1966); and Peter Van Ness, *Revolution and China's Foreign Policy: Peking's Support for Wars of National Liberation* (Berkeley, 1970).

Writings which take a generally moderate view of Chinese foreign policy include Richard Harris, "China and the World," *International Affairs* 35 (April 1959): 161–169; Charles B. McLane, "China's Role in the Communist Bloc," *Current History* 43 (September 1962): 129–135, 180; Bernard B. Fall, "Red China's Aims in South Asia," ibid.: 136–141, 181; Allen S. Whiting, "The Logic of Communist China's Policy: The First Decade," *The Yale Review* 50 (September 1960): 1–27; V. P. Dutt, *China and the World: An Analysis of Communist China's Foreign Policy* (New York, 1966); A. Doak Barnett, *Communist China and Asia* (New York, 1960); Roderick MacFarquhar, "The Chinese Model and the Underdeveloped World," *International Affairs* 39 (July 1963): 372–385; and Jane S. Little, "Communist China's Use of Nationalism in Its Policies Toward the Third World," *Public Policy* 16 (1967): 76–111. John K. Fairbank made a special appeal for better United States-Chinese relations in his presidential address before the American Historical Association, "Assignment for the '70's," *American Historical Review* 74 (February 1969): 861–879.

For a good overview of the American experience in the Far East after 1945, see Dick Wilson, "The American Quarter-Century in Asia," *Foreign Affairs* 51 (July 1973): 811–830. For Wilson, an English scholar, the major errors of the United States were in its policies toward China and Indochina where official misinterpretation of communism became a major factor.

What have the American people learned from their Chinese and Vietnamese experience? In his article, "Have We Learned, Or Only Failed?" *The New York Times Magazine,* April 1, 1973, George W. Ball recognizes the danger that they might have learned very little.

Similarly Richard Holbrooke notes the limits of the Vietnam lessons in "Escaping the Domino Trap," ibid., September 7, 1975. For others no lessons were essential. One article which attributes the stability of Asia in the 1970s in part to the American effort in Vietnam is Donald E. Nuechterlein, "Southeast Asia in International Politics: A 1975 Perspective," *Asian Survey* 15 (July 1975): 574–585.